Contents

Unit		
1	A new you!	page 4
2	Rule the school	page 15
Time to revise 1		page 25
3	Room for improvement!	page 26
4	Festival fever	page 36
Time to revise 2		page 45
5	Extreme behaviour!	page 46
6	Stay in or go out?	page 56
Time to revise 3		page 66
7	Horrible history	page 67
8	Communication breakdown	page 76
Time to revise 4		page 86
9	Getting on ...	page 87
10	Planet Earth	page 95
Time to revise 5		page 106
11	Get fit, have fun	page 107
12	Thrills and chills	page 115
Time to revise 6		page 123
Wordlist		page 124

1 A new you!

Reading: Pages 8–9

1.1 **chef** (n) /ʃef/ = a skilled cook, especially the main cook in a hotel or restaurant. *a **chef** at a famous restaurant*
σεφ, αρχιμάγειρος

1.2 **manager** (n) /ˈmænɪdʒə/ = sb who is in charge of training and organising a sports team. *the **manager** of the football team* ➤ manage (v), management (n)
προπονητής-ρια

1.3 **surfer** (n) /ˈsɜːfə/ = sb who rides on waves while standing on a special board. *The **surfer** had a wonderful day at the beach.* ➤ surf (v)
αυτός-ή που κάνει σερφ

1.4 **web designer** (n phr) /web dɪˌzaɪnə/ = sb who plans and makes websites, especially for businesses or organisations. *Sylvia is a **web designer** and knows a lot about computers.*
ιστογραφίστας-ρια (σχεδιαστής-ρια ιστοσελίδων)

1.5 **fun** (adj) /fʌn/ = enjoyable and amusing. *We had a **fun** evening at the amusement park.* ➤ fun (n), funny (adj)
διασκεδαστικός-ή-ό, ευχάριστος-η-ο

1.6 **main** (adj) /meɪn/ = bigger or more important than all other things, ideas, etc. of the same kind. *Tell me the **main** ideas only.*
κύριος-α-ο, βασικός-ή-ό

1.7 **quite** (adv) /kwaɪt/ = fairly; a little or a lot, but not completely. *The film was **quite** good but the book was better.*
αρκετά

1.8 **topic** (n) /ˈtɒpɪk/ = a subject that people talk or write about. *Fashion is a popular **topic** in girls' magazines.*
θέμα

1.9 **fake** (v) /feɪk/ = to pretend to be interested, ill, etc. when you are not. *Was she really crying or just **faking** it?* ➤ fake (n, adj)
παίζω θέατρο
◆ fake it = προσποιούμαι ότι είμαι/κάνω κάτι

1.10 **skill** (n) /skɪl/ = an ability to do sth well, especially because you have learned and practised it. *You must learn new **skills** to do this job.* ➤ skilled (adj)
δεξιοτεχνία, επιδεξιότητα

1.11 **DJ** (n) /ˌdiː ˈdʒeɪ/ = sb who plays records on a radio show or in a club where you can dance. *Sean will be the **DJ** at the party tonight.*
ντι τζέι, παρουσιαστής-ρια δίσκων
Also: disc jockey

1.12 **transformation** (n) /ˌtrænsfəˈmeɪʃən/ = a complete change in sb or sth. *the **transformation** from an ugly room to a beautiful one* ➤ transform (v)
μεταμόρφωση, μετατροπή

1.13 **challenge** (n) /ˈtʃælənd ʒ/ = sth difficult that tests your skill, strength or ability, especially in an interesting way. *Learning a musical instrument is a **challenge**.* ➤ challenge (v), challenging (adj)
πρόκληση (στις ικανότητες, κλπ.)

1.14 **contestant** (n) /kənˈtestənt/ = sb who takes part in a quiz or competition. *We have two **contestants** in our quiz show tonight.* ➤ contest (n)
αγωνιζόμενος-η

1.15 **series** (n) /ˈsɪəriːz/ = a set of television or radio programmes that have the same characters or deal with the same type of subject and are usually broadcast every week or several times a week. *a new comedy **series***
σειρά
Plural: series

1.16 **convince** (v) /kənˈvɪns/ = to make sb feel certain that sth is true. *You will have to **convince** me that you can do it.* ➤ convincing (adj)
πείθω
◆ convince sb (that); convince sb of sth

1.17 **professional** (adj) /prəˈfeʃənəl/ = doing a job, sport or activity for money, rather than just for fun. *Mary is a **professional** singer.* ➤ professional (n), profession (n)
επαγγελματίας, επαγγελματικός-ή-ό
Opp: amateur

1.18 **impression** (n) /ɪmˈpreʃən/ = the opinion or feeling you have about sb or sth because of the way they seem. *The actor made a good **impression** in his first film.* ➤ impress (v), impressive (adj)
εντύπωση
◆ make an impression

1.19 **admit** (v) /ədˈmɪt/ = to accept the truth; to agree unwillingly that sth is true or that sb is right. *She **admitted** that she was wrong.*
παραδέχομαι
◆ admit (that)

1.20 **house music** (n phr) /haʊs ˌmjuːzɪk/ = a type of popular dance music. *My brother loves **house music**.*
χάους (είδος μουσικής)

1.21 **stay up** (phr v) /steɪ ˈʌp/ = to not go to bed at the time you would normally go to bed. *Our parents let us **stay up** late on Fridays.*
ξαγρυπνώ μέχρι αργά

Chrysoula Davaki

Activate!

B1
Study Companion

Abbreviations and symbols used in the Study Companion

Abbreviation	Full term	Meaning	Example
adj	adjective	επίθετο	main
adv	adverb	επίρρημα	completely
Irr v	irregular verb	ανώμαλο ρήμα	let–let–let
n	noun	ουσιαστικό	transformation
n phr	noun phrase	ονοματική φράση	web designer
n pl	noun plural	ουσιαστικό στον πληθυντικό	lyrics
Opp	opposite	αντίθετο	professional Opp: amateur
phr	phrase	φράση	there's no going back
phr v	phrasal verb	φραστικό ρήμα	pick up
prep	preposition	πρόθεση	including
prep phr	prepositional phrase	φράση με πρόθεση	in progress
sb	somebody	κάποιος-α	somebody
sth	something	κάτι	something
Syn	synonym	συνώνυμο	frequently Syn: often
v	verb	ρήμα	convince
v phr	verb phrase	ρηματική φράση	take part
◆	special note	ειδική σημείωση	convince ◆ convince sb (that); convince sb of sth
➤	derivative	παράγωγο ή ομόριζη λέξη	arrange (v) ➤ arrangement (n)

1 A new you!

1.22 be about to do sth (v phr) /bi əˌbaʊt tə ˈduː ˌsʌmθɪŋ/ = if sb is about to do sth, or if sth is about to happen, they will do it or it will happen very soon. *The film **is about to start**, so switch on the TV.*
είμαι έτοιμος-η-ο να κάνω κάτι

1.23 completely (adv) /kəmˈpliːtli/ = to the greatest degree possible. *We changed the colour of our bedroom walls **completely** – from blue to yellow.* ➤ complete (adj, v)
εντελώς

1.24 transform (v) /trænsˈfɔːm/ = to completely change the appearance, form or character of sth or sb, especially in a way that improves it. *The manager **transformed** the football team into champions.*
μεταμορφώνω, μετατρέπω
◆ transform sb/sth into sb/sth

1.25 be in for (v phr) /bi ˈɪn fə, fɔː/ = if sb is in for sth unpleasant, it is going to happen to them. *He thinks it's easy but he'**s in for** a surprise!*
με περιμένει (κάτι δυσάρεστο)

1.26 smart (adj) /smɑːt/ = smart clothes, buildings, etc. are clean, tidy and attractive. *She was wearing a **smart** suit.*
κομψός-ή-ό

1.27 cello (n) /ˈtʃeləʊ/ = a musical instrument like a large violin that you hold between your knees and play by pulling a bow (= a special stick) across the strings. *How long have you been playing the **cello**?*
(βιολον)τσέλο
◆ play the cello

1.28 thoughts (n pl) /θɔːts/ = a person's ideas or opinions about sth or sb. *Tell us your **thoughts** on the subject.*
➤ think (v)
γνώμη, σκέψη
◆ thoughts on

1.29 stare (v) /steə/ = to look at sth or sb for a long time without moving your eyes, for example because you are surprised, angry or bored. *What are you **staring** at?*
➤ stare (n)
κοιτάζω επίμονα
◆ stare at

1.30 disbelief (n) /ˌdɪsbɪˈliːf/ = a feeling that sth is not true or does not exist. *She looked at him in **disbelief**.*
➤ disbelieve (v)
δυσπιστία, σκεπτικισμός
◆ in disbelief = με δυσπιστία. Opp: belief

1.31 there's no going back (phr) /ðeəz ˌnəʊ ɡəʊɪŋ ˈbæk/ = used to say that you cannot make a situation the same as it was before. *Things have changed and **there's no going back**.*
δεν υπάρχει επιστροφή

1.32 keen (adj) /kiːn/ = wanting to do sth or wanting sth to happen very much. *John is **keen** to join the team.*
ενθουσιώδης-ες
◆ keen to do sth; keen on

1.33 record (n) /ˈrekɔːd/ = a round flat piece of plastic with a hole in the middle that music and sound used to be stored on before the CD was invented. *My grandparents still listen to their old **records**.*
δίσκος (μουσικής)
◆ mix records = to join a number of songs together so that they are pleasant to listen and dance to

1.34 success (n) /səkˈses/ = when you successfully do or complete what you want. *The concert was a **success**.*
➤ succeed (v), successful (adj)
επιτυχία
Opp: failure

1.35 wearily (adv) /ˈwɪərəli/ = in a way which shows that you are very tired or bored, especially because you have been doing sth for a long time. *She sat down and smiled **wearily**.* ➤ weary (adj), weariness (n)
κουρασμένα

1.36 pressure (n) /ˈpreʃə/ = a way of working or living that causes you worry or stress, especially because you feel you have too many things to do. *Mark is under a lot of **pressure** at work.*
πίεση
◆ under pressure

1.37 professional (n) /prəˈfeʃənəl/ = sb who earns money by doing a job, sport or activity that many other people do just for fun. *She danced as well as a real **professional**.*
επαγγελματίας
Opp: amateur

1.38 fashionable (adj) /ˈfæʃənəbəl/ = popular, especially for a short period of time. *Dark colours are **fashionable** at the moment.* ➤ fashion (n)
της μόδας, μοντέρνος-α-ο
Opp: unfashionable

1.39 image (n) /ˈɪmɪdʒ/ = the way that sb or sth is seen by other people. *Singers worry a lot about their **image**.*
εικόνα, ίματζ

1.40 couple (n) /ˈkʌpəl/ = a small number of things. *This will only take a **couple** of minutes.*
μερικοί-ές-ά
◆ a couple of

1.41 on your own (prep phr) /ɒn jər ˈəʊn/ = alone; without anybody's help. *I can manage **on my own**, thanks.*
μόνος-η μου

1.42 audience (n) /ˈɔːdiəns/ = a group of people who come to watch and listen to sb speaking or performing in public. *The **audience** began clapping and cheering.*
ακροατήριο, ακροατές, θεατές

1.43 terrified (adj) /ˈterəfaɪd/ = very scared. *He was **terrified** and began to cry.* ➤ terrify (v), terrifying (adj), terror (n)
τρομοκρατημένος-η-ο
◆ terrified of

A new you! 1

1.44 **tear** (n) /tɪə/ = a drop of liquid that flows from your eye, especially when you are sad or in pain. *There were **tears** in her eyes.*
δάκρυ
◆ be in tears = κλαίω

1.45 **arrange** (v) /əˈreɪndʒ/ = to make it possible for sb to have or do sth. *We will **arrange** for a taxi to meet you at the airport.* ➤ arrangement (n)
κανονίζω

1.46 **voice** (n) /vɔɪs/ = the quality of sound you produce when you sing. *Please sing – you've got a lovely **voice**.*
φωνή

1.47 **movement** (n) /ˈmuːvmənt/ = when sb or sth changes position or moves from one place to another. *a dancer's graceful **movements*** ➤ move (v)
κίνηση

1.48 **coach** (n) /kəʊtʃ/ = sb who trains a person or team in a sport. *Rob is a tennis **coach**.* ➤ coach (v)
προπονητής-ρια

1.49 **confident** (adj) /ˈkɒnfɪdənt/ = sure that you have the ability to do things well or deal with situations successfully. *If you want to pass your test, you have to be calm and **confident**.* ➤ confidence (n)
που έχει αυτοπεποίθηση

1.50 **at last** (prep phr) /ət ˈlɑːst/ = finally. *It was a long journey but they arrived **at last**.*
επιτέλους

1.51 **final** (adj) /ˈfaɪnəl/ = last in a series of actions, events, parts of a story, etc. *The **final** song of the concert was the best.*
τελικός-ή-ό

1.52 **nervous** (adj) /ˈnɜːvəs/ = worried or frightened about sth and unable to relax. *Sam's **nervous** about his test.*
νευρικός-ή-ό

1.53 **do your best** (phr) /ˌduː jə ˈbest/ = to try as hard as you can to do sth. *If you **do your best**, you'll succeed.*
καταβάλλω κάθε δυνατή προσπάθεια

1.54 **shy** (adj) /ʃaɪ/ = nervous and embarrassed about meeting and speaking to other people, especially people you do not know. *She was a quiet, **shy** girl.*
➤ shyness (n), shyly (adv)
ντροπαλός-ή-ό

1.55 **take part** (v phr) /teɪk ˈpɑːt/ = to be involved in an activity, sport, event, etc. with other people. *Are you **taking part** in the competition?*
συμμετέχω
◆ take part in

1.56 **surprising** (adj) /səˈpraɪzɪŋ/ = unusual or unexpected. *A **surprising** number of people came to the concert.*
➤ surprise (v, n), surprised (adj)
εκπληκτικός-ή-ό

1.57 **frightened** (adj) /ˈfraɪtnd/ = feeling afraid. *Don't be **frightened**. We won't hurt you.* ➤ frighten (v), fright (n), frightening (adj)
φοβισμένος-η-ο

1.58 **situation** (n) /ˌsɪtʃuˈeɪʃən/ = a combination of all the things that are happening and all the conditions that exist at a particular time in a particular place. *I found myself in a difficult **situation**.*
κατάσταση

1.59 **ability** (n) /əˈbɪləti/ = sb's level of skill at doing sth. *The **ability** to sing well is rare.* ➤ able (adj)
ικανότητα
Opp: inability

1.60 **complete** (adj) /kəmˈpliːt/ = used to emphasise that a quality or situation is as great as it could possibly be. *The discovery was a **complete** surprise.* ➤ complete (v)
παντελής-ές

1.61 **elegant** (adj) /ˈelɪɡənt/ = beautiful, attractive or graceful. *Sarah is an **elegant** young woman.*
➤ elegance (n)
κομψός-ή-ό

1.62 **attractive** (adj) /əˈtræktɪv/ = sb who is attractive is good looking, especially in a way that makes you interested in them. *Many girls find him **attractive**.*
➤ attract (v), attraction (n)
ελκυστικός-ή-ό
Opp: unattractive

1.63 **noisy** (adj) /ˈnɔɪzi/ = sb or sth that is noisy makes a lot of sounds, especially ones that are loud, unpleasant or frightening. *Please tell those **noisy** children to be quiet.*
➤ noise (n)
θορυβώδης-ες

1.64 **summarise** (v) /ˈsʌməraɪz/ = to make a short statement giving only the main information and not the details of a plan, event, report, etc. *The writer **summarised** his ideas in a few words.* ➤ summary (n)
συνοψίζω

1.65 **be coming up** (v phr) /bi ˌkʌmɪŋ ˈʌp/ = to be going to happen soon. *Christmas **is coming up** and I must buy some presents.*
έρχεται, πλησιάζει

Vocabulary: Page 10

1.66 **organise** (v) /ˈɔːɡənaɪz/ = to make the necessary arrangements so that sth can happen with good results. *Clara and Joan are **organising** the school concert.*
➤ organised (adj), organisation (n)
οργανώνω

1.67 **train** (v) /treɪn/ = to teach sb the skills of a particular job or activity. *She **trains** people to sing.* ➤ training (n), trainer (n)
εκπαιδεύω

1 A new you!

1.68 outdoors (adv) /ˌaʊtˈdɔːz/ = outside, not in a building. *He likes working **outdoors** in the fresh air.*
στο ύπαιθρο
Opp: indoors

1.69 plant (n) /plɑːnt/ = a living thing that has leaves and roots and grows in earth. *She is watering the **plants** in the garden.* ➤ plant (v)
φυτό

1.70 create (v) /kriˈeɪt/ = to invent or design sth. *The artist **created** a beautiful painting.* ➤ creation (n), creative (adj)
δημιουργώ

1.71 board (n) /bɔːd/ = a long piece of plastic, wood, etc. that you stand on when you go surfing. *The surfer stood on his **board** and rode the waves.*
σανίδα σερφ
Also: surfboard

1.72 do well (phr) /ˌduː ˈwel/ = to be successful, especially in work or business. *She's **doing well** at college.*
(τα) πηγαίνω καλά

1.73 experienced (adj) /ɪkˈspɪəriənst/ = having skills or knowledge because you have done sth often or for a long time. *an **experienced** DJ* ➤ experience (n, v)
πεπειραμένος-η-ο
Opp: inexperienced

1.74 way (n) /weɪ/ = the manner or style in which sb does sth or in which sth happens. *speak in a friendly **way***
τρόπος
◆ in a (friendly) way

1.75 decision (n) /dɪˈsɪʒən/ = a choice that you make after a period of thinking about it. *It wasn't easy for me to make a **decision**.* ➤ decide (v)
απόφαση
◆ make a decision

1.76 particular (adj) /pəˈtɪkjʊlə/ = a particular thing or person is the one that you are talking about, and not any other. *I like this **particular** song.*
συγκεκριμένος-η-ο

1.77 memorise (v) /ˈmeməraɪz/ = to learn words, music, etc. so that you know them perfectly. ***Memorise** the words of this song.* ➤ memory (n)
απομνημονεύω, αποστηθίζω

Grammar: Page 11

1.78 permanently (adv) /ˈpɜːmənəntli/ = always; for a very long time. *Jill has come to live here **permanently**.* ➤ permanent (adj)
μόνιμα

1.79 habit (n) /ˈhæbɪt/ = sth that you do regularly or usually, often without thinking about it because you have done it so many times before. *good and bad **habits***
συνήθεια

1.80 repeated (adj) /rɪˈpiːtɪd/ = done or happening again and again. ***repeated** mistakes* ➤ repeat (v), repetition (n)
επανειλημμένος-η-ο

1.81 including (prep) /ɪnˈkluːdɪŋ/ = used to introduce sth or sb that is part of a larger group that you have just mentioned. *Many of my friends, **including** Ann and Bob, were at the party.* ➤ include (v)
συμπεριλαμβανόμενος

1.82 sense (n) /sens/ = one of the five natural powers of sight, hearing, feeling, taste and smell, that give us information about the things around us. *a good **sense** of smell* ➤ sense (v), sensitive (adj)
αίσθηση

1.83 horrible (adj) /ˈhɒrəbəl/ = very unpleasant or upsetting. *That's a **horrible** thing to say!*
φρικτός-ή-ό

1.84 go well (phr) /ˌgəʊ ˈwel/ = to happen in a successful way. *The party **went well**.*
(τα) πηγαίνω καλά

1.85 course (n) /kɔːs/ = a series of lessons in a subject. *I want to do a **course** in Chinese.*
σειρά μαθημάτων
◆ do a course

1.86 expert (n) /ˈekspɜːt/ = sb who has a special skill or special knowledge of a subject, gained as a result of training or experience. *Marion is an **expert** on classical music.*
ειδήμονας, ειδικός
◆ expert on

1.87 behave (v) /bɪˈheɪv/ = to do things that are good, bad, etc. *He **behaves** badly in class.* ➤ behaviour (n)
συμπεριφέρομαι

1.88 appearance (n) /əˈpɪərəns/ = the way sb or sth looks to other people. *Would you like to change your **appearance**?* ➤ appear (v)
εμφάνιση

1.89 personality (n) /ˌpɜːsəˈnæləti/ = sb's character, especially the way they behave towards other people. *She has a great **personality**.* ➤ personal (adj), person (n)
προσωπικότητα

Listening: Page 12

1.90 conversation (n) /ˌkɒnvəˈseɪʃən/ = an informal talk in which people exchange news, feelings and thoughts. *an interesting **conversation** with my friend*
συζήτηση, κουβέντα

1.91 expect (v) /ɪkˈspekt/ = to think that sth will happen because it seems likely or has been planned. *I **expect** to be back next week.*
αναμένω, περιμένω

A new you! 1

1.92 **mood** (n) /muːd/ = the way you feel at a particular time. *I'm in a good **mood** this morning.* ➤ moody (adj)
(ψυχική) διάθεση
◆ be in a (good) mood

1.93 **calm** (adj) /kɑːm/ = relaxed and quiet, not angry, nervous or upset. *How can you be so **calm** in a situation like this?* ➤ calm (v, n)
ήρεμος-η-ο

1.94 **serious** (adj) /ˈsɪəriəs/ = important and needing a lot of thought or attention. *a **serious** book*
σοβαρός-ή-ό

1.95 **lively** (adj) /ˈlaɪvli/ = sb who is lively has a lot of energy and is very active. *Kim is a **lively** teenager with a lot of energy.* ➤ live (v), life (n)
ζωηρός-ή-ό

Speaking: Page 13

1.96 **spot** (n) /spɒt/ = a short period of time when sb can speak or perform on radio or television. *He was given a five-minute **spot** after the news.*
σύντομο ραδιοφωνικό/τηλεοπτικό πρόγραμμα

1.97 **local** (adj) /ˈləʊkəl/ = relating to the particular area you live in or are talking about. *a **local** radio station*
➤ local (n)
τοπικός-ή-ό

1.98 **statement** (n) /ˈsteɪtmənt/ = sth you say or write, especially officially, to let people know your opinion or to record facts. *true or false **statements*** ➤ state (v)
δήλωση

1.99 **energy** (n) /ˈenədʒi/ = the power and ability to be active with body or mind. *Tom has a lot of **energy**.*
➤ energetic (adj)
ενέργεια

1.100 **sense of humour** (n phr) /ˌsens əv ˈhjuːmə/ = the ability to understand and enjoy things that are funny. *I like Pam – she has a great **sense of humour**.*
αίσθηση του χιούμορ

1.101 **attention** (n) /əˈtenʃən/ = the interest that people show in sth or sb. *Ben loves being the centre of **attention**.*
προσοχή
◆ the centre of attention

1.102 **apply** (v) /əˈplaɪ/ = to make a formal request, usually written, for sth such as a job, a place in a university or permission to do sth. *I have **applied** for a job.*
➤ application (n)
κάνω αίτηση
◆ apply for; apply to do sth

1.103 **surname** (n) /ˈsɜːneɪm/ = family name; last name. *Her **surname** is Smith.*
επώνυμο

1.104 **nickname** (n) /ˈnɪkneɪm/ = a name given to sb, especially by their friends or family, that is not their real name and is often connected with what they look like or sth they have done. *We have **nicknames** for all our teachers.*
παρατσούκλι

1.105 **enthusiastic** (adj) /ɪnˌθjuːziˈæstɪk/ = feeling or showing a lot of interest and excitement about sth. *Everybody was **enthusiastic** about Wendy's performance.*
➤ enthusiasm (n)
ενθουσιασμένος-η-ο
◆ enthusiastic about

1.106 **white lie** (n phr) /ˌwaɪt ˈlaɪ/ = a lie that is not serious, told to avoid upsetting sb. *Don't be angry – it was just a little **white lie**!*
αθώο ψέμα

1.107 **be into** (v phr) /bi ˈɪntə, ˈɪntʊ/ = to like and be interested in sth. *Greg **is into** rapping.*
μου αρέσει

Use your English: Pages 14–15

1.108 **bored** (adj) /bɔːd/ = tired and impatient because you do not think sth is interesting, or because you have nothing to do. *After a while I got **bored** and left.* ➤ bore (v), boring (adj), boredom (n)
(αυτός-ή-ό) που βαριέται/πλήττει
◆ bored with

1.109 **frightening** (adj) /ˈfraɪtnɪŋ/ = making you feel afraid or nervous. *It was a **frightening** experience.*
τρομακτικός-ή-ό

1.110 **surprised** (adj) /səˈpraɪzd/ = having a feeling of surprise. *He looked **surprised** when he saw me.*
έκπληκτος-η-ο
◆ surprised at/by

1.111 **annoyed** (adj) /əˈnɔɪd/ = slightly angry; irritated. *I'll be **annoyed** if we don't win the race.* ➤ annoy (v), annoying (adj)
ενοχλημένος-η-ο
◆ annoyed with/by

1.112 **annoying** (adj) /əˈnɔɪ-ɪŋ/ = making you feel a bit angry. *an **annoying** noise*
ενοχλητικός-ή-ό

1.113 **can't stand** (v phr) /kɑːnt ˈstænd/ = used to say that you do not like sb or sth at all, or that you think that sth is extremely unpleasant. *My father **can't stand** rap music.*
δεν αντέχω
◆ can't stand sth/doing sth

1.114 **lyrics** (n pl) /ˈlɪrɪks/ = the words of a song. *a song with great **lyrics***
στίχοι τραγουδιού

1 A new you!

1.115 **amazed** (adj) /əˈmeɪzd/ = very surprised. *I'm **amazed** you've never heard of the Rolling Stones.* ➤ amaze (v), amazing (adj), amazement (n)
έκπληκτος-η-ο
◆ amazed at/by

1.116 **amazing** (adj) /əˈmeɪzɪŋ/ = very good, especially in an unexpected way. *She's an **amazing** piano player.*
εκπληκτικός-ή-ό

1.117 **boring** (adj) /ˈbɔːrɪŋ/ = not interesting in any way. *It was a **boring** book and I couldn't finish it.*
βαρετός-ή-ό

1.118 **worried** (adj) /ˈwʌrid/ = unhappy because you keep thinking about a problem or about sth bad that might happen. *I'm **worried** about my test.* ➤ worry (v, n), worrying (adj)
ανήσυχος-η-ο
◆ worried about

1.119 **fed up** (adj) /ˌfed ˈʌp/ = annoyed or bored and wanting sth to change. *I'm **fed up** with my noisy neighbours.*
αγανακτισμένος-η-ο
◆ fed up with

1.120 **chew** (v) /tʃuː/ = to bite sth continuously in order to taste it or because you are nervous. *The dog was **chewing** an old shoe.*
μασώ

1.121 **gum** (n) /gʌm/ = a type of sweet that you chew for a long time but do not swallow. *I always have some **gum** after a meal.*
τσίκλα
Also: chewing gum

1.122 **phobia** (n) /ˈfəʊbiə/ = a strong unreasonable fear of sth. *Mum has a **phobia** about snakes.*
φοβία
◆ phobia about

1.123 **practical joke** (n phr) /ˌpræktɪkəl ˈdʒəʊk/ = a trick that is intended to give sb a surprise or shock, or to make them look stupid. *They played a **practical joke** on me.*
φάρσα
◆ play a practical joke on sb

1.124 **truth** (n) /truːθ/ = the true facts about sth, rather than what is untrue, imagined or guessed. *Are you telling the **truth**?* ➤ true (adj), truthful (adj)
αλήθεια
◆ tell the truth

1.125 **lie** (n) /laɪ/ = sth that you say or write that you know is untrue. *I don't believe it! It's a **lie**!* ➤ lie (v), liar (n)
ψέμα
◆ tell a lie

1.126 **honest** (adj) /ˈɒnəst/ = sb who is honest always tells the truth and does not cheat or steal. *He was a hard-working, **honest** man.* ➤ honesty (n)
έντιμος-η-ο, τίμιος-α-ο
Opp: dishonest

1.127 **spot** (v) /spɒt/ = to notice sb or sth, especially when they are difficult to see or recognise. *Can you **spot** the differences between these two pictures?*
εντοπίζω, επισημαίνω

1.128 **result** (n) /rɪˈzʌlt/ = sth that happens or exists because of sth else. *Her success was the **result** of hard work.*
αποτέλεσμα

1.129 **tiny** (adj) /ˈtaɪni/ = extremely small. *a **tiny** mark on the paper*
μικροσκοπικός-ή-ό

1.130 **expression** (n) /ɪkˈspreʃən/ = a look on sb's face that shows what they are thinking or feeling. *Her **expression** changed when she heard the bad news.* ➤ express (v), expressive (adj)
έκφραση

1.131 **liar** (n) /ˈlaɪə/ = sb who knowingly says things which are not true. *Are you calling me a **liar**?*
ψεύτης-ρα

1.132 **blush** (v) /blʌʃ/ = to become red in the face, usually because you are nervous and uncomfortable. *Wilson saw she was watching him and **blushed**.* ➤ blush (n)
κοκκινίζω

1.133 **bright** (adj) /braɪt/ = (of colours) strong and easy to see. *a **bright** red dress* ➤ brightness (n)
έντονος-η-ο, φωτεινός-ή-ό

1.134 **ground** (n) /graʊnd/ = the surface that you walk on when you are outdoors. *She lay on the **ground** and looked at the sky.*
έδαφος

1.135 **common** (adj) /ˈkɒmən/ = happening often and to many people or in many places. *A fear of spiders is **common**.*
κοινός-ή-ό, συνήθης-ες
Opp: rare

1.136 **lie detector** (n phr) /ˈlaɪ dɪˌtektə/ = a piece of equipment used especially by the police to check whether sb is lying, by measuring sudden changes in their heart rate. *Have you ever taken a **lie detector** test?*
ανιχνευτής ψεύδους

1.137 **pick up** (phr v) /ˌpɪk ˈʌp/ = if a machine picks up a sound, movement or signal, it is able to notice it or receive it. *The animal's ears can **pick up** very small sounds.*
πιάνω, εντοπίζω

1.138 **heart rate** (n phr) /ˈhɑːt reɪt/ = the number of times your heart beats over a period of time. *His **heart rate** is normal.*
παλμός

1.139 **skin** (n) /skɪn/ = the natural outer layer of a person's or animal's body. *a lovely soft **skin***
δέρμα, επιδερμίδα

A new you! 1

1.140 heat (n) /hiːt/ = the quality of being warm or hot. *I couldn't stand the **heat** of the fire.* ➤ heat (v), hot (adj)
(υψηλή) θερμοκρασία, ζέστη

1.141 find out (phr v) /ˌfaɪnd ˈaʊt/ = to get information after trying to discover it or by chance. *I **found out** that he had lied to us.*
μαθαίνω, ανακαλύπτω

1.142 measure (v) /ˈmeʒə/ = to find the size, length or amount of sth, using standard units such as inches, metres, etc. *We **measured** the children to see if they had grown.* ➤ measurement (n)
μετρώ

1.143 activity (n) /ækˈtɪvəti/ = a situation in which a lot of things are happening or a lot of things are being done. *Physical **activity** helps you stay fit and healthy.* ➤ active (adj), act (v, n)
δραστηριότητα

1.144 brain (n) /breɪn/ = the organ inside your head that controls how you think, feel and move. *Dolphins have large **brains**.*
εγκέφαλος

1.145 certain (adj) /ˈsɜːtn/ = used to talk about a particular person or thing without saying exactly who or what they are. *The library is open at **certain** times of the day.*
ορισμένος-η-ο

1.146 form (v) /fɔːm/ = to make sth exist. *How do we **form** the present continuous?* ➤ form (n)
σχηματίζω

1.147 order (n) /ˈɔːdə/ = the way that things or events are arranged in relation to each other, for example showing whether sth is first, second, third, etc. *Put these books in **order**.*
σειρά

1.148 frequently (adv) /ˈfriːkwəntli/ = very often or many times. *Sheila is **frequently** late for class.* ➤ frequent (adj), frequency (n)
συχνά, τακτικά
Syn: often

1.149 rarely (adv) /ˈreəli/ = not often. *I **rarely** have breakfast before ten at weekends.* ➤ rare (adj)
σπάνια

1.150 occasionally (adv) /əˈkeɪʒənəli/ = sometimes, but not regularly and not often. *We see each other **occasionally**.* ➤ occasional (adj), occasion (n)
περιστασιακά

1.151 sweet (n) /swiːt/ = a small piece of sweet food made of sugar or chocolate. *Our teacher doesn't let us eat **sweets** in class.* ➤ sweet (adj)
καραμέλα, γλυκό

1.152 awake (adj) /əˈweɪk/ = not sleeping. *He was tired and he couldn't stay **awake**.* ➤ wake (v)
ξύπνιος-α-ο

1.153 underneath (prep) /ˌʌndəˈniːθ/ = directly under another object or covered by it; on the lower surface of sth. *There's something **underneath** the table.*
κάτω από

1.154 let (v) /let/ = to allow sb to do sth. *Please **let** me go out with my friends tonight, Mum.*
αφήνω, επιτρέπω
◆ let sb do sth. Irr v: let–let–let

1.155 covered (adj) /ˈkʌvəd/ = having a layer of sth on top. *The floor was **covered** in dust.* ➤ cover (v, n)
σκεπασμένος-η-ο
◆ covered in/with

1.156 celebrity (n) /səˈlebrəti/ = a famous living person. *a popular **celebrity***
διασημότητα

1.157 public (adj) /ˈpʌblɪk/ = a public place usually has a lot of people in it. *There were posters for the concert in many **public** places.* ➤ public (n), publicity (n)
δημόσιος-α-ο

1.158 stuck (adj) /stʌk/ = impossible or unable to move from a particular position. *What is that **stuck** on your blouse?* ➤ stick (v)
κολλημένος-η-ο
◆ get stuck

1.159 swallow (v) /ˈswɒləʊ/ = to make food or drink go down your throat and towards your stomach. *I **swallowed** my coffee and left the restaurant.*
καταπίνω

Writing: Pages 16–17

1.160 talk show (n phr) /ˈtɔːk ʃəʊ/ = a television show in which famous people answer questions about themselves. *Guess who's on tonight's **talk show**!*
τηλεοπτική συζήτηση

1.161 chance (n) /tʃɑːns/ = a time or situation that you can use to do sth that you want to do. *Ralph was waiting for the **chance** to introduce himself.*
ευκαιρία

1.162 giant (adj) /ˈdʒaɪənt/ = extremely big. *A **giant** tortoise was crawling towards us.* ➤ giant (n)
γιγαντιαίος-α-ο

1.163 unforgettable (adj) /ˌʌnfəˈɡetəbəl/ = an unforgettable experience, sight, etc. leaves such strong emotions that you will never forget it, especially because it is particularly good or beautiful. *The rock concert was **unforgettable**.* ➤ forget (v)
αξέχαστος-η-ο

1.164 experience (n) /ɪkˈspɪəriəns/ = sth that happens to you or sth you do, especially when this has an effect on what you feel or think. *a frightening **experience*** ➤ experience (v), experienced (adj)
εμπειρία

1 A new you!

1.165 nan (n) /næn/ = grandmother. *My **nan** is visiting us next week.*
γιαγιά
Also: grandmother

1.166 look forward to (phr v) /lʊk 'fɔːwəd tə, tʊ/ = to be excited and pleased about sth that is going to happen. *I'm **looking forward to** the party.*
προσβλέπω σε, ευελπιστώ σε
◆ look forward to sth/doing sth

1.167 especially (adv) /ɪˈspeʃəli/ = much more than usual, or much more than other people or things. *A lot of tourists come here, **especially** in the summer.*
ιδιαίτερα

1.168 look after (phr v) /lʊk 'ɑːftə/ = to take care of sb or sth by helping them, giving them what they need or keeping them safe. *Don't worry. I'll **look after** the kids for you.*
φροντίζω

1.169 fascinating (adj) /ˈfæsəneɪtɪŋ/ = extremely interesting. *That was a **fascinating** book.* ➤ fascinate (v), fascinated (adj), fascination (n)
γοητευτικός-ή-ό, συναρπαστικός-ή-ό

1.170 actually (adv) /ˈæktʃuəli, -tʃəli/ = used to add new information to what you have just said, to give your opinion or to start a new conversation. *I know Harry well. **Actually**, I've known him since we were kids.*
όντως, πραγματικά

1.171 feed (v) /fiːd/ = to give food to a person or animal. *Have you **fed** the cat?*
ταΐζω

1.172 human (n) /ˈhjuːmən/ = a person. *Monkeys look like **humans** in some ways.*
ανθρώπινο πλάσμα
Also: human being

1.173 grow up (phr v) /ˌɡrəʊ 'ʌp/ = to develop from being a child to being an adult. *What do you want to be when you **grow up**?*
μεγαλώνω, ενηλικιώνομαι

1.174 vet (n) /vet/ = sb who is trained to give medical care and treatment to sick animals. *We took our sick dog to the **vet**.*
κτηνίατρος

1.175 PS (abbreviation) /ˌpiː 'es/ = a note written at the end of a letter, adding more information. *Best wishes, Zoe. **PS** My brother says 'hi'.*
υστερόγραφο

1.176 by the way (prep phr) /baɪ ðə 'weɪ/ = used when saying sth that is not connected with what you were talking about before. ***By the way**, I saw Marie yesterday.*
παρεμπιπτόντως

1.177 ahead (adv) /əˈhed/ = before an event happens. *Can you tell me if you're coming a few hours **ahead** of your arrival?*
έγκαιρα, νωρίτερα

1.178 well (interjection) /wel/ = used to emphasise sth you are saying. ***Well**, I don't think that's a good idea.*
που λες

1.179 in fact (prep phr) /ɪn 'fækt/ = used to add sth surprising or unusual that is true. *It looks difficult but **in fact**, it's easy.*
στην πραγματικότητα

1.180 introduce (v) /ˌɪntrəˈdjuːs/ = if you introduce sb to another person, you tell them each other's names for the first time. *Let me **introduce** you to Karl.* ➤ introduction (n)
συστήνω

1.181 captain (n) /ˈkæptən/ = sb who leads a team or other group of people. *Neville is **captain** of the basketball team.*
αρχηγός, ηγέτης

1.182 polite (adj) /pəˈlaɪt/ = behaving or speaking in a way that is correct for the social situation you are in and showing that you are careful to consider other people's needs and feelings. *a **polite** young man* ➤ politeness (n)
ευγενικός-ή-ό
Opp: impolite, rude

1.183 check (v) /tʃek/ = to do sth in order to find out whether sth really is correct, true or in good condition. ***Check** the facts to make sure they are correct.* ➤ check (n)
ελέγχω

1.184 punctuation (n) /ˌpʌŋktʃuˈeɪʃən/ = the marks used to divide a piece of writing into sentences, phrases, etc. *Pay attention to the **punctuation** in your letter.*
στίξη

WORDZONE SPECIAL

Some adjectives are usually followed by certain prepositions.

annoyed **with/by**	bored **with**	frightened **of**	interested **in**	surprised **at/by**
bad **at**	fed up **with**	good **at**	keen **on**	worried **about**

A new you! 1

Vocabulary and grammar practice

1 Complete the sentences with these adjectives.

common   confident   elegant   enthusiastic   lively   local   professional   terrified

1 Tim is so .... about learning to play the piano that he practises every day.
2 If you want to be a(n) .... dancer, you must be very talented.
3 My brother plays for the .... football team.
4 Beth is a(n) .... young woman, so she isn't scared of speaking in public.
5 It is a(n) .... mistake to think that classical music is boring. It isn't – it can be very exciting.
6 I can't believe you're .... of such a tiny spider!
7 Sandy looks after her clothes and always looks ....
8 Danny is a very .... and active child. He never sits still!

2 Choose the correct words to complete the sentences.

1 I'm *fed up / bored* with my noisy neighbours! They have parties every night!
2 Vickie's *nickname / surname* is Pinky because she always wears pink.
3 You really need to *make / do* your best if you want to pass your exams.
4 When you eat, you should *chew / swallow* your food well.
5 It was a *frightening / frightened* film and I was terrified.
6 We're *looking after / looking forward to* seeing you at the concert tomorrow!
7 If you want to be successful, you must plan *ahead / underneath*.
8 Ten *experts / contestants* took part in the quiz but only two won prizes.

3 Complete the sentences with the correct form of the words in capitals.

1 Did you see the .... on her face? She looked sad. **EXPRESS**
2 I think the baby's .... Listen! He's crying. **WAKE**
3 The clothes in this shop are not very .... **FASHION**
4 I think Linda is more .... than Carol. **ATTRACT**
5 I think History is a .... subject. **FASCINATE**
6 Ricky loves Australia and wants to live there .... **PERMANENT**
7 The singer made a good first .... **IMPRESS**
8 Pam has a natural .... to entertain people. **ABLE**

4 Match the words 1–7 with the words a–g. Then complete the sentences.

1 chewing ☐   a detector
2 heart ☐   b gum
3 house ☐   c lies
4 lie ☐   d music
5 public ☐   e places
6 talk ☐   f rate
7 white ☐   g show

1 A new you!

1 Smoking is not allowed in .... in England.
2 My favourite .... is on television and I don't want to miss it.
3 My brother never listens to .... He thinks it's terrible.
4 Oh, no! There's a piece of .... stuck in my hair!
5 Our .... is usually slower when we are resting.
6 The police sometimes use a .... to see if somebody is telling the truth or not.
7 Did you tell me the truth or was that one of your little .... ?

5 Present simple, present continuous, stative verbs
Complete the text with the correct form of the verbs in brackets. Use the present simple or present continuous.

Dear Sarah,

I'm sorry for not writing sooner. How are you? I guess you're back at school now and busy with the volleyball team. 1) .... (you / practise) every day?

I'm OK here. London is an exciting city but it 2) .... (rain) very often and I 3) .... (miss) home! Today the sun 4) .... (shine), though, and it's great to be outside!

I 5) .... (love) my new dancing school. I have a wonderful teacher. He 6) .... (think) I'm talented. I 7) .... (usually / practise) with eight other girls. I share a flat with one of them. Her name is Suzie and she's very nice. But this week I'm on my own – Suzie 8) .... (visit) her parents.

Well, I'd better go now. Don't forget to say hello to your parents and write back soon!

Love, Christina

6 Adverbs of frequency
Put the words in the correct order.

1 shopping / do / alone. / rarely / I / the
....

2 Mary / dance / at parties? / never / Does
....

3 on the radio. / often / I / different kinds of music / listen to
....

4 sometimes / Why / Philip / is / late / for class?
....

5 basketball practice / The children / after school. / go to / usually
....

6 go / don't / to bed / They / always / late.
....

A new you! 1

Test yourself!

Choose the word or phrase that best completes the conversation or sentence.

1. 'What time ...... to bed?'
   'At about ten o'clock on weekdays.'
   A you usually go
   B are you going usually
   C do you usually go
   D you are usually going

2. The young man ...... himself to us as Jake Thomas.
   A appeared
   B introduced
   C offered
   D guessed

3. You're very talented and I'm going to ...... some singing lessons for you.
   A expect
   B cover
   C admit
   D arrange

4. I ...... my homework after eight o'clock in the evening.
   A do never
   B am never doing
   C never doing
   D never do

5. That was one of the most ...... films I've ever seen!
   A frightening
   B frightened
   C frighten
   D fright

6. 'What do you think of the soup?'
   'It ...... delicious!'
   A taste
   B is tasting
   C tastes
   D has taste

7. Eve is doing ...... at school.
   A well
   B good
   C best
   D successful

8. ...... so much energy?
   A You have always
   B Are you always having
   C Have always you
   D Do you always have

9. This machine can ...... even tiny changes in the sound of your voice.
   A come up
   B pick up
   C stay up
   D take part

10. 'Could I speak to Sean, please?'
    'I'm afraid not. He ...... a shower at the moment.'
    A has
    B have
    C having
    D is having

11. Angela ...... of taking piano lessons.
    A thinks
    B does think
    C is thinking
    D thinking

12. Luke looks very ...... in his new suit.
    A local
    B smart
    C polite
    D common

13. 'Is your sister still keen ...... volleyball?'
    'Yes. She's captain of the school team.'
    A on
    B for
    C with
    D to

14. 'Brian, ... gum again?'
    'Sorry, miss. I'll throw it in the bin.'
    A are you chewing
    B you are chewing
    C do you chew
    D you chew

2 Rule the school

Reading: Pages 18–19

2.1 **rule** (v) /ruːl/ = to have the power to control. **rule** a country ➤ rule (n), ruler (n)
κυβερνώ

2.2 **text-messaging** (n) /tekst ˌmesədʒɪŋ/ = the act of sending sb a written message on a mobile phone. *Most teenagers know everything about **text-messaging**.*
στέλνω μήνυμα σε κινητό τηλέφωνο

2.3 **break dancing** (n phr) /ˈbreɪk ˌdɑːnsɪŋ/ = a type of modern street dance. *Wayne showed me some cool **break dancing** moves.*
είδος χορού

2.4 **subject** (n) /ˈsʌbdʒɪkt/ = sth that you study at school or university. *My favourite **subject** is Science.*
(σχολικό) μάθημα

2.5 **computer gaming** (n phr) /kəmˈpjuːtə ˌgeɪmɪŋ/ = the act of playing games on a computer. *Katy loves **computer gaming** and surfing the internet.*
παιχνίδια σε ηλεκτρονικό υπολογιστή

2.6 **discuss** (v) /dɪˈskʌs/ = to talk about sth with sb in order to exchange ideas or decide sth. *We're meeting to **discuss** our Science project.* ➤ discussion (n)
συζητώ

2.7 **detail** (n) /ˈdiːteɪl/ = a single feature, fact or piece of information about sth. *Describe the picture in **detail**.*
λεπτομέρεια
◆ in detail = με λεπτομέρειες

2.8 **slow down** (phr v) /ˌsləʊ ˈdaʊn/ = to become slower or to make sth slower. *The icy roads **slowed** us **down**.*
επιβραδύνω

2.9 **head teacher** (n phr) /ˌhed ˈtiːtʃə/ = the teacher who is in charge of a school. *The **head teacher** spoke to the students.*
διευθυντής-ρια σχολείου

2.10 **secondary school** (n phr) /ˈsekəndəri ˌskuːl/ = a school for children between the ages of 11 and 18. *Derek finished **secondary school** and went to college.*
γυμνάσιο και λύκειο

2.11 **advert** (n) /ˈædvɜːt/ = an advertisement. *an **advert** for private lessons in the newspaper*
αγγελία, διαφήμιση
Also: advertisement

2.12 **twist** (n) /twɪst/ = a sudden change in a story or situation that you did not expect. *There's a **twist** at the end of the film.*
μεταβολή, νέα τροπή

2.13 **adult** (n) /ˈædʌlt, əˈdʌlt/ = a person or animal that has finished growing. *When you are an **adult**, you have a lot of responsibilities.* ➤ adult (adj)
ενήλικος
Syn: grown-up

2.14 **real-life** (adj) /ˌrɪəl ˈlaɪf/ = actually happening in life, not taken from a story or book. ***real-life** problems*
πραγματικός-ή-ό

2.15 **aim** (n) /eɪm/ = sth that you want to do or get. *My **aim** is to start my own business.* ➤ aim (v)
σκοπός, στόχος

2.16 **cool** (adj) /kuːl/ = attractive, fashionable or interesting in a way that people admire. *You look **cool** in those clothes.*
φίνος-α-ο, θαυμάσιος-α-ο

2.17 **curriculum** (n) /kəˈrɪkjələm/ = the subjects that students learn at a school or college. *Chinese will be on the **curriculum** next term.*
διδακτέα ύλη

2.18 **include** (v) /ɪnˈkluːd/ = if one thing includes another, the second thing is part of the first. *The price of the holiday **includes** transport to the hotel.* ➤ including (prep)
περιλαμβάνω

2.19 **funky** (adj) /ˈfʌŋki/ = modern, fashionable and interesting. ***funky** new clothes*
της μόδας

2.20 **excuse** (n) /ɪkˈskjuːs/ = a reason, often one that is not true, that you give in order to do sth or avoid doing sth. *He tried to think of an **excuse** to leave the class early.* ➤ excuse (v)
δικαιολογία

2.21 **examination** (n) /ɪgˌzæmɪˈneɪʃən/ = an official test of knowledge in a subject. *I passed all my **examinations**.* ➤ examine (v)
εξέταση

2.22 **uniform** (n) /ˈjuːnɪfɔːm/ = a type of clothing worn by all the members of an organisation or all the children at a school. *Do you wear a school **uniform**?*
στολή

2.23 **three-quarter** (adj) /ˌθriːˈkwɔːtə/ = having three of the four equal parts of the full size or length of sth. *a **three-quarter** length coat*
τριών τετάρτων

2.24 **length** (n) /leŋθ/ = the measurement of how long sth is from one end to the other. *Measure the **length** of the room.* ➤ lengthen (v), long (adj)
μήκος

Rule the school 2

2.25 **top** (n) /tɒp/ = a piece of clothing that you wear on the upper part of your body. *Put on a warm **top**.*
ρούχο προοριζόμενο για το άνω μέρος του κορμού

2.26 **trainer** (n) /ˈtreɪnə/ = a type of shoe that you wear for sport. *I put on my **trainers** and went running.*
αθλητικό παπούτσι

2.27 **ridiculous** (adj) /rɪˈdɪkjʊləs/ = very silly. *That's a **ridiculous** idea!*
γελοίος-α-ο

2.28 **complain** (v) /kəmˈpleɪn/ = to say that you are not satisfied with sth or not happy about sth. *'Nobody ever tells me anything!' Lynn **complained**.* ➤ complaint (n)
παραπονούμαι
◆ complain about

2.29 **chat** (v) /tʃæt/ = to talk in a friendly and informal way, especially about unimportant things. *Pete and I were **chatting** in the kitchen.* ➤ chat (n)
κουβεντιάζω

2.30 **deal with** (phr v) /ˈdiːl wɪð, wɪθ/ = to do what is necessary, especially in order to solve a problem. *Don't worry. I'll **deal with** the problem.*
αντιμετωπίζω
Irr v: deal with–dealt with–dealt with

2.31 **assembly** (n) /əˈsembli/ = a regular meeting of all the students and teachers in a school. *We have **assembly** every day at nine.* ➤ assemble (v)
συνέλευση

2.32 **immediately** (adv) /ɪˈmiːdiətli/ = without delay. *Open this door **immediately**!* ➤ immediate (adj)
αμέσως

2.33 **make a fool of yourself** (phr) /ˌmeɪk ə ˈfuːl əv jəˌself/ = to do sth silly or embarrassing. *She was worried that she might **make a fool of herself**.*
γελοιοποιούμαι

2.34 **giggle** (v) /ˈgɪgəl/ = to laugh in a silly way, especially because you are nervous or embarrassed. *The little girls couldn't stop **giggling**.* ➤ giggle (n)
χαζογελώ

2.35 **carry on** (phr v) /ˌkæri ˈɒn/ = to continue doing sth. *I told them to keep quiet but they **carried on** talking.*
συνεχίζω
◆ carry on doing sth

2.36 **immature** (adj) /ˌɪməˈtʃʊə/ = behaving like a younger person. *Some students are **immature** when they start college.*
ανώριμος-η-ο
Opp: mature

2.37 **punish** (v) /ˈpʌnɪʃ/ = to do sth unpleasant to sb because they have done sth wrong. *His dad **punished** him for lying.* ➤ punishment (n)
τιμωρώ

2.38 **detention** (n) /dɪˈtenʃən/ = a school punishment in which you have to stay at school after the other students have left. *Does your teacher give **detentions**?*
τιμωρία μαθητή με παραμονή στο σχολείο επί ορισμένο χρονικό διάστημα μετά το σχόλασμα

2.39 **make up** (phr v) /ˌmeɪk ˈʌp/ = to think of a story, explanation, excuse, etc. that is not true. *The children **made up** stories.*
επινοώ

2.40 **misbehave** (v) /ˌmɪsbɪˈheɪv/ = to behave badly. *Students who **misbehave** will have to leave the room.*
παρεκτρέπομαι
Opp: behave

2.41 **headphones** (n pl) /ˈhedfəʊnz/ = a piece of equipment that you wear over your ears to listen to a radio, recorded music, etc. *Ada put on **headphones** to listen to music.*
ακουστικά

2.42 **towards** (prep) /təˈwɔːdz/ = used to say that sb or sth moves, looks, faces, etc. in the direction of sb or sth. *A strange woman was coming **towards** me.*
προς

2.43 **beg** (v) /beg/ = to ask for sth in a way that shows you want or need it very much. *She **begged** me to stay.*
εκλιπαρώ, ικετεύω
◆ beg sb to do sth

2.44 **turn off** (phr v) /ˌtɜːn ˈɒf/ = to make a machine, light, etc. stop working, using its controls. *He **turned off** the computer and went to bed.*
διακόπτω (λειτουργία, παροχή, κλπ.), κλείνω
Opp: turn on

2.45 **promise** (v) /ˈprɒmɪs/ = to say that you will definitely do or give sth. *They **promised** to call us.* ➤ promise (n)
υπόσχομαι
◆ promise to do sth; promise sb (that)

2.46 **gradually** (adv) /ˈgrædʒuəli/ = slowly, over a long period of time. ***Gradually**, the sick child got better.* ➤ gradual (adj)
σταδιακά

2.47 **improvement** (n) /ɪmˈpruːvmənt/ = the act of making sth better, or the state of being better. *There was an **improvement** in their behaviour.* ➤ improve (v)
βελτίωση

2.48 **concentrate** (v) /ˈkɒnsəntreɪt/ = to think very carefully about sth you are doing. ***Concentrate** on your work.* ➤ concentration (n)
εστιάζω την προσοχή μου, συγκεντρώνομαι
◆ concentrate on

2.49 **move** (n) /muːv/ = when sb moves for a short time in a particular direction. *The dancers practised their **moves** many times before the performance.* ➤ move (v), movement (n)
κίνηση

2 Rule the school

2.50 essay (n) /ˈeseɪ/ = a short piece of writing about a particular subject. *I wrote an **essay** about Shakespeare.*
έκθεση (ιδεών)

2.51 though (adv) /ðəʊ/ = used after adding a fact, opinion or question which seems surprising after what you have just said, or which makes what you have just said seem less true. *It's a beautiful bag. It's expensive, **though**.*
παρά ταύτα, ωστόσο

2.52 grown-up (n) /ˈɡrəʊn ʌp/ = an adult. *Ask a **grown-up** to help you.*
ενήλικος
Syn: adult

2.53 revise (v) /rɪˈvaɪz/ = to prepare for a test by studying books and notes from your lessons. *She's **revising** for her History exam.* ➤ revision (n)
κάνω επανάληψη

2.54 pass (v) /pɑːs/ = to succeed in an examination or test. *Did you **pass** your exams?*
περνώ

2.55 however (adv) /haʊˈevə/ = used when you are adding a fact or piece of information that seems surprising or seems very different from what you have just said. *It's a beautiful bag. **However**, it's expensive.*
ωστόσο, όμως

2.56 educational (adj) /ˌedjʊˈkeɪʃənəl/ = teaching you sth. *Working in Africa was a very **educational** experience.* ➤ education (n), educate (v)
εκπαιδευτικός-ή-ό, μορφωτικός-ή-ό

2.57 unpopular (adj) /ʌnˈpɒpjʊlə/ = not liked by most people. *an **unpopular** teacher* ➤ unpopularity (n)
που δεν αρέσει στο κοινό, μη δημοφιλής-ές
Opp: popular

2.58 silly (adj) /ˈsɪli/ = stupid or not sensible. *a **silly** idea* ➤ silliness (n)
ανόητος-η-ο, χαζός-ή-ό

2.59 lazy (adj) /ˈleɪzi/ = sb who is lazy does not like working or doing things that need effort. *a **lazy** student who doesn't do any homework* ➤ laziness (n)
τεμπέλικος-η-ο

2.60 mixed (adj) /mɪkst/ = consisting of a lot of different types of things, people, ideas, etc. *Amy had **mixed** feelings about going to college.* ➤ mix (v), mixture (n)
ανάμικτος-η-ο

2.61 top mark (n phr) /ˌtɒp ˈmɑːk/ = the highest letter or number given by a teacher to show how good a student's work is. *He usually gets **top marks**.*
(ως βαθμολογία) άριστα

2.62 unexpected (adj) /ˌʌnɪkˈspektɪd/ = sth that is unexpected is surprising because you did not expect it to happen. *an **unexpected** visit from my cousins*
απρόοπτος-η-ο
Opp: expected

2.63 solve (v) /sɒlv/ = to find or provide a way of dealing with a problem. ***solve** a problem* ➤ solution (n)
λύνω

2.64 invent (v) /ɪnˈvent/ = to make or design a new type of thing. *Alexander Bell **invented** the telephone.* ➤ invention (n)
εφευρίσκω, επινοώ

Vocabulary: Page 20

2.65 regular (adj) /ˈreɡjələ/ = happening every hour, every week, every month, etc., usually with the same amount of time in between. ***Regular** exercise is good for you.*
τακτικός-ή-ό
Opp: irregular

2.66 stay behind (phr v) /ˌsteɪ bɪˈhaɪnd/ = to stay in a place after the other people have left. *I **stayed behind** after school.*
μένω πίσω

2.67 hall (n) /hɔːl/ = a building or large room for public events such as meetings or dances. *an assembly **hall***
αίθουσα

2.68 corridor (n) /ˈkɒrɪdɔː/ = a long narrow area between two rows of rooms. *Her office is at the end of the **corridor**.*
διάδρομος

2.69 orchestra (n) /ˈɔːkɪstrə/ = a large group of musicians who play different kinds of musical instruments together. *He plays the violin in the school **orchestra**.*
ορχήστρα

2.70 lab (n) /læb/ = a room or building in which people do scientific work. *the school science **lab***
εργαστήριο
Also: laboratory

2.71 staff (n) /stɑːf/ = the people who work for an organisation. *The members of **staff** had a meeting.*
(το) προσωπικό, επιτελείο

2.72 caretaker (n) /ˈkeəˌteɪkə/ = sb whose job is to look after a building, especially a school. *The **caretaker** lets us in when we are late.*
επιστάτης, θυρωρός κτιρίου

2.73 clear up (phr v) /ˌklɪər ˈʌp/ = to tidy or empty a place by removing things. ***Clear up** this mess!*
τακτοποιώ, συγυρίζω

2.74 messy (adj) /ˈmesi/ = dirty or untidy. *a **messy** room* ➤ mess (n)
ακατάστατος-η-ο

2.75 sensibly (adv) /ˈsensəbli/ = in a way that shows good judgement or good ideas. *If you don't behave **sensibly**, you will be punished.* ➤ sensible (adj), sense (n)
λογικά, συνετά

Rule the school 2

2.76 **educate** (v) /'edjʊkeɪt/ = to teach sb in a school or college. *He was **educated** at Westminster School.* ➤ education (n), educated (adj), educational (adj)
μορφώνω, εκπαιδεύω

2.77 **embarrassment** (n) /ɪmˈbærəsmənt/ = the feeling of being nervous or uncomfortable about what other people think of you. *Erica's face was red with **embarrassment**.* ➤ embarrass (v), embarrassing (adj), embarrassed (adj)
αμηχανία

2.78 **fair** (adj) /feə/ = reasonable, right and accepted by most people. *It's not **fair** to expect me to do all the work.*
δίκαιος-α-ο
Opp: unfair

2.79 **poor** (adj) /pɔː/ = not as good as it should be or could be. *The team's performance was **poor**.*
που υστερεί, αδύνατος-η-ο, κακός-ή-ό

2.80 **disappoint** (v) /ˌdɪsəˈpɔɪnt/ = to make sb feel unhappy because sth they hoped for did not happen or was not as good as they expected. *The result **disappointed** me.* ➤ disappointment (n), disappointed (adj), disappointing (adj)
απογοητεύω

2.81 **entrance** (n) /ˈentrəns/ = the right to go into a place or join an organisation, college, etc. ***Entrance** to the museum is free.* ➤ enter (v), entry (n)
είσοδος, εισαγωγή

Grammar: Page 21

2.82 **in progress** (prep phr) /ɪn ˈprəʊɡres/ = happening now. *The lesson is still **in progress**, so be quiet.*
σε εξέλιξη

2.83 **interrupt** (v) /ˌɪntəˈrʌpt/ = to make a process or activity stop temporarily. *She arrived late and **interrupted** the class.* ➤ interruption (n)
διακόπτω

2.84 **definition** (n) /ˌdefəˈnɪʃən/ = a phrase or sentence that says what a word means. *There is more than one **definition** of the word 'right'.* ➤ define (v)
(προσδι)ορισμός, καθορισμός έννοιας

2.85 **naughty** (adj) /ˈnɔːti/ = a naughty child behaves badly. *Barney has been **naughty** today.* ➤ naughtiness (n)
άτακτος-η-ο

2.86 **private** (adj) /ˈpraɪvət/ = for only one person or group to use. *a room with a **private** bath* ➤ privacy (n)
ιδιωτικός-ή-ό

2.87 **recently** (adv) /ˈriːsəntli/ = not long ago. *Have you seen Carolyn **recently**?* ➤ recent (adj)
πρόσφατα

2.88 **abolish** (v) /əˈbɒlɪʃ/ = to officially end a law, system, etc. *plans to **abolish** the death penalty*
καταργώ

2.89 **several** (determiner) /ˈsevərəl/ = more than a few, but not a lot. *I called her **several** times.*
μερικοί-ές-ά

2.90 **university** (n) /ˌjuːnɪˈvɜːsəti/ = an educational institution at the highest level, where you study for a degree. *go to **university***
πανεπιστήμιο

2.91 **report** (n) /rɪˈpɔːt/ = a written or spoken description of a situation or event. *The scientist wrote a **report**.* ➤ report (v)
έκθεση, αναφορά

2.92 **anxious** (adj) /ˈæŋkʃəs/ = worried about sth. *I'm **anxious** about my exams.* ➤ anxiety (n)
ανήσυχος-η-ο
◈ anxious about

2.93 **conclusion** (n) /kənˈkluːʒən/ = sth you decide after considering all the information you have. *Their **conclusion** is that she's lying.* ➤ conclude (v)
συμπέρασμα

Listening: Page 22

2.94 **wash up** (phr v) /ˌwɒʃ ˈʌp/ = to wash the plates, dishes, etc. after a meal. *Will you help me **wash up**?*
πλένω τα πιάτα, τα μαχαιροπίρουνα, κλπ.

2.95 **mention** (v) /ˈmenʃən/ = to talk or write about sth without giving many details. *He **mentioned** your name.*
αναφέρω

2.96 **specific** (adj) /spəˈsɪfɪk/ = detailed and exact. *She gave us **specific** instructions.*
συγκεκριμένος-η-ο

2.97 **intonation** (n) /ˌɪntəˈneɪʃən/ = the way in which the level of your voice changes as you speak. *speak with correct **intonation***
διακύμανση του τόνου εκφοράς, επιτονισμός

Speaking: Page 23

2.98 **according to** (prep) /əˈkɔːdɪŋ tə, tʊ/ = as shown by sth or said by sb. *I didn't do the exam but **according to** Martha, the questions were difficult.*
σύμφωνα με

2.99 **survey** (n) /ˈsɜːveɪ/ = a set of questions that you ask a large number of people in order to find out about their opinions or behaviour. *We did a **survey** of students at our school.*
επισκόπηση, περισκόπηση

2.100 **imaginative** (adj) /ɪˈmædʒənətɪv/ = having or showing imagination. *an **imaginative** writer* ➤ imagine (v), imagination (n), imaginary (adj)
που χαρακτηρίζεται από φαντασία, ευρηματικός-ή-ό
Opp: unimaginative

2 Rule the school

2.101 **be bothered** (v phr) /bi ˈbɒðəd/ = (in negative) used to say that sth is not important to you. *'What shall we eat?' 'I'm not bothered.'*
σκοτίζομαι

2.102 **miss** (v) /mɪs/ = to be too late for sth. *Hurry up or we'll miss the train!*
χάνω

2.103 **fall asleep** (v phr) /fɔːl əˈsliːp/ = to begin to sleep. *I fell asleep watching TV.*
αποκοιμιέμαι

2.104 **stress** (v) /stres/ = to say one word or part of a word more loudly than others. *stress a word* ➤ stress (n)
τονίζω

Use your English: Pages 24–25

2.105 **keep an eye on sb/sth** (phr) /kiːp ən ˈaɪ ɒn ˌsʌmbədi, ˌsʌmθɪŋ/ = to look after sb or sth to make sure they are safe. *Please keep an eye on the children while I'm out.*
παρακολουθώ, έχω το νου μου, φροντίζω

2.106 **pressure** (n) /ˈpreʃə/ = attempts to make sb do sth by threatening them or making them believe that they should do it. *Her family are putting pressure on her to stay at home.*
πίεση
◆ put pressure on sb

2.107 **separately** (adv) /ˈsepərətli/ = not joined or together. *They arrived at the party separately.*
➤ separate (adj, v)
χωριστά

2.108 **take off** (phr v) /ˌteɪk ˈɒf/ = to remove a piece of clothing. *She took off her shoes.*
βγάζω
Opp: put on

2.109 **remove** (v) /rɪˈmuːv/ = to take sth away from, out of or off the place where it is. *Remove your shoes from the table!*
βγάζω

2.110 **make for** (phr v) /meɪk fə, fɔː/ = to go towards a place. *He made for the door.*
(ξε)κινώ για, πηγαίνω προς

2.111 **keep on** (phr v) /ˌkiːp ˈɒn/ = to continue doing sth, or to do sth many times. *She kept on trying.*
συνεχίζω
◆ keep on doing sth

2.112 **put on** (phr v) /ˌpʊt ˈɒn/ = to put clothes on your body. *Put your coat on – it's cold.*
βάζω, φορώ
Opp: take off

2.113 **get dressed** (v phr) /ˌget ˈdrest/ = to put your clothes on. *Hurry up and get dressed for the party!*
ντύνομαι

2.114 **take up** (phr v) /ˌteɪk ˈʌp/ = to start doing a new job or activity. *I've taken up golf.*
αρχίζω (να ασχολούμαι με κάτι)

2.115 **take care of** (v phr) /teɪk ˈkeər əv, ɒv/ = to look after sb or sth. *Who's taking care of the baby?*
φροντίζω

2.116 **make sure** (v phr) /ˌmeɪk ˈʃɔː/ = to check that sth is true or that sth has been done. *Can you make sure the door's locked?*
διασφαλίζω, σιγουρεύω

2.117 **make up** (phr v) /ˌmeɪk ˈʌp/ = to invent a story or an excuse. *Rosa made up an excuse.*
επινοώ, εφευρίσκω

2.118 **keep up with** (phr v) /ˌkiːp ˈʌp wɪð, wɪθ/ = to do sth as well or as quickly as other people. *Dave can't keep up with the rest of the class.*
συμβαδίζω με, προφταίνω

2.119 **record** (n) /ˈrekɔːd/ = information that is written down or stored on computer so that it can be looked at in the future. *Keep a record of everything you spend.*
καταγραφή

2.120 **put up with** (phr v) /ˌpʊt ˈʌp wɪð, wɪθ/ = to accept a bad situation without complaining. *put up with the noise*
ανέχομαι

2.121 **put your heart into sth** (phr) /ˌpʊt jə ˈhɑːt ˌɪntə ˌsʌmθɪŋ/ = to do sth with enthusiasm. *She puts her heart into her work because she loves her job.*
κάνω κάτι με τη ψυχή μου

2.122 **graffiti** (n) /grəˈfiːti/ = writing and pictures that are drawn illegally on the walls of buildings, trains, etc. *Who painted the graffiti on these walls?*
γκράφιτι

2.123 **make** (v) /meɪk/ = to cause sth to happen. *My parents make me go to bed early.*
υποχρεώνω, εξαναγκάζω
◆ make sb do sth

2.124 **in case of** (prep phr) /ɪn ˈkeɪs əv/ = if or when sth happens. *In case of fire, leave the room quickly.*
κατά το ενδεχόμενο, σε περίπτωση

2.125 **emergency** (n) /ɪˈmɜːdʒənsi/ = a dangerous situation that happens suddenly and in which people might be hurt or killed. *Call a doctor! It's an emergency!*
έκτακτη ή επείγουσα ανάγκη

2.126 **indoor** (adj) /ˈɪndɔː/ = used or happening inside a building. *an indoor swimming pool* ➤ indoors (adv)
εσωτερικός-ή-ό, κλειστός-ή-ό
Opp: outdoor

Rule the school 2

2.127 outdoor (adj) /ˈaʊtdɔː/ = existing, happening or used outside, not inside a building. *I love **outdoor** sports.* ➤ outdoors (adv)
υπαίθριος-α-ο, εξωτερικός-ή-ό

2.128 rollerblading (n) /ˈrəʊləˌbleɪdɪŋ/ = skating while wearing boots with a single row of wheels fixed under them. *We went **rollerblading** in the park.*
πατινάζ με τροχοπέδιλα

2.129 uni-cycling (n) /ˈjuːniˌsaɪklɪŋ/ = riding a vehicle that is like a bicycle but has only one wheel. ***Uni-cycling** is more difficult than riding a bicycle.*
ποδηλασία με μονόκυκλο

2.130 appreciate (v) /əˈpriːʃieɪt/ = to understand how good or useful sb or sth is. *We **appreciated** his kindness and generosity.* ➤ appreciation (n)
εκτιμώ

2.131 meanwhile (adv) /ˈmiːnwaɪl/ = while sth else is happening, or in the time between two events. *Bill took the dogs out. **Meanwhile**, I fed the cats.*
στο μεταξύ

2.132 varied (adj) /ˈveərid/ = including many different types of things. *a **varied** diet* ➤ vary (v), variety (n), various (adj)
ποικίλος-η-ο

2.133 separate (adj) /ˈsepərət/ = not joined to or touching another thing. *The library isn't in this building. It's in a **separate** building.* ➤ separate (v)
χωριστός-ή-ό, ξεχωριστός-ή-ό

2.134 timetable (n) /ˈtaɪmˌteɪbəl/ = a list of times of classes in a school or college. *Have they given you your school **timetable** yet?*
πρόγραμμα σχολής

2.135 atmosphere (n) /ˈætməsfɪə/ = the feeling that a place, situation or event gives you. *a hotel with a pleasant **atmosphere***
περιβάλλον, ατμόσφαιρα

2.136 relaxed (adj) /rɪˈlækst/ = a situation or attitude that is relaxed is informal and not strict. *There's a **relaxed** atmosphere in this school.* ➤ relax (v), relaxation (n)
χαλαρός-ή-ό

2.137 choice (n) /tʃɔɪs/ = if you have a choice, you can choose between several things. *I can't make a **choice** – I like them all.* ➤ choose (v)
επιλογή

2.138 freedom (n) /ˈfriːdəm/ = the right to do what you want without being controlled. *The people fought for their **freedom**.* ➤ free (adj)
ελευθερία

2.139 refer to (phr v) /rɪˈfɜː tə, tʊ/ = to mention sb or sth. *He **referred to** her several times.*
αναφέρομαι σε

2.140 omit (v) /əʊˈmɪt, ə-/ = to not include sth; to leave out. *Important details were **omitted**.*
παραλείπω

2.141 old-fashioned (adj) /ˌəʊld ˈfæʃənd/ = not modern or not fashionable any more. *Her clothes look **old-fashioned**.*
παλιομοδίτικος-η-ο

2.142 Dutch (n) /dʌtʃ/ = the language that is spoken in the Netherlands. *He speaks **Dutch**.*
ολλανδική γλώσσα

2.143 look (n) /lʊk/ = the act of looking at sth. *Let me have a **look** at that – I think it's mine.* ➤ look (v)
ματιά
◆ have a look

2.144 last (v) /lɑːst/ = to continue for a particular length of time. *The hot weather **lasted** for two weeks.*
διαρκώ

2.145 league (n) /liːg/ = a group of sports teams or players who play games against each other. *They play in the football **league**.*
αθλητικοί όμιλοι μετέχοντες πρωταθλήματος

2.146 belong to (phr v) /bɪˈlɒŋ tə, tʊ/ = if sth belongs to you, you own it. *Does this umbrella **belong to** you?*
ανήκω

2.147 Chemistry (n) /ˈkemɪstri/ = the study of chemicals and what happens to them when they change or combine with each other. *Who is teaching us **Chemistry** this year?* ➤ chemical (n, adj)
Χημεία

2.148 Religion (n) /rɪˈlɪdʒən/ = a system of belief in one or more gods as taught in school. *I always get full marks in **Religion**.* ➤ religious (adj)
Θρησκευτικά

2.149 fail (v) /feɪl/ = if you fail a test, you do not pass it. *Brenda **failed** her Maths test.* ➤ failure (n)
αποτυγχάνω
Opp: pass

Writing: Pages 26–27

2.150 tummy (n) /ˈtʌmi/ = your stomach. *The child has a sore **tummy**, so he can't go to school.*
κοιλίτσα

2.151 rumble (v) /ˈrʌmbəl/ = if your stomach rumbles, it makes a noise because you are hungry. *My stomach is **rumbling**. Let's have something to eat.*
γουργουρίζω

2.152 function (n) /ˈfʌŋkʃən/ = the purpose that sth has. *In this job I perform a number of **functions**.* ➤ function (v)
σκοπός, λειτουργία

2 Rule the school

2.153 suitable (adj) /ˈsuːtəbəl, ˈsjuː-/ = having the right qualities for a particular person, purpose or situation. *We found a **suitable** place to live.* ➤ suit (v)
κατάλληλος-η-ο
Opp: unsuitable

2.154 fault (n) /fɔːlt/ = if sth bad that happens is your fault, you are responsible for it happening. *The accident was my **fault**.* ➤ faulty (adj)
φταίξιμο, σφάλμα

2.155 bump into (phr v) /bʌmp ˈɪntə, ˈɪntʊ/ = to meet sb when you were not expecting to. *Guess who I **bumped into** this morning!*
ανταμώνω κατά τύχη

2.156 drop (v) /drɒp/ = to let sth you are holding fall to the ground. *Tessa **dropped** her bag on the floor.*
μου πέφτει, ρίχνω

2.157 luckily (adv) /ˈlʌkəli/ = fortunately. ***Luckily**, I had my keys with me.* ➤ lucky (adj), luck (n)
ευτυχώς

2.158 shocking (adj) /ˈʃɒkɪŋ/ = very upsetting, wrong or immoral. ***shocking** behaviour* ➤ shock (v, n)
σκανδαλώδης-ες

2.159 PE (abbreviation) /ˌpiː ˈiː/ = sport and physical activity taught as a school subject. *I hated **PE** when I was at school.*
σωματική αγωγή
❖ PE = Physical Education

2.160 realise (v) /ˈrɪəlaɪz/ = to know and understand sth, or suddenly begin to understand it. *I closed the door and then **realised** that I didn't have my keys with me.*
συνειδητοποιώ, καταλαβαίνω

2.161 spare (adj) /speə/ = an extra key, tyre, etc. that you have so that it is available if it is needed. *Don't forget to take **spare** clothes with you.*
ανταλλακτικός-ή-ό, εφεδρικός-ή-ό, δεύτερος-η-ο

2.162 fall down (phr v) /ˌfɔːl ˈdaʊn/ = to drop down towards the ground. *The glass **fell down** and broke.*
πέφτω

2.163 pants (n pl) /pænts/ = a piece of underwear that covers the area between your waist and the top of your legs. *three pairs of **pants***
σώβρακο

2.164 show (v) /ʃəʊ/ = if sth shows, it is easy to see. *If you wear a pullover over your shirt, the dirty mark won't **show**.*
φαίνομαι

2.165 sign (n) /saɪn/ = a piece of wood, metal, plastic, etc. with words or pictures on it to give people information. *a 'No Smoking' **sign***
πινακίδα, ταμπέλα

2.166 loo (n) /luː/ = a toilet. *I need to go to the **loo**.*
αποχωρητήριο

2.167 rush (v) /rʌʃ/ = to move or go somewhere quickly. *It was late, so we **rushed** to the train station.* ➤ rush (n)
σπεύδω

2.168 lock (n) /lɒk/ = sth you use to fasten a door, drawer, etc. and that you usually open with a key. *I put my key in the **lock**.* ➤ lock (v)
κλειδαριά

2.169 stuck (adj) /stʌk/ = if sth is stuck, it cannot move. *I tried to open the window but it was **stuck**.* ➤ stick (v)
κολλημένος-η-ο

2.170 out of order (prep phr) /ˌaʊt əv ˈɔːdə/ = if a machine is out of order, it has stopped working. *The photocopier is **out of order** again.*
εκτός λειτουργίας

2.171 formal (adj) /ˈfɔːməl/ = suitable for official or serious occasions. *a **formal** party*
επίσημος-η-ο
Opp: informal

2.172 entry (n) /ˈentri/ = sth that you write, make, do, etc. in order to try and win a competition. *Her **entry** came second in the competition.*
συμμετοχή

2.173 past (prep) /pɑːst/ = up to and beyond a person or place, without stopping. *I saw them as they drove **past** in their new car.*
πέρα από

2.174 scruffy (adj) /ˈskrʌfi/ = dirty and untidy. *a **scruffy** pair of jeans*
ατημέλητος-η-ο και βρώμικος-η-ο

2.175 beard (n) /bɪəd/ = hair that grows around a man's chin and cheeks. *The old man had a long white **beard**.*
γενειάδα

2.176 burst out (phr v) /ˈbɜːst aʊt/ = to suddenly start to laugh, cry, etc. *They **burst out** laughing when they heard the joke.*
ξεσπώ
❖ burst out laughing/crying

2.177 nearly (adv) /ˈnɪəli/ = almost. *We've **nearly** finished.*
σχεδόν

2.178 in the end (prep phr) /ɪn ði ˈend/ = after a period of time or after everything has been done. *What did you decide **in the end**?*
τελικά

2.179 narrative (n) /ˈnærətɪv/ = the description of events in a story. *read an exciting **narrative***
αφήγηση

Rule the school 2

WORDZONE SPECIAL

Easily confused words: subject, lesson, course

subject
A subject is an area of knowledge that you study at a school or university.
My favourite **subjects** are History and Latin. My best friend is not good at these **subjects**. However, she's very good at Physics and Chemistry.

lesson
A lesson is a period of time in which school students are taught a particular subject.
Lessons start at nine and finish at two. I have a music **lesson** at four.

course
A course is a series of lessons in a particular subject.
The local college offers some interesting **courses** for adults in the evenings. Next year I want to do a **course** in Chinese.

Vocabulary and grammar practice

 Choose the correct verb to complete the sentences.

1 We *complained / discussed* to our neighbours about their noisy children.
2 Dave *rushed / rumbled* past me in a hurry without saying hello.
3 Lisa *revised / passed* all her university entrance exams with top marks.
4 'Stop *misbehaving / concentrating* or I'll send you outside!' the teacher said angrily.
5 There was a lot of traffic and I *failed / missed* my plane.
6 Greta was *educated / examined* at an expensive private school in England.
7 Thomas Edison *abolished / invented* the electric light bulb.
8 We are meeting tomorrow to *discuss / mention* our Science project.

 Complete the sentences with the correct form of these phrasal verbs.

burst out   deal with   keep up with   make for   make up   put on   put up with   take up

1 My sister .... laughing when she saw me covered in ketchup.
2 We need to find a way to .... the problem.
3 As soon as the film ended, the audience .... the exit.
4 I didn't know you had .... cooking as a hobby.
5 Some students are very good at .... excuses.
6 William .... his trainers and left for basketball practice.
7 'Your behaviour is unacceptable and I won't .... it!' said Jenny's mother.
8 Please slow down! We can't .... you!

2 Rule the school

 Complete the text with the correct form of the words in capitals.

A few months ago at school 1) .... , something very 2) .... happened. Mr Collins, our head teacher, was telling us about an 3) .... trip to a museum when I heard my mobile phone ringing. Unfortunately, my ring tone is a rock song! I went bright red with 4)	ASSEMBLE EMBARRASS EDUCATE EMBARRASS
'Who is that 5) .... student?' Mr Collins said angrily. As a 6) .... , he told me to stay behind after school. 7) .... , my French teacher Ms Stephens explained to Mr Collins that I never 8) .... in class and that the same thing had happened to her once! Of course, I apologised to Mr Collins and in the end, I didn't get a detention.	MATURE PUNISH LUCKY BEHAVED

 Past simple and past continuous
Complete the sentences with the correct form of the verbs in brackets. Use the past simple or past continuous.

1 While I .... (wash) my hair, the doorbell .... (ring).
2 What time .... (Timothy / leave) the house yesterday?
3 We .... (not go) out a lot when we were teenagers.
4 What .... (you / eat) when your tooth .... (break)?
5 Sally .... (clear up) the mess and then .... (take) a shower.
6 While I .... (study) for my History test, my mother .... (prepare) dinner.
7 Last summer they .... (spend) nearly every day at the beach.
8 He .... (fail) his Biology test last Tuesday.

 Relative clauses
Complete the sentences with the correct relative pronouns. Omit the relative pronoun if it is not necessary.

1 Mrs Feathers, ... is our new Science teacher, makes us study hard.
2 I am still looking for the notebook .... I lost yesterday.
3 Is that the boy .... you met at volleyball practice yesterday?
4 The school library, ... has lots of books, is a great place to study.
5 Most of us like our new football coach, ... is very young.
6 The subjects .... I passed with top marks are English and Geography.
7 The girl .... sits next to me in class is from England.
8 The city of York, ... has a good university, is in the north of England.
9 That's the girl .... father is my music teacher.
10 Luckily, I wasn't on the bus .... had the accident.

23

Rule the school 2

Test yourself!

Choose the word or phrase that best completes the conversation or sentence.

1 If I do the cooking, will you …… after dinner?
   A make up
   B slow down
   C wash up
   D deal with

2 The teacher said we could find all the …… for our History project on the Internet.
   A aims
   B details
   C signs
   D excuses

3 'Why …… me about the Biology test?'
   'Sorry, I forgot.'
   A weren't you telling
   B you not tell
   C didn't you tell
   D you not told

4 I think you should …… the problem with the head teacher.
   A discuss
   B revise
   C abolish
   D mention

5 That's the teacher …… organised the school trip.
   A who
   B which
   C what
   D she

6 While Lily was writing an email, her sister …… on the phone with a friend.
   A chatted
   B were chatting
   C would chat
   D was chatting

7 Sorry I interrupted you, Adam. Please …… .
   A carry on
   B keep on
   C put on
   D take off

8 Text-messaging, …… is so popular with teenagers, was unknown in the past.
   A that
   B who
   C what
   D which

9 'Katie, where are your school books?'
   'I'm afraid I …… them on the bus, sir.'
   A leave
   B left
   C was leaving
   D did leave

10 Harry dealt with the situation very …… .
   A recently
   B sensibly
   C immediately
   D separately

11 'Why do you look so scared?'
   'I was studying when somebody …… on the door.'
   A knocked
   B was knocking
   C knocking
   D was knocked

12 You were lucky you didn't get …… for the way you behaved in class!
   A top mark
   B report
   C punishment
   D detention

13 Jamie took a quick shower and …… to college.
   A was going
   B did go
   C went
   D would go

14 Do these break dancing DVDs …… to you?
   A refer
   B compare
   C belong
   D appreciate

Time to revise 1 | Units 1–2

1 **Complete the sentences with these nouns.**

ability   curriculum   grown-up   image   impression   secondary school   tears   twist

1 My brother is only fourteen but he looks like a(n) .... in my father's old clothes.
2 When I finish .... , I want to study modern languages at university.
3 We were surprised by the unexpected .... in the story.
4 She has an amazing .... to make people laugh.
5 I think more languages should be included in the school ....
6 The child was crying and .... were running down her face.
7 The young man made an excellent .... at the job interview.
8 The singer changed her .... and became a great success.

2 **Choose the correct word to complete the sentences.**

1 We looked for some *funky / fake* clothes to wear for the dance competition.
2 Why don't you ask the *adult / caretaker* if the lift is still out of order?
3 We could hear the little girls *giggling / blushing* in the room next door.
4 Oh, good! Here are the pizzas we ordered *at last / in the end* !
5 My sister prefers *outdoors / outdoor* sports. She likes being in the fresh air.
6 The *aim / skill* of this report is to find the best solution to our problem.
7 The boy was *terrified / terrifying* when he saw the huge spider.
8 I am doing some interesting *lessons / courses* at college this term.
9 When I saw the photograph, I stared at it *at / in* disbelief.
10 Why do I have to do all the hard work? It isn't *fair / poor* !

3 **Complete the second sentence so that it has a similar meaning to the first sentence, using the word given. Do not change the word given. You must use between two and five words, including the word given.**

1 Molly usually passes her tests at school.   **OFTEN**

   Molly .... fail her tests at school.

2 Please check if the children are in bed.   **SURE**

   Please .... that the children are in bed.

3 All my classmates participated in the competition.   **PART**

   All my classmates .... in the competition.

4 If you try your hardest, you will succeed.   **BEST**

   If you .... , you will succeed.

5 I refuse to tolerate such immature behaviour!   **UP**

   I won't .... such immature behaviour!

6 They were angry when they discovered the truth.   **OUT**

   They were angry when they .... the truth.

25

3 Room for improvement!

Reading: Pages 30–31

3.1 room for improvement (phr) /ˌruːm fər ɪmˈpruːvmənt/ = used to say that sth is not perfect and needs to be improved. *Your work is quite good but there's **room for improvement**.*
περιθώριο για βελτίωση

3.2 identity (n) /aɪˈdentəti/ = the qualities that sb has that make them different from other people. *Ewa lives in England but she has a strong sense of her Polish **identity**.* ➤ identification (n), identify (v)
ταυτότητα

3.3 matter (v) /ˈmætə/ = to be important. *It doesn't **matter** if you're late.*
έχω σημασία
◆ it doesn't matter

3.4 iPod (n) /ˈaɪpɒd/ = a small piece of electronic equipment for playing music, made by the Apple computer company. *Victor never leaves the house without his **iPod**.*

3.5 tune (n) /tjuːn/ = a series of musical notes that are nice to listen to. *She played a **tune** on the piano.*
μελωδία

3.6 What is … like? (phr) /wɒt ɪz … ˈlaɪk/ = used when asking sb to describe or give their opinion of a person or thing. ***What's** your new computer **like**?*
Πώς είναι ο/η/το … ;

3.7 gadget (n) /ˈgædʒɪt/ = a small tool or machine that helps you do sth. *a handy little **gadget** for opening bottles*
μικρό εργαλείο ή συσκευή

3.8 second-hand (adj) /ˌsekənd ˈhænd/ = sth that is second-hand is not new but has already been owned by sb else when you buy it. *We bought a cheap **second-hand** car.*
μεταχειρισμένος-η-ο, από δεύτερο χέρι

3.9 come round (phr v) /kʌm ˈraʊnd/ = to visit sb. *Paula is **coming round** to my house for coffee.*
επισκέπτομαι

3.10 average (adj) /ˈævərɪdʒ/ = having qualities that are typical of most people or things. *He's an **average** teenager, like most of his friends.* ➤ average (n)
μέσος-η-ο

3.11 console (n) /ˈkɒnsəʊl/ = a flat board that contains the controls for a machine, piece of electrical equipment, computer, etc. *a games **console** that connects to a computer*
κονσόλα

3.12 waste (v) /weɪst/ = to use sth in a way that is not sensible or useful, or use more of it than you should. *They **wasted** a lot of time trying to fix it themselves.* ➤ waste (n)
χαραμίζω, χάνω

3.13 end up (phr v) /ˌend ˈʌp/ = to finally be in a particular place, situation or state without intending to. *I didn't like him at first but we **ended up** being friends.*
καταλήγω
◆ end up doing sth

3.14 scary (adj) /ˈskeəri/ = frightening. *a **scary** film* ➤ scare (v, n), scared (adj)
τρομακτικός-ή-ό

3.15 whole (adj) /həʊl/ = all of sth. *We spent the **whole** day at the beach.*
ολόκληρος-η-ο, όλος-η-ο

3.16 get a life (phr) /ˌget ə ˈlaɪf/ = used to tell sb that they are boring and should find more exciting things to do. *Stop complaining and **get a life**!*
βρίσκω ενδιαφέροντα

3.17 soft toy (n phr) /ˌsɒft ˈtɔɪ/ = a toy for young children that is made of cloth and filled with soft material. *There were lots of **soft toys** on her bed.*
(παιχνίδι) χνουδωτό ζωάκι

3.18 wardrobe (n) /ˈwɔːdrəʊb/ = a piece of furniture like a large cupboard that you hang clothes in. *Hang your clothes in the **wardrobe**.*
ντουλάπα (για ρούχα)

3.19 sort out (phr v) /ˌsɔːt ˈaʊt/ = to organise sth that is untidy or in the wrong order. *I must **sort out** my papers.*
τακτοποιώ

3.20 nag (v) /næg/ = to keep asking sb to do sth in an annoying way. *She keeps **nagging** me to fix the lamp.*
γκρινιάζω συνεχώς, μουρμουρίζω

3.21 throw out (phr v) /ˌθrəʊ ˈaʊt/ = to get rid of sth. *The milk was bad and I **threw** it **out**.*
πετώ

3.22 gross (adj) /grəʊs/ = very unpleasant to look at or think about. *His jokes are really **gross**.*
απδιαστικός-ή-ό

3.23 stand (v) /stænd/ = to be able to accept or deal with sth unpleasant or difficult. *She couldn't **stand** the pain any longer.*
αντέχω
◆ can't stand sth/doing sth

3 Room for improvement!

3.24 no wonder (phr) /nəʊ ˈwʌndə/ = used to say that sth does not surprise you. *He ate a whole box of chocolates.* **No wonder** *he feels sick!*
δεν είναι απορίας άξιον το ότι, πολύ φυσικό να

3.25 pocket money (n phr) /ˈpɒkɪt ˌmʌni/ = a small amount of money that parents give regularly to their children, usually every week or month. *How much* **pocket money** *do you get?*
χαρτζιλίκι

3.26 cushion (n) /ˈkʊʃən/ = a bag filled with soft material that you put on a chair or the floor to make it more comfortable. *She put some* **cushions** *on the sofa.*
μαξιλάρι (καθίσματος)

3.27 chill out (phr v) /tʃɪl ˈaʊt/ = to relax and rest, especially after going to a party, club, etc. *My friends and I like to* **chill out** *at home on Sunday afternoons.*
χαλαρώνω

3.28 cheque (n) /tʃek/ = a printed piece of paper that you sign and use to pay for things. *Can I pay by* **cheque**?
επιταγή
◆ pay for sth by cheque

3.29 reward (n) /rɪˈwɔːd/ = sth, especially money, that is given to sb to thank them for doing sth. *She offered a £50* **reward** *for news about her lost cat.* ➤ reward (v)
αμοιβή

3.30 take up (phr v) /teɪk ˈʌp/ = to accept an offer, suggestion or idea. *Rick* **took up** *the challenge and cycled 250 miles alone.*
αποδέχομαι
◆ take up a challenge

3.31 earn (v) /ɜːn/ = to receive money for work that you do. *She* **earns** *£47,000 a year.*
κερδίζω, βγάζω (χρήματα)

3.32 work out (phr v) /wɜːk ˈaʊt/ = to think about sth and manage to understand it. *The puzzle is complicated – it will take you hours to* **work** *it* **out**.
κατανοώ, λύνω

3.33 similar (adj) /ˈsɪmələ/ = almost the same. *They are sisters and they look* **similar**. ➤ similarity (n)
παρόμοιος-α-ο
◆ similar to

3.34 typical (adj) /ˈtɪpɪkəl/ = having the usual features or qualities of a particular group or thing. *On a* **typical** *weekday I wake up at six.*
χαρακτηριστικός-ή-ό

3.35 nasty (adj) /ˈnɑːsti/ = unpleasant or unkind. *That was a* **nasty** *thing to say!*
κακός-ή-ό, που έχει κακία

3.36 task (n) /tɑːsk/ = a piece of work that must be done, especially one that is difficult or unpleasant or that must be done regularly. *do a difficult* **task**
δουλειά

3.37 advice (n) /ədˈvaɪs/ = the things you say to sb when you tell them what you think they should do. *Beth asked her doctor for* **advice** *about her health.* ➤ advise (v)
συμβουλή

3.38 advise (v) /ədˈvaɪz/ = to tell sb what you think they should do. *The doctor* **advised** *me to take more exercise.*
συμβουλεύω
◆ advise sb to do sth

Vocabulary: Page 32

3.39 save up (phr v) /seɪv ˈʌp/ = to keep sth instead of spending it so that you can use or enjoy it in the future. *George is* **saving up** *to buy an iPod.*
εξοικονομώ, αποταμιεύω

3.40 item (n) /ˈaɪtəm/ = a single thing, especially one thing in a list, group or set of things. *They took out every* **item** *in the cupboard.*
αντικείμενο, επί μέρους στοιχείο περιεχομένων

3.41 print (v) /prɪnt/ = to produce words or pictures on paper using a machine. *I'm* **printing** *the document now.*
➤ printer (n)
τυπώνω (με στοιχειοθεσία και μελάνι)

3.42 sign (v) /saɪn/ = to write your name on sth to show that you wrote it, agree with it or were present. *She* **signed** *the letter.* ➤ signature (n)
υπογράφω

3.43 cash (n) /kæʃ/ = money in the form of coins and notes. *I need some* **cash** *to buy her a present.*
(χρήμα σε) μετρητά
◆ pay for sth in cash

3.44 change (n) /tʃeɪndʒ/ = the money you get back when you pay more than sth costs. *Here's your* **change**, *sir.*
(επιστρεφόμενα) ρέστα

3.45 credit card (n phr) /ˈkredɪt kɑːd/ = a small plastic card that you use to buy goods or services and pay for them later. *Let's pay in cash, not with a* **credit card**.
πιστωτική κάρτα

3.46 afford (v) /əˈfɔːd/ = to have enough money to pay for sth. *I wish we could* **afford** *a new computer.*
➤ affordable (adj)
έχω τη δυνατότητα να αγοράσω, διαθέτω χρήματα για
◆ can/can't afford sth; can/can't afford to do sth

3.47 lend (v) /lend/ = to let sb borrow money or sth that belongs to you. *Could you* **lend** *me ten euros?*
δανείζω

3.48 owe (v) /əʊ/ = to have to pay sb because they have let you borrow money from them. *Bob* **owes** *me twenty euros.*
οφείλω, χρωστώ

Room for improvement! 3

3.49 terror (n) /ˈterə/ = a feeling of extreme fear. *She screamed in terror.* ➤ terrible (adj), terrify (v), terrified (adj), terrifying (adj)
τρόμος

3.50 fame (n) /feɪm/ = when a lot of people know about you because of what you have achieved. *He won fame as a singer.* ➤ famous (adj)
φήμη

3.51 harm (n) /hɑːm/ = damage, hurt or injury. *We must protect our children from harm.* ➤ harm (v), harmful (adj), harmless (adj)
βλάβη, κακό, ζημιά

3.52 notice (v) /ˈnəʊtɪs/ = to see, feel or hear sb or sth. *I said 'hello' but she didn't notice.* ➤ notice (n), noticeable (adj)
δίνω προσοχή, προσέχω

3.53 scare (v) /skeə/ = to make sb feel frightened. *The fireworks will scare the animals.*
φοβίζω, τρομάζω

3.54 sense (n) /sens/ = good understanding and judgement, especially about practical things. *I hope they have enough sense to come home early tonight!* ➤ sensible (adj)
λογική, σύνεση

3.55 scratch (v) /skrætʃ/ = to make a long thin cut on sb's skin with your nails, or a mark on sth with a sharp object. *The cat scratched my hand.* ➤ scratch (n)
προξενώ αμυχή, χαρακιά, νυχιά ή ξυσιά

3.56 mark (n) /mɑːk/ = a small area of dirt or damage on sth. *Her shoes left dirty marks on the carpet.* ➤ mark (v)
σημάδι

3.57 cross (adj) /krɒs/ = annoyed. *Are you cross with me for losing your book?*
φουρκισμένος-η-ο

Grammar: Page 33

3.58 prediction (n) /prɪˈdɪkʃən/ = when you say what you think will happen in the future. *It's hard to make a prediction about who'll win the championship.* ➤ predict (v)
πρόβλεψη
◆ make a prediction

3.59 unplanned (adj) /ˌʌnˈplænd/ = not planned or expected. *an unplanned trip*
απρογραμμάτιστος-η-ο
Opp: planned

3.60 base on (phr v) /ˈbeɪs ɒn/ = to use sth as the thing you develop sth else from. *The film is based on a true story.*
βασίζω, στηρίζω

3.61 intention (n) /ɪnˈtenʃən/ = sth you plan to do. *I have no intention of getting married.* ➤ intentional (adj), intend (v)
πρόθεση

3.62 fixed (adj) /fɪkst/ = fixed times, amounts, meanings, etc. cannot be changed. *Classes begin and end at fixed times.* ➤ fix (v)
προκαθορισμένος-η-ο

3.63 arrangement (n) /əˈreɪndʒmənt/ = plans and preparations that you must make so that sth can happen in the future. *Have you made all the arrangements for the party?* ➤ arrange (v)
σχέδιο

3.64 suggestion (n) /səˈdʒestʃən/ = an idea, plan or possibility that sb suggests. *Can I make a suggestion?* ➤ suggest (v)
πρόταση
◆ make a suggestion

3.65 give sb a hand (phr) /ˌɡɪv sʌmbədi ə ˈhænd/ = to help sb with sth. *This box is heavy and I can't lift it. Can you give me a hand?*
βοηθώ κάποιον-α, δίνω ένα χέρι βοήθειας

3.66 honestly (adv) /ˈɒnəstli/ = used to try to make sb believe that what you have just said is true. *I'll bring you the DVD tomorrow, honestly!* ➤ honest (adj), honesty (n)
ειλικρινά

3.67 vacuum clean (v phr) /ˌvækjʊm ˈkliːn/ = to clean the floor with a vacuum cleaner. *I need to vacuum clean the carpet.* ➤ vacuum cleaner (n phr)
καθαρίζω με ηλεκτρική σκούπα
Also: vacuum

3.68 part-time (adj) /ˌpɑːt ˈtaɪm/ = sb who has a part-time job works for only part of each day or week. *I have a part-time job.*
μερικής απασχόλησης
Opp: full-time

3.69 equip (v) /ɪˈkwɪp/ = to provide sb with the tools or equipment they need. *They equipped themselves with the right tools before starting the job.* ➤ equipment (n)
εξοπλίζω

3.70 fully (adv) /ˈfʊli/ = completely. *I fully understand the problem.* ➤ full (adj)
πλήρως

3.71 function (v) /ˈfʌŋkʃən/ = to work in the correct or intended way. *Scientists are learning how our brains function.* ➤ function (n)
λειτουργώ

3.72 discotheque (n) /ˈdɪskətek/ = a place or social event at which people dance to recorded popular music. *Let's go dancing at the discotheque tonight.*
ντίσκο
Also: disco

3 Room for improvement!

3.73 **smoke** (n) /sməʊk/ = white, grey or black gas that is produced by sth burning. *We could see the **smoke** from the fire.* ➤ smoke (v)
καπνός

3.74 **make it** (phr) /meɪk ɪt/ = to be successful at sth, for example in your job. *If you work hard, you'll **make it**.*
πετυχαίνω, τα καταφέρνω

3.75 **fire brigade** (n phr) /faɪə brɪˌɡeɪd/ = the organisation that works to prevent fires and stop them from burning. *They saw the fire and called the **fire brigade**.*
πυροσβεστική υπηρεσία

3.76 **intend** (v) /ɪnˈtend/ = to have sth in your mind as a plan or purpose. *What do you **intend** to do about the problem?*
προτίθεμαι, σκοπεύω
◆ intend to do sth; intend doing sth

Listening: Page 34

3.77 **offer** (n) /ˈɒfə/ = when sth is sold at a lower price than usual. *Don't miss our special **offer** – two DVDs for the price of one.*
προσφορά
◆ special offer

3.78 **half price** (n phr) /ˌhɑːf ˈpraɪs/ = half the usual price. *The shoes in this shop are **half price**.*
μισή τιμή

3.79 **sale** (n) /seɪl/ = a time when a shop sells its goods at lower prices than usual. *There's a great **sale** on at the shop this week.* ➤ sell (v)
εκπτώσεις

3.80 **discount** (n) /ˈdɪskaʊnt/ = a reduction in the usual price of sth. *If you pay in cash, you will get a **discount**.*
έκπτωση

3.81 **bargain** (n) /ˈbɑːɡən/ = sth you buy cheaply or for less than its usual price. *The table was a real **bargain** – sixty percent off.*
ευκαιρία, κελεπούρι

3.82 **off** (adv) /ɒf/ = used to say that a price is reduced by a particular amount. *We'll sell the equipment for eighty euros. That's twenty percent **off** the usual price of a hundred euros.*
μείον

3.83 **refuse** (v) /rɪˈfjuːz/ = to say firmly that you will not do or accept sth. *I **refuse** to tell you anything.* ➤ refusal (n)
αρνούμαι
◆ refuse to do sth

3.84 **persuade** (v) /pəˈsweɪd/ = to make sb decide to do sth by telling them why it is a good idea. *John tried to **persuade** me to stay.* ➤ persuasion (n)
πείθω
◆ persuade sb to do sth

3.85 **possession** (n) /pəˈzeʃən/ = sth that you own. *His car is his favourite **possession**.* ➤ possess (v)
απόκτημα, περιουσιακό στοιχείο

3.86 **raise money** (phr) /reɪz ˈmʌni/ = to get people to give money that will be used to help other people or to do a particular job. *The event will **raise money** for charity.*
συγκεντρώνω χρήματα

Speaking: Page 35

3.87 **change** (n) /tʃeɪndʒ/ = a situation or experience that is different from what happened before, and is usually interesting or enjoyable. *Let's go out tonight for a **change**.*
αλλαγή
◆ for a change

3.88 **respond** (v) /rɪˈspɒnd/ = to answer. *How did she **respond** to your questions?* ➤ response (n)
απαντώ, αποκρίνομαι
◆ respond to

3.89 **would rather** (phr) /wʊd ˈrɑːðə/ = if you would rather do or have sth, you would prefer to do or have it. *I hate doing nothing. I'**d rather** work.*
θα προτιμούσα
◆ would rather do sth

3.90 **stuff** (n) /stʌf/ = several different things, used when you want to talk about them in general. *Where shall we put all this **stuff**?*
αντικείμενα, πράγματα

3.91 **rack** (n) /ræk/ = a frame or shelf with bars where you can put or keep things. *a luggage **rack***
σχάρα, θήκη ή ράφι με στοιχεία στήριξης ή ανάρτησης

Use your English: Pages 36–37

3.92 **inexpensive** (adj) /ˌɪnɪkˈspensɪv/ = cheap but good. *an **inexpensive** holiday*
φθηνός-ή-ό, ολιγοδάπανος-η-ο
Opp: expensive

3.93 **dependent** (adj) /dɪˈpendənt/ = needing sb or sth in order to exist, be successful, healthy, etc. *The economy is **dependent** on tourism.* ➤ dependence (n), depend (v)
εξαρτημένος-η-ο, εξαρτώμενος-η-ο
◆ dependent on. Opp: independent

3.94 **visible** (adj) /ˈvɪzəbəl/ = sth that is visible can be seen or noticed. *The lights of the city were **visible** in the distance.* ➤ visibility (n), vision (n)
ορατός-ή-ό
Opp: invisible

Room for improvement! 3

3.95 **fit** (adj) /fɪt/ = healthy and strong, especially because you exercise regularly. *Jogging helps me keep **fit**.*
➤ fitness (n)
σε φόρμα
Opp: unfit

3.96 **mature** (adj) /məˈtʃʊə/ = behaving in a reasonable way like an adult. *Barney is very **mature** for his age.*
➤ maturity (n)
ώριμος-η-ο
Opp: immature

3.97 **practical** (adj) /ˈpræktɪkəl/ = useful and suitable for a particular purpose. *She is **practical** and sensible.*
πρακτικός-ή-ό
Opp: impractical

3.98 **unable** (adj) /ʌnˈeɪbəl/ = not able to do sth. *She was **unable** to sleep, so she watched TV instead.*
ανίκανος-η-ο, ανήμπορος-η-ο
◆ unable to do sth. Opp: able

3.99 **acceptable** (adj) /əkˈseptəbəl/ = if a kind of behaviour is acceptable, people approve of it and think that it should be allowed. *Behaviour like that is not **acceptable**!* ➤ accept (v)
αποδεκτός-ή-ό, παραδεκτός-ή-ό
Opp: unacceptable

3.100 **appropriate** (adj) /əˈprəʊpriət/ = suitable for a particular time, situation or purpose. *Take **appropriate** clothes with you.*
κατάλληλος-η-ο
Opp: inappropriate

3.101 **reliable** (adj) /rɪˈlaɪəbəl/ = if sb or sth is reliable, you can trust and depend on them. *Vanessa is hard-working and **reliable**.* ➤ rely (v)
αξιόπιστος-η-ο
Opp: unreliable

3.102 **patient** (adj) /ˈpeɪʃənt/ = able to stay calm and not become angry when you are waiting for sth or doing sth difficult. *Be **patient** and wait.* ➤ patience (n)
υπομονετικός-ή-ό
Opp: impatient

3.103 **laziness** (n) /ˈleɪzinəs/ = the quality of not liking work and physical activity, or not making any effort to do anything. *I didn't do any work today. It wasn't **laziness** – I was ill.* ➤ lazy (adj)
τεμπελιά

3.104 **hormone** (n) /ˈhɔːməʊn/ = a chemical substance that your body produces naturally, which makes it develop in a particular way. *Growth **hormones** make animals grow.*
ορμόνη

3.105 **difference** (n) /ˈdɪfərəns/ = a way in which two or more people or things are not like each other. *a **difference** in price* ➤ different (adj), differ (v)
διαφορά

3.106 **cause** (n) /kɔːz/ = a person, event or thing that makes sth happen. *Careless driving is a common **cause** of accidents.* ➤ cause (v)
αιτία

3.107 **suffer** (v) /ˈsʌfə/ = to experience physical or emotional pain. *David **suffers** from terrible headaches.*
➤ suffering (n)
υποφέρω
◆ suffer from

3.108 **lack** (n) /læk/ = when there is not enough of sth or none of it. *a **lack** of time*
έλλειψη

3.109 **moody** (adj) /ˈmuːdi/ = annoyed or unhappy. *You look **moody**. What's wrong?* ➤ mood (n)
κακόκεφος-η-ο

3.110 **delay** (v) /dɪˈleɪ/ = to wait until a later time to do sth. *I'm sorry I'm late. I was **delayed** by the traffic.*
➤ delay (n)
καθυστερώ

3.111 **certainty** (n) /ˈsɜːtnti/ = when you are completely sure about sth. *She knew with **certainty** that he was lying.*
➤ certain (adj)
βεβαιότητα, σιγουριά

3.112 **probability** (n) /ˌprɒbəˈbɪləti/ = how likely it is that sth will happen. *What's the **probability** of an accident happening?* ➤ probable (adj)
πιθανότητα

3.113 **possibility** (n) /ˌpɒsəˈbɪləti/ = sth that may happen or may be true. *the **possibility** of winning a prize*
➤ possible (adj)
δυνατότητα

3.114 **definitely** (adv) /ˈdefənətli/ = without any doubt; certainly. *I'm tired. I **definitely** need a holiday!*
➤ definite (adj)
οπωσδήποτε

3.115 **in time** (prep phr) /ɪn ˈtaɪm/ = early enough, before sth happens. *Bob wants to get home **in time** to watch the match.*
εγκαίρως

3.116 **switch off** (phr v) /swɪtʃ ˈɒf/ = to turn off a machine, light, etc. using a switch. *I **switched off** my mobile phone.*
σβήνω, διακόπτω τη λειτουργία

3.117 **madness** (n) /ˈmædnəs/ = very stupid and often dangerous behaviour. *It would be **madness** to go sailing in this bad weather.* ➤ mad (adj)
παραφροσύνη, τρέλα

3.118 **beep** (v) /biːp/ = if a machine beeps, it makes a short high sound. *The machine started **beeping**.* ➤ beep (n)
ηχώ

30

3 Room for improvement!

3.119 research (n) /rɪˈsɜːtʃ/ = serious and detailed study of a subject in order to find out new information. *the latest scientific **research*** ➤ research (v), researcher (n)
(επιστημονική) έρευνα

3.120 affect (v) /əˈfekt/ = to cause a change in sb or sth, or to change the situation they are in. *I hope this new job will not **affect** your schoolwork.*
επηρεάζω

3.121 pattern (n) /ˈpætən/ = the regular way in which sth happens. *Weather **patterns** have changed recently.*
μόρφωμα, διαμόρφωση, σχήμα

3.122 catch up (phr v) /kætʃ ˈʌp/ = to do what needs to be done because you have not been able to do it until now. *I must **catch up** on some work this weekend.*
καλύπτω την καθυστέρηση/διαφορά από
◆ catch up on

3.123 major (adj) /ˈmeɪdʒə/ = very large or important. *Traffic is a **major** problem in this city.*
μείζων
Opp: minor

3.124 impact (n) /ˈɪmpækt/ = the effect or influence that sth or sb has. *He had a big **impact** on my life.*
αντίκτυπος, επίπτωση
◆ have an impact on

3.125 quality (n) /ˈkwɒləti/ = how good or bad sth is. *The **quality** of the water is poor.*
ποιότητα

3.126 solution (n) /səˈluːʃən/ = a way of solving a problem or dealing with a difficult situation. *There's a problem and we have to find a **solution**.* ➤ solve (v)
λύση

3.127 fact (n) /fækt/ = sth that is true. *It's a well-known **fact** that they're very rich.*
δεδομένο, γεγονός

3.128 vote (n) /vəʊt/ = when sb shows that they support a particular person, party, plan, etc. by making a mark on a piece of paper, raising their hands, etc. *Let's take a **vote**.* ➤ vote (v)
ψήφος
◆ take a vote

Writing: Pages 38–39

3.129 makeover (n) /ˈmeɪkəʊvə/ = when you change the way a building, room, etc. looks. *Let's give this room a **makeover**.*
μεταμόρφωση

3.130 underline (v) /ˌʌndəˈlaɪn/ = to draw a line under a word to show that it is important. ***Underline** the important information.*
υπογραμμίζω

3.131 clutter (n) /ˈklʌtə/ = things that fill a space in an untidy way. *I hate **clutter** – let's put these toys away.* ➤ clutter (v)
περιττά ή ανεπιθύμητα αντικείμενα σωριασμένα φύρδην-μίγδην

3.132 producer (n) /prəˈdjuːsə/ = sb whose job is to control the preparation of a play, film or broadcast but who does not direct the actors. *She's a film **producer**.* ➤ produce (v), production (n)
παραγωγός

3.133 application (n) /ˌæplɪˈkeɪʃən/ = a formal request, usually in writing, for sth such as a job, a university place or permission to do sth. *I completed an **application** for the job.* ➤ apply (v)
αίτηση

3.134 form (n) /fɔːm/ = an official document with spaces where you give information. *Fill in the application **form** using a pen.*
έντυπο, φόρμα
◆ application form

3.135 assistant (n) /əˈsɪstənt/ = sb whose job is to help sb more important. *My **assistant** will write the email for me.* ➤ assist (v)
βοηθός

3.136 de-clutter (v) /diː ˈklʌtə/ = to get rid of things that fill a space in an untidy way. *First, we'll **de-clutter** the office and throw out what we don't need.*
πετώ ότι είναι περιττό

3.137 available (adj) /əˈveɪləbəl/ = if sth is available, you can have it, buy it or use it. *Tickets are **available** from the box office.* ➤ availability (n)
διαθέσιμος-η-ο
Opp: unavailable

3.138 convenient (adj) /kənˈviːniənt/ = a convenient time is good for you because you are not doing anything else then. *Is ten o'clock a **convenient** time to meet?* ➤ convenience (n)
βολικός-ή-ό
Opp: inconvenient

3.139 contact (v) /ˈkɒntækt/ = to write to or telephone sb. *How can we **contact** you? By phone or email?* ➤ contact (n)
έρχομαι σε επαφή, επικοινωνώ

3.140 look forward to (phr v) /lʊk ˈfɔːwəd tə, tʊ/ = to be excited and happy about sth that is going to happen. *I'm **looking forward to** going to Japan.*
προσβλέπω σε, ευελπιστώ σε
◆ look forward to sth/doing sth

3.141 postage (n) /ˈpəʊstɪdʒ/ = the money charged for sending a letter or package by post. *How much is the **postage** for a letter?* ➤ post (v, n)
ταχυδρομικά τέλη

Room for improvement! 3

3.142 polite (adj) /pəˈlaɪt/ = speaking or behaving in a way that shows respect for other people. *A **polite** young man opened the door for me.* ➤ politeness (n)
ευγενικός-ή-ό
Opp: impolite, rude

3.143 conference (n) /ˈkɒnfərəns/ = a large formal meeting in which people discuss important things. *There were about a hundred scientists at the **conference**.*
συνέδριο

3.144 timetable (n) /ˈtaɪmˌteɪbəl/ = a list of the times of buses, trains, etc. *the train **timetable***
πίνακας δρομολογίων

3.145 depart (v) /dɪˈpɑːt/ = to leave. *The train will **depart** from Platform 4.* ➤ departure (n)
αναχωρώ
❖ depart from

3.146 fare (n) /feə/ = the amount you pay to travel by train, plane, bus, etc. *How much is the bus **fare** into town?*
επιβατικός ναύλος
❖ return fare = the amount you pay to travel by train, plane, bus, etc. to a place and back again

3.147 per (prep) /pə, pɜː/ = for each. *The hotel room costs 100 euros **per** night.*
για κάθε, ανά

3.148 option (n) /ˈɒpʃən/ = sth that you can choose to do. *There are two **options**: we can go to the beach or stay at home.*
εναλλακτική δυνατότητα, επιλογή

3.149 reply (n) /rɪˈplaɪ/ = sth that is said, written or done as a way of answering. *What was Stephen's **reply** to your question?* ➤ reply (v)
απάντηση, απόκριση

3.150 semi (prefix) /ˈsemi/ = partly but not completely. *a **semi**-formal letter*
ημι-, μισο-

WORDZONE SPECIAL

Easily confused words: cheque, check

cheque
A cheque is a printed piece of paper that you sign and use to pay for things. *They gave me a **cheque** for £250.*

check
In British English, a check is an examination to find out if sth is correct, true or safe. *Let's do a **check** and see if everything is all right.*

Note: cheque (British English) = check (American English)

Vocabulary and grammar practice

 Complete the sentences with these adjectives.

average   fit   gross   inexpensive   possible   reliable   similar   visible

1 Will it be .... to tidy up the mess before Mum comes home?
2 Max exercises regularly and is very ....
3 The .... adult doesn't usually like that kind of music.
4 Sonia is very .... You can depend on her.
5 My mother bought some pretty but .... floor cushions for our flat.
6 The two brothers are very .... They look almost like twins!
7 What is that horrible stuff all over the floor? It looks .... !
8 The moon is sometimes .... in the sky during the day.

3 Room for improvement!

2 Complete the puzzle with words related to money.

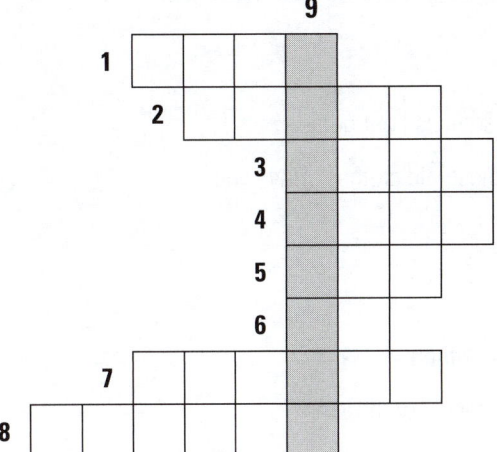

1 Please can you …… me your dictionary?
2 This chair was a bargain. I bought it half …….
3 The …… starts on Monday and there will be lots of bargains.
4 How do you want to pay? In …… or by credit card?
5 I borrowed some money from my friend and now I …… her about sixty euros.
6 I can't afford a new computer at the moment. I must save …… first.
7 I gave the shop assistant ten euros and he gave me two euros …….
8 How much …… money do your parents give you every week?
9 The shop offered us a twenty percent …….

3 Choose the correct word to complete the sentences.

1 Look at all these papers on your desk! Let's *clutter / de-clutter* the place so you can work better.
2 The iPod in the shop was fantastic but I can't *earn / afford* it.
3 'What time is the train leaving?' 'I don't know. Let's look at the *timetable / calendar*.'
4 Why are you looking so *convenient / cross*? Did I say anything wrong?
5 Marian gave me some excellent *advice / advise* on how to find the best bargains.
6 You shouldn't *raise / waste* money on silly things like that.
7 The experience had a huge *impact / mark* on the children.
8 Liam likes looking for interesting little *patterns / gadgets* in the sales.

4 Complete the sentences with the correct form of the words in capitals.

1 How much is the ………………………… for a small package to London?   **POST**
2 This beautiful painting is my favourite ………………………… .   **POSSESS**
3 What's the ………………………… between house music and hip hop?   **DIFFER**
4 It would be ………………………… to go out in this terrible weather.   **MAD**
5 Teenagers can be very ………………………… sometimes.   **MOOD**
6 I'd like to be a film ………………………… when I grow up.   **PRODUCE**
7 My Aunt Jo's ………………………… about the weather are always right!   **PREDICT**
8 We stayed in last night and watched a ………………………… movie on TV.   **SCARE**

33

Room for improvement! 3

 5 **The future**
Complete the dialogues with the correct form of the verbs in brackets. Use *will*, *shall*, *going to* or the present continuous.

1. **A:** Have a good trip and drive safely.
   B: Thanks. I .... (call) you as soon as I get home.

2. **A:** What .... (you / do) with those old clothes? Have you decided?
   B: I think I .... (give) them away.

3. **A:** That lamp is lovely!
   B: Do you think so? I .... (buy) it then.

4. **A:** What time .... (you / play) tennis with Helen?
   B: At three.

5. **A:** Watch out! You .... (trip) over these boxes.
   B: I'd better move them before I break my neck.

6. **A:** I love this chair but I can't afford it.
   B: .... (I / lend) you some money? You can pay me back later.

 6 **Modal verbs**
Choose the correct words to complete the letter.

Dear Olivia,

I need your help. It's about my friend Sally. She used to be a sensible girl but recently her behaviour has changed and I think something **1)** *must / should* be wrong. She won't speak to me about it, so I don't know what the problem **2)** *could / must* be.

Sally used to be a good student but now she is late for school every day. She says she misses the bus and it **3)** *ought to / might* be true. I don't really believe that, though. She doesn't study any more and has failed three important tests already. When I asked her about this, she said she had forgotten to do her homework but I know that **4)** *ought to / can't* be true. I think there **5)** *should / may* be a problem at home with her family. Her father **6)** *might / should* be ill again and perhaps Sally is under a lot of pressure. But if there is a problem, there **7)** *ought to / can't* be a solution, don't you think?

Can you give me some advice? If I can help Sally, it **8)** *can't / should* bring us closer again.

Worried in Worcester

3 Room for improvement!

Test yourself!

Choose the word or phrase that best completes the conversation or sentence.

1 'Oh, no! I've lost my bus ticket.'
   'Don't worry. …… you a new one.'
   A   I'm buying
   B   I'll buy
   C   I'm going to buy
   D   I buy

2 Let's …… these clothes and see which ones you want to keep.
   A   sort out
   B   throw out
   C   chill out
   D   work out

3 'How long will it take us to get to Manchester?'
   'We …… be there by seven.'
   A   can't
   B   should
   C   have
   D   ought

4 Pete keeps …… me to lend him my laptop.
   A   beeping
   B   scratching
   C   owing
   D   nagging

5 Can I give you a …… ? I don't have enough cash to pay you.
   A   reward
   B   cheque
   C   bargain
   D   discount

6 Sylvia can't join us tomorrow afternoon because she …… her aunt in hospital.
   A   will visit
   B   shall visit
   C   visits
   D   is visiting

7 That …… be Nick's iPod. He left with his five minutes ago.
   A   can't
   B   may
   C   must
   D   should

8 I'm afraid ten o'clock is not a(n) …… time. Can we meet half an hour later?
   A   similar
   B   typical
   C   convenient
   D   average

9 'What do you think of the group's new CD?'
   'I'm sure it …… a success.'
   A   is being
   B   shall be
   C   going to be
   D   will be

10 I …… Billy to come to the cinema with me.
   A   improved
   B   persuaded
   C   noticed
   D   sensed

11 You've been cleaning the house for hours. You …… be exhausted.
   A   could
   B   can't
   C   must
   D   ought

12 Please write your personal details on the application …… .
   A   rack
   B   reply
   C   form
   D   topic

13 Watch out! You …… the vase if you're not careful.
   A   are dropping
   B   will drop
   C   shall drop
   D   drop

14 …… you couldn't wake up this morning. You went to bed very late last night!
   A   No wonder
   B   It's typical
   C   In time
   D   It doesn't matter

4 Festival fever

Reading: Pages 40–41

4.1 **festival** (n) /ˈfestɪvəl/ = an occasion when there are performances of many films, plays, pieces of music, etc. *the Cannes Film **Festival***
φεστιβάλ, γιορτή

4.2 **fever** (n) /ˈfiːvə/ = a situation in which people feel very excited or anxious. *football **fever***
(συνήθως πρόσκαιρος μεταδοτικός) ενθουσιασμός, (παροδική) τρέλα

4.3 **put up** (phr v) /pʊt ˈʌp/ = to raise sth so that it is upright. *The kids **put up** a tent in the garden.*
στήνω

4.4 **tent** (n) /tent/ = a temporary structure used for camping, which is made of cloth or plastic and is supported by poles and ropes. *Have you ever slept in a **tent**?*
σκηνή

4.5 **along with** (phr) /əˈlɒŋ wɪð, wɪθ/ = together with sb or sth else. *We went to the festival **along with** thousands of other people.*
μαζί με

4.6 **queue** (n) /kjuː/ = a line of people or vehicles that are waiting for sth. *There was a long **queue** outside the cinema.* ➤ queue (v)
ουρά, σειρά (προτεραιότητας)

4.7 **laid-back** (adj) /ˌleɪd ˈbæk/ = relaxed and not seeming to worry about anything. *He is very **laid-back** and doesn't worry about things.*
χαλαρωμένος-η-ο, άνετος-η-ο

4.8 **backstage** (adj) /ˌbækˈsteɪdʒ/ = belonging to or working behind the stage in a theatre. *the **backstage** equipment* ➤ backstage (adv)
παρασκηνιακός-ή-ό

4.9 **crew** (n) /kruː/ = a group of people who work together on sth. *the television **crew** who made the programme*
συνεργείο, πλήρωμα

4.10 **tune up** (phr v) /ˌtjuːn ˈʌp/ = when musicians tune up, they prepare their instruments so they will play the correct notes. *Listen! I can hear the orchestra **tuning up**.*
κουρδίζω, χορδίζω (μουσικό όργανο)

4.11 **run** (v) /rʌn/ = to continue to be performed or used for a period of time. *The play was very successful and **ran** for three years.*
(για θεατρικό έργο, ταινία, κλπ.) παίζω

4.12 **organiser** (n) /ˈɔːɡənaɪzə/ = sb who plans and arranges an event. *the **organisers** of the festival* ➤ organise (v), organisation (n)
οργανωτής

4.13 **book** (v) /bʊk/ = to arrange for sb to perform at a particular place and time. *We've **booked** a jazz band for the wedding.* ➤ booking (n)
κλείνω

4.14 **band** (n) /bænd/ = a group of musicians who play popular music together. *He plays the guitar in a **band**.*
μπάντα, μουσικό συγκρότημα

4.15 **crowd** (n) /kraʊd/ = a large group of people in one place. *There was a large **crowd** at the stadium watching the match.* ➤ crowded (adj)
πλήθος

4.16 **act** (n) /ækt/ = a short piece of entertainment on television or stage. *We enjoyed the comedy **act**.* ➤ act (v), actor (n), actress (n)
παράσταση

4.17 **body painting** (n phr) /ˈbɒdi ˌpeɪntɪŋ/ = the act of drawing pictures on your body using paint. *Some people believe **body painting** is a form of art.*
μακιγιάζ σώματος

4.18 **craft** (n) /krɑːft/ = an activity for which you need skill, especially with your hands. *I'd love to learn a **craft** like making baskets.*
τέχνη

4.19 **workshop** (n) /ˈwɜːkʃɒp/ = a meeting at which people try to improve their skills by working together. *I want to go to the **workshop** on story writing next week.*
εργαστήρι

4.20 **square** (n) /skweə/ = an open area with buildings around it in the middle of a town. *There are many cafés around the town **square**.*
πλατεία

4.21 **tension** (n) /ˈtenʃən/ = a nervous and anxious feeling. *The **tension** as we waited for the news was terrible.* ➤ tense (adj)
ένταση

4.22 **build up** (phr v) /ˌbɪld ˈʌp/ = if a feeling builds up, it gradually increases. *Excitement was **building up** before the match.*
αυξάνομαι σταδιακά

4.23 **local** (n) /ˈləʊkəl/ = sb who lives in the place that you are talking about. *I asked a **local** for directions to the station.* ➤ local (adj)
ντόπιος

4 Festival fever

4.24 gather (v) /ˈɡæðə/ = if people gather somewhere, or if sb gathers them, they come together in the same place. *A crowd **gathered** to watch the performance.* ➤ gathering (n)
μαζεύω-ομαι, συγκεντρώνω-ομαι

4.25 splash (v) /splæʃ/ = if a liquid splashes, or if you splash it, it falls on sth or hits it. *She **splashed** water on her face.* ➤ splash (n)
πιτσιλίζω

4.26 fountain (n) /ˈfaʊntən/ = a structure that sends water up into the air. *There was a **fountain** in the garden.*
σιντριβάνι

4.27 annual (adj) /ˈænjuəl/ = happening once every year. *the school's **annual** concert*
ετήσιος-α-ο

4.28 event (n) /ɪˈvent/ = a performance, competition, party, etc. that has been arranged for a particular date or time. *The festival is an important annual **event**.*
εκδήλωση

4.29 firework (n) /ˈfaɪəwɜːk/ = a small object that explodes or burns with a coloured light, used for celebrating special events. *Everybody likes watching **fireworks**.*
πυροτέχνημα

4.30 spray (v) /spreɪ/ = to scatter small drops or pieces through the air. *The glass broke and tiny pieces **sprayed** everywhere.* ➤ spray (n)
ραντίζω, σκορπίζω

4.31 shower (n) /ˈʃaʊə/ = a lot of small things in the air or falling. *A **shower** of small flowers fell from the tree.* ➤ shower (v)
βροχή

4.32 scream (v) /skriːm/ = to make a loud high noise because you are hurt, frightened, angry or excited. *There was a bang and people started **screaming**.* ➤ scream (n)
ουρλιάζω

4.33 set off (phr v) /ˌset ˈɒf/ = to leave and start going somewhere. *We'd better **set off** before it gets dark.*
ξεκινώ

4.34 coast (n) /kəʊst/ = the land next to the sea. *They live in a cottage on the **coast**.*
ακτή

4.35 stall (n) /stɔːl/ = a large table on which you put things you want to sell. *a market **stall***
(υπαίθριος) πάγκος

4.36 dip (v) /dɪp/ = to put sth into a liquid for a short time and lift it out again. *Janet **dipped** her feet into the water.* ➤ dip (n)
βουτώ

4.37 massage (n) /ˈmæsɑːʒ/ = the action of pressing and rubbing sb's body with your hands to reduce pain or make them relax. *My back hurt, so she gave me a **massage**.* ➤ massage (v)
μασάζ

4.38 factory (n) /ˈfæktəri/ = a building where goods are produced in large quantities. *They make chocolate in this **factory**.*
εργοστάσιο

4.39 arts (n pl) /ɑːts/ = art, music, theatre, film, literature, etc., all considered together. *Are young people interested in the **arts**?*
τέχνες

4.40 turn into (phr v) /ˌtɜːn ˈɪntə, ˈɪntʊ/ = to become different, or to make sb or sth become different. *The producer **turned** the shy young actress **into** a star.*
μεταβάλλω-ομαι σε, μεταμορφώνω-ομαι

4.41 international (adj) /ˌɪntəˈnæʃənəl/ = relating to or involving more than one country. ***international** football matches*
διεθνής-ές

4.42 parade (n) /pəˈreɪd/ = a public celebration when musical bands, decorated vehicles, etc. move down the street. *There were hundreds of children in costumes in the **parade**.* ➤ parade (v)
παρέλαση

4.43 costume (n) /ˈkɒstjʊm/ = a set of clothes worn by an actor, or to make sb look like a particular type of person, animal, etc. *The actors wore beautiful **costumes**.*
αμφίεση, στολή

4.44 amphitheatre (n) /ˈæmfɪˌθɪətə/ = a large circular building without a roof and with many rows of seats around a central space, used for performances. *They performed the play in the **amphitheatre**.*
αμφιθέατρο

4.45 stage (n) /steɪdʒ/ = the raised floor in a theatre where actors perform a play. *The actor walked onto the **stage** and the audience cheered.*
σκηνή
◈ on stage = επί σκηνής

4.46 require (v) /rɪˈkwaɪə/ = to need sth. *Pets **require** a lot of care.* ➤ requirement (n)
χρειάζομαι, απαιτώ

4.47 shelter (n) /ˈʃeltə/ = a small building or covered place that protects you from bad weather or from attack. *a bus **shelter*** ➤ shelter (v)
στέγαστρο

4.48 cloth (n) /klɒθ/ = material made from cotton, wool, etc. that is used for making clothes, sheets, etc. *a dress made of cotton **cloth***
ύφασμα, πανί

Festival fever 4

4.49 rope (n) /rəʊp/ = very strong thick string. *Tie the horse to the tree with this **rope**.*
σχοινί

4.50 line (n) /laɪn/ = a number of people or things behind or next to each other. *a **line** of trees at the side of the road*
σειρά

4.51 amount (n) /əˈmaʊnt/ = how much of sth there is. *I have a large **amount** of work to do.*
ποσότητα

4.52 reduce (v) /rɪˈdjuːs/ = to make sth become less in size, amount, price, etc. *They **reduced** the amount of rubbish they throw out every day.* ➤ reduction (n)
ελαττώνω, μειώνω

4.53 pain (n) /peɪn/ = the feeling you have when part of your body hurts. *She had a **pain** in her stomach, so she went to the doctor.* ➤ painful (adj), painless (adj)
πόνος

4.54 press (v) /pres/ = to push sth firmly. *What will happen if I **press** this button?* ➤ pressure (n)
πιέζω

4.55 prefer (v) /prɪˈfɜː/ = to like or want sb or sth more than sb or sth else. *Would you **prefer** a hot or a cold drink?* ➤ preference (n)
προτιμώ
❖ prefer to do sth; prefer doing sth; prefer sth to sth

Vocabulary: Page 42

4.56 carnival (n) /ˈkɑːnɪvəl/ = a public event when people play music, wear special clothes and dance in the streets. ***carnival** time in Rio*
καρναβάλι

4.57 come on (phr v) /kʌm ˈɒn/ = to come onto a stage or sports field. *He scored a goal two minutes after he'd **come on**.*
εμφανίζομαι επί σκηνής, μπαίνω στο γήπεδο

4.58 clap (v) /klæp/ = to hit your hands together several times to show that you approve of sth. *The concert ended and we **clapped** and cheered.* ➤ clap (n)
χειροκροτώ

4.59 light up (phr v) /laɪt ˈʌp/ = to make a place become light or bright. *They **light up** the Parthenon at night.*
φωτίζω

4.60 opportunity (n) /ˌɒpəˈtjuːnəti/ = a chance to do sth. *I would like to take this **opportunity** to thank you.*
ευκαιρία

4.61 cause (n) /kɔːz/ = an organisation or aim that a group of people support or fight for. *I don't mind giving money if it's for a good **cause**.*
καλός σκοπός

4.62 odd (adj) /ɒd/ = strange or different from what you expected. *Olivia wears **odd** clothes sometimes and her parents don't like it.*
αλλόκοτος-η-ο, παράξενος-η-ο
❖ the odd one out = sb or sth that is different from the other people or things in a group

4.63 spectator (n) /spekˈteɪtə/ = sb who watches an event, especially a sports event. *There were about 40,000 **spectators** at the stadium.* ➤ spectacle (n)
θεατής

4.64 participant (n) /pɑːˈtɪsəpənt/ = sb who takes part in an activity or event. *the number of **participants** in the competition* ➤ participate (v)
συμμέτοχος

4.65 religious (adj) /rɪˈlɪdʒəs/ = relating to religion. *We don't have the same **religious** beliefs.* ➤ religion (n)
θρησκευτικός-ή-ό

4.66 tradition (n) /trəˈdɪʃən/ = a custom, belief or way of doing sth that has existed for a long time. *It's an old German **tradition**.* ➤ traditional (adj)
παράδοση

4.67 theme park (n phr) /ˈθiːm pɑːk/ = a place where you can have fun riding on big machines, which are all based on one subject such as water or space travel. *The children enjoyed themselves at the **theme park**.*
λούνα παρκ όπου οι δραστηριότητες βασίζονται σε ένα συγκεκριμένο θέμα

4.68 sample (n) /ˈsɑːmpəl/ = a small part or amount of sth that is examined or tried to find out what the rest is like. *free **samples** of a new shampoo* ➤ sample (v)
δείγμα

4.69 apparently (adv) /əˈpærəntli/ = used to say that you have heard that sth is true although you are not completely sure about it. ***Apparently**, it's not the first time he's done something like that.* ➤ apparent (adj), appear (v), appearance (n)
κατά τα φαινόμενα, προφανώς

4.70 water slide (n phr) /ˈwɔːtə slaɪd/ = a slide that goes down into a swimming pool, usually with water running down it. *The children played on the big **water slide**.*
τσουλήθρα νερού

4.71 fitness (n) /ˈfɪtnəs/ = when you are healthy or strong enough to do hard work or sports. *You must exercise to improve your physical **fitness**.* ➤ fit (adj)
καλή φυσική κατάσταση

4.72 disaster (n) /dɪˈzɑːstə/ = a complete failure. *The actor forgot his words and the play was a **disaster**.* ➤ disastrous (adj)
πλήρης αποτυχία, καταστροφή

4.73 cheer (v) /tʃɪə/ = to shout approval, encouragement, etc. *The spectators **cheered** when he scored the goal.* ➤ cheer (n)
ζητωκραυγάζω, επευφημώ

4 Festival fever

4.74 go off (phr v) /ɡəʊ ˈɒf/ = to stop working. *The lights went off and we were in the dark.*
σβήνω, παύω να λειτουργώ

4.75 boo (v) /buː/ = to shout 'boo' to show that you do not like a person, performance, etc. *The musicians played badly and the audience booed.* ➤ boo (n)
γιουχάρω, αποδοκιμάζω

4.76 compound noun (n phr) /ˌkɒmpaʊnd ˈnaʊn/ = a noun that is made up of two or more words. *'Science fiction' is a compound noun.*
σύνθετο ουσιαστικό

4.77 neon (n) /ˈniːɒn/ = a gas that is used in tubes in electric lights and signs. *neon lights*
(το αέριο) νέον
◆ neon light

Grammar: Page 43

4.78 continue (v) /kənˈtɪnjuː/ = to not stop happening, existing or doing sth. *Don't stop. Please continue.*
συνεχίζω

4.79 recent (adj) /ˈriːsənt/ = having happened or begun to exist only a short time ago. *a recent photo*
πρόσφατος-η-ο

4.80 fabulous (adj) /ˈfæbjʊləs/ = very good. *You look fabulous in those clothes!*
έξοχος-η-ο, φανταστικός-ή-ό

4.81 lover (n) /ˈlʌvə/ = sb who likes sth very much. *My uncle is a music lover and goes to concerts nearly every week.* ➤ love (v, n)
λάτρης

4.82 chocolate-coated (adj) /ˌtʃɒklət ˈkəʊtɪd/ = covered with chocolate. *We bought some chocolate-coated peanuts.*
καλυμμένος-η-ο με σοκολάτα

4.83 bug (n) /bʌɡ/ = a small insect. *I'm scared of bugs and spiders.*
έντομο, ζουζούνι

4.84 fried (adj) /fraɪd/ = cooked in hot oil. *fried mushrooms* ➤ fry (v)
τηγανητός-ή-ό

4.85 association (n) /əˌsəʊsiˈeɪʃən, əˌsəʊʃi-/ = an organisation for people who do the same kind of work or have the same interests. *the Association of University Lecturers*
➤ associate (v)
σύλλογος

4.86 dish (n) /dɪʃ/ = food cooked or prepared in a particular way. *a wonderful pasta dish*
πιάτο

4.87 stew (n) /stjuː/ = a meal made by cooking meat or fish and vegetables together slowly for a long time. *We're having beef stew for dinner tonight.* ➤ stew (v)
ραγού, στιφάδο

4.88 wide (adj) /waɪd/ = including a large variety of different people, things, etc. *We offer a wide range of vegetarian dishes.*
ευρύς-εία -ύ

4.89 prove (v) /pruːv/ = to show that sth is definitely true. *You're wrong and I can prove it.* ➤ proof (n)
αποδεικνύω-ομαι

4.90 tasty (adj) /ˈteɪsti/ = food that is tasty has a nice taste but is not sweet. *This pizza is tasty!* ➤ taste (v, n)
νόστιμος-η-ο

Listening: Page 44

4.91 exhibition (n) /ˌeksəˈbɪʃən/ = a public show where people can go and see paintings, photographs, etc. *an exhibition of historical photographs*
➤ exhibit (v, n)
έκθεση

4.92 in advance (prep phr) /ɪn ədˈvɑːns/ = before sth happens or is expected to happen. *I'm warning you in advance: I'm not a good dancer.*
εκ των προτέρων, από πριν

Speaking: Page 45

4.93 cancel (v) /ˈkænsəl/ = to decide that sth that was planned will not happen, or to tell sb this. *I was ill, so I cancelled my trip to Rome.* ➤ cancellation (n)
ακυρώνω

4.94 financial (adj) /fɪˈnænʃəl, faɪ-/ = relating to money or the management of money. *He doesn't have enough money and he has financial problems.* ➤ finance (n)
οικονομικός-ή-ό

4.95 attraction (n) /əˈtrækʃən/ = sth that is interesting or enjoyable to see or do. *The beautiful beaches are the island's main attraction.* ➤ attract (v), attractive (adj)
θέλγητρο

4.96 set up (phr v) /ˌset ˈʌp/ = to place or build sth somewhere, especially sth that is not permanent. *We set up stalls for the bazaar.*
στήνω

4.97 break down (phr v) /ˌbreɪk ˈdaʊn/ = if a car or a machine breaks down, it stops working. *My car broke down on the way to work.*
παύω να λειτουργώ, μένω από βλάβη

Festival fever 4

4.98 mayor (n) /meə/ = the person who is elected to lead the government of a town or city. *the **mayor** of the town*
δήμαρχος

4.99 blow (v) /bləʊ/ = to move in the wind, or to make sth move somewhere in the wind. *The strong wind **blew** the tent away.*
φυσώ
◆ blow off = to violently remove sth

4.100 wig (n) /wɪg/ = artificial hair that you wear on your head. *Aunt Agatha was wearing a blond **wig**.*
περούκα

Use your English: Pages 46–47

4.101 sensation (n) /senˈseɪʃən/ = extreme excitement or interest, or sth that causes this. *The singer caused a **sensation**. She was fantastic!*
αίσθηση, εντύπωση

4.102 compete (v) /kəmˈpiːt/ = to try to win sth or to be more successful than sb else. *Eight runners are **competing** in the race.* ➤ competition (n), competitor (n), competitive (adj)
ανταγωνίζομαι, συναγωνίζομαι

4.103 wannabe (n) /ˈwɒnəbi/ = sb who tries to look or behave like a famous or popular person. *Tom Cruise **wannabes***
επίδοξος-η-ο

4.104 judge (v) /dʒʌdʒ/ = to decide who has won a competition. *She is going to **judge** a talent contest.* ➤ judge (n), judgement (n)
κρίνω

4.105 industry (n) /ˈɪndəstri/ = all the companies that work in one particular type of trade or service. *She works in the music **industry**.* ➤ industrial (adj)
βιομηχανία

4.106 succeed (v) /səkˈsiːd/ = to achieve what you have been trying to do. *Did you **succeed** in finding a place to stay?* ➤ success (n), successful (adj)
επιτυγχάνω, πετυχαίνω
◆ succeed in doing sth

4.107 alternative (adj) /ɔːlˈtɜːnətɪv/ = different from what is usual or accepted. *an **alternative** lifestyle*
εναλλακτικός-ή-ό

4.108 obvious (adj) /ˈɒbviəs/ = easy to notice or understand. *It was **obvious** that Gina was lying.*
προφανής-ές, ολοφάνερος-η-ο

4.109 impress (v) /ɪmˈpres/ = to make sb feel admiration and respect. *His talent **impressed** the judges.*
➤ impression (n), impressive (adj)
εντυπωσιάζω

4.110 loyalty (n) /ˈlɔɪəlti/ = when sb always supports sb or sth. *I expect **loyalty** from my family.* ➤ loyal (adj)
πίστη, αφοσίωση

4.111 enthusiasm (n) /ɪnˈθjuːziæzəm/ = a strong feeling of interest and enjoyment. *He shares your **enthusiasm** for jazz.* ➤ enthusiastic (adj)
ενθουσιασμός

4.112 finalist (n) /ˈfaɪnəl-ɪst/ = one of the people or teams that reaches the last part of a competition. *She was one of the **finalists** of the competition.* ➤ final (n, adj)
φιναλίστας

4.113 independent (adj) /ˌɪndɪˈpendənt/ = an independent organisation is not owned or controlled by, or does not receive money from, another organisation or the government. *He owns a small **independent** bookshop.*
➤ independence (n)
ανεξάρτητος-η-ο

4.114 support (n) /səˈpɔːt/ = help and encouragement that you give to a person or group of people. *Thank you for your **support**. I wouldn't have succeeded without it.*
➤ support (v)
στήριξη

4.115 suspiciously (adv) /səˈspɪʃəsli/ = in a way that shows you do not trust sb or sth. *He looked at me **suspiciously**.* ➤ suspicious (adj), suspicion (n), suspect (v)
καχύποπτα

4.116 reserve (v) /rɪˈzɜːv/ = to arrange for a place in a hotel, on a plane, etc. to be kept for you to use. *I'd like to **reserve** a table for two.* ➤ reservation (n)
προκρατώ, κλείνω

4.117 technician (n) /tekˈnɪʃən/ = sb whose job is to do practical work connected with science or technology. *a laboratory **technician***
τεχνίτης, τεχνικός

4.118 fix (v) /fɪks/ = to repair sth. *She **fixed** my computer and it's working again.*
επισκευάζω

4.119 stallholder (n) /ˈstɔːlˌhəʊldə/ = sb who rents and keeps a market stall. *Several market **stallholders** gave away sweets to children.*
μικροπωλητής

4.120 serve (v) /sɜːv/ = to give sb food or drinks as part of a meal. *Mother will **serve** dinner at eight.*
σερβίρω

Writing: Pages 48–49

4.121 enormous (adj) /ɪˈnɔːməs/ = very big in size, amount or degree. *The team made an **enormous** effort and won.*
τεράστιος-α-ο

4 Festival fever

4.122 guest (n) /gest/ = sb who you invite to stay in your home or to go to an event. *How many **guests** are coming to your party?*
καλεσμένος-η, προσκεκλημένος-η

4.123 come along (phr v) /kʌm əˈlɒŋ/ = to follow sb or go with them. *Can I **come along** with you? I don't want to go alone.*
έρχομαι μαζί

4.124 chatty (adj) /ˈtʃæti/ = having a friendly, informal style. *She wrote me a funny, **chatty** letter.* ➤ chat (n, v)
συζητητικός-ή-ό

4.125 jammed (adj) /dʒæmd/ = full of people or things. *The hall was **jammed** with people and there were no empty seats.*
κατάμεστος-η-ο
◈ jammed with

4.126 journalist (n) /ˈdʒɜːnəl-ɪst/ = sb who writes reports for newspapers, magazines, television or radio. *The **journalist** interviewed the singer and then wrote an article for the magazine.*
δημοσιογράφος

4.127 conversational (adj) /ˌkɒnvəˈseɪʃənəl/ = a conversational style, phrase, etc. is informal and commonly used in talk between two or more people, especially friends. *The article was written in **conversational** language.* ➤ conversation (n)
συζητητικός-ή-ό
◈ conversational language = καθομιλουμένη

4.128 poster (n) /ˈpəʊstə/ = a large notice, picture, etc. used to advertise sth or as a decoration. *She put up **posters** of rock stars in her bedroom.*
αφίσα

4.129 register (n) /ˈredʒɪstə/ = a way of speaking or writing that is formal, informal, humorous, etc. which you use when you are in a particular situation. *Emails to friends are written in an informal **register**.*
(συγγραφικό) ύφος

4.130 sound (v) /saʊnd/ = the way sth sounds is how it seems to you when you listen to it or hear about it. *I spoke to him yesterday and he **sounded** sad.* ➤ sound (n)
ακούγομαι

WORDZONE SPECIAL

Some nouns refer to a group of people or things: *audience, band, crew, crowd, team*.
They can be followed by a singular or plural verb but there is a small difference in meaning.
The **crew** of the ship **was** large. (the crew as a group)
The **crew were** working hard. (each person in the crew)

Vocabulary and grammar practice

1 Complete the sentences with these nouns.

organiser   queue   samples   stall   tension   tradition   wannabe   workshop

1 The .... of the art festival is a famous painter himself.
2 There was a long .... outside the cinema and we waited for hours to buy tickets.
3 In our family it is a(n) .... to have roast goose for Christmas dinner.
4 We could feel the .... in the room as the teacher read out the exam results.
5 There was a(n) .... selling fresh strawberries at the market.
6 Let's ask Mary to come to the painting .... with us. She's always wanted to learn how to paint.
7 Russell has a nice voice but he is just another Justin Timberlake ...., I'm afraid.
8 You should take .... of your work to the job interview and show people what you can do.

Festival fever 4

2 **Match the phrasal verbs 1–8 with their meaning a–h. Then complete the sentences with the correct form of the phrasal verbs.**

1 put up
2 turn into
3 come along
4 break down
5 build up
6 set off
7 tune up
8 light up

a to make a place become bright or light
b to raise sth so that it is upright
c to leave and start going somewhere
d to stop working
e to make sth become different
f to increase gradually and become stronger
g to prepare an instrument so it will play the correct notes
h to follow sb or go with them

1 The fireworks were amazing and .... the whole sky.
2 My car has .... again. I think it's time to buy a new one.
3 We're going to that new Mexican restaurant tonight. Would you like to .... ?
4 They .... the spare bedroom .... a study.
5 Everybody was excited and you could feel the tension .... before the play.
6 The musicians were already .... when we arrived at the concert hall.
7 Why are the neighbours .... a new wall? What was wrong with the old one?
8 If we .... early, we should be there by ten o'clock.

3 **Complete the sentences with these words.**

body painting   chocolate-coated   food lover   laid-back   music industry
neon lights   theme park   water slide

1 If you bring your swimming things, we can try out the .... at the amusement park.
2 As we drove into the city, we could see the colourful .... that lit up the streets.
3 The children were eating .... nuts as they were watching the film.
4 Joanne is a songwriter and has worked in the .... for years.
5 I saw a documentary about .... yesterday. Some people had amazing drawings on their skin.
6 I know you're a .... but you're putting on weight, so be careful!
7 We enjoyed the .... atmosphere at the arts and crafts festival.
8 The new .... that opened last week has some fantastic rides!

4 Festival fever

4 **Choose the correct word to complete the sentences.**

1 The people at the festival were dressed in colourful *costumes / crafts*.
2 The band played so badly that the audience started *booing / clapping*.
3 The children *sprayed / dipped* their feet in the cold water but didn't dive into the pool.
4 Organising the school play will be a wonderful *sensation / opportunity* for you to gain some experience.
5 The *spectators / participants* cheered as their teams walked onto the field.
6 My favourite *dish / stew* is spaghetti carbonara. What's yours?
7 Music festivals like these *reserve / require* a lot of planning.
8 We enjoy the *recent / annual* carnival parade and watch it every year.

5 **Present perfect simple and continuous**
Complete the text with the correct form of the verbs in brackets. Use the present perfect simple or continuous.

Hello, listeners, and welcome to the Notting Hill Carnival, brought to you live from the streets of West London. Of course, Londoners 1) .... (look forward to) this event for months but this year the carnival 2) .... (also / attract) a record number of visitors from overseas. Maria and José Santes, for example, who are standing next to me, 3) .... (come) all the way from Spain!

The atmosphere today is amazing. The bands 4) .... (play) since early this morning and people are dancing and having a wonderful time.

Earlier today I spoke to John Witham, who 5) .... (be) one of the festival organisers for ten years. He tells me that the carnival takes weeks to organise and that some of the participants 6) .... (prepare) their costumes for months.

6 **Direct and indirect objects**
Put the words in the correct order.

1 me / you / show / Can / the way to the station / ?
....

2 his mother / a beautiful picture / drew / for / The little boy
....

3 dinner / Lynn / because it was her birthday / everybody / bought
....

4 the newspaper / her father / gave / She / to
....

5 sent / Have / yet / you / the tickets / they / ?
....

6 my friends / showed / my new costume / I / to
....

Festival fever 4

Test yourself!

Choose the word or phrase that best completes the conversation or sentence.

1 'Why is your face so red?'
   'Because I ....'
   A ran
   B have run
   C am running
   D have been running

2 People ...... in the streets to watch the fireworks.
   A gathered
   B reserved
   C competed
   D cancelled

3 Melanie is a member of a(n) ...... that encourages young people to learn local crafts.
   A audience
   B crowd
   C crew
   D association

4 That's my ticket! Give ...... !
   A to me it
   B it to me
   C it me
   D me it

5 In some countries people catch ...... and eat them!
   A bugs
   B ropes
   C samples
   D wigs

6 'Is Susan a friend of yours?'
   'Oh, yes. We ...... each other for years.'
   A know
   B knew
   C have known
   D have been knowing

7 The show was ...... and we had a fantastic time.
   A fabulous
   B obvious
   C enormous
   D tasty

8 My grandmother always bakes ...... when we visit her.
   A for us a cake
   B a cake for us
   C to us a cake
   D a cake to us

9 'I ...... to phone you for hours!'
   'Oh, sorry. My mobile was switched off.'
   A am trying
   B have tried
   C have been trying
   D tried

10 The play is very successful. It has been ...... for three years.
   A acting
   B booking
   C continuing
   D running

11 The singer fell ill, so they had to ...... the concert.
   A reduce
   B pass
   C cancel
   D reserve

12 Ms Scott ...... the office. Would you like to leave a message?
   A has just left
   B just left
   C has just been leaving
   D has been just leaving

13 Why are you looking at me so ...... ? Don't you believe me?
   A apparently
   B obviously
   C suspiciously
   D tidily

14 Have you sent ...... yet?
   A an invitation Sarah
   B an invitation to Sarah
   C to Sarah an invitation
   D for Sarah an invitation

44

Time to revise 2 | Units 3–4

1 Complete the sentences with the correct form of these verbs.

contact   earn   get   improve   owe   respond   stand   waste

1 Michaela .... a lot of money and she can afford an expensive car like that.
2 You can .... me by email or by calling me on my mobile phone.
3 Ben can't .... waking up early. That's why he's often late for school.
4 Have they .... to your email yet?
5 My school work has .... a lot and I get good marks now.
6 We've got a lot to do before the festival, so we mustn't .... any time.
7 She's so boring! She should .... a life.
8 How much money does he .... you?

2 Choose the correct word to complete the sentences.

1 It was raining, so they *delayed / cancelled* the parade and everybody went home.
2 That was a very *nasty / tasty* thing to say! You hurt her feelings.
3 His stamp collection is his favourite *possession / sensation*.
4 We're having beef *crew / stew* for dinner tonight.
5 Please can you *check / cheque* those numbers for me?
6 Can I *give / take* you a hand with those heavy boxes?
7 The audience cheered when the band finally came *on / along*.
8 I've got a problem and I need your *advise / advice*.

3 Complete the letter with the correct form of the words in capitals.

Dear Chris,	
Goods news! Our 1) .... was a success. As you know,	**EXHIBIT**
our 2) .... was to raise money for some new	**INTEND**
equipment for the computer room and thanks to the hard	
work of the 3) .... , we succeeded!	**ORGANISE**
There were hundreds of visitors and the hall was 4)	**JAM**
every day for two weeks. 5) .... , everybody was	**APPARENT**
impressed by the quality of the students' work. And guess what!	
The pictures I drew were one of the main 6) .... ! My	**ATTRACT**
painting of a carnival caused a 7) .... and the mayor	**SENSE**
bought it for 400 euros! He says he's going to hang it in the	
town hall! I know I'm 8) .... but I can't wait to see	**PATIENT**
it there!	

45

5 Extreme behaviour!

Reading: Pages 52–53

5.1 **extreme** (adj) /ɪkˈstriːm/ = extreme opinions, behaviour, situations, etc. are unusual and different from what most people consider to be reasonable. ***Extreme*** *sports are very dangerous.*
ακραίος-α-ο

5.2 **react** (v) /riˈækt/ = to behave in a particular way because of what sb has done or said to you or because of the situation you are in. *The audience **reacted** by shouting and booing.* ➤ reaction (n)
αντιδρώ
◆ react to

5.3 **unfair** (adj) /ˌʌnˈfeə/ = not right or fair. *It's **unfair** to give money to her and not to me.*
άδικος-η-ο
Opp: fair

5.4 **accidentally** (adv) /ˌæksɪˈdentl-i/ = if you accidentally do sth, you do it without meaning to do it or planning to do it. *I'm sorry. I broke the window **accidentally**.* ➤ accidental (adj), accident (n)
τυχαία

5.5 **fall over** (phr v) /fɔːl ˈəʊvə/ = to fall to the ground. *I **fell over** a bag on the floor and hurt myself.*
πέφτω

5.6 **apologise** (v) /əˈpɒlədʒaɪz/ = to tell sb that you are sorry that you have upset them or caused them problems. *He **apologised** for being late.* ➤ apology (n)
απολογούμαι, ζητώ συγγνώμη
◆ apologise for sth/doing sth

5.7 **rude** (adj) /ruːd/ = speaking or behaving in a way that is not polite. *Don't make **rude** comments about people!* ➤ rudeness (n)
αγενής-ες

5.8 **comment** (n) /ˈkɒment/ = an opinion that you give about sb or sth. *The teacher made some **comments** about my work.* ➤ comment (v)
παρατήρηση, σχόλιο

5.9 **get** (v) /get/ = to change to a new state, feeling or situation; to become. *Children **get** bored easily.*
γίνομαι
◆ get bored/angry/upset, etc.

5.10 **upset** (adj) /ʌpˈset/ = unhappy because sth unpleasant has happened so that you feel shocked or want to cry. *I failed my test and I'm **upset**.* ➤ upset (v)
στενοχωρημένος-η-ο
◆ upset about

5.11 **ignore** (v) /ɪgˈnɔː/ = to deliberately not pay attention to sb or sth. *I said 'hello' but she **ignored** me.*
➤ ignorance (n)
αγνοώ

5.12 **sort out** (phr v) /ˌsɔːt ˈaʊt/ = if you sort out a problem, you deal with it. *I'll **sort out** the problem for you.*
επιλύω, αντιμετωπίζω

5.13 **get involved in sth** (phr) /ˌget ɪnˈvɒlvd ɪn ˌsʌmθɪŋ/ = to take part in an activity or event. ***get involved in*** *a fight*
εμπλέκομαι

5.14 **bully** (n) /ˈbʊli/ = sb who deliberately frightens or upsets a person who is smaller or weaker than they are. *Don't let those **bullies** scare you.* ➤ bully (v)
τραμπούκος

5.15 **tease** (v) /tiːz/ = if you tease sb, you say amusing or slightly unkind things to them about their appearance, behaviour, etc. *My sister **teases** me about my big ears but I don't mind.*
πειράζω

5.16 **bully** (v) /ˈbʊli/ = to frighten sb or threaten to hurt them, especially if they are weaker or smaller than you. *The older kids sometimes **bully** the younger ones.*
τυραννώ, καταδυναστεύω, εκφοβίζω

5.17 **ages** (n pl) /ˈeɪdʒɪz/ = a long time. *It will take **ages** to finish the job!*
μεγάλο χρονικό διάστημα

5.18 **posh** (adj) /pɒʃ/ = from or belonging to a high social class, or behaving or speaking in a way that is typical of people from a high social class. *They live in a huge house in a **posh** neighbourhood.*
σικ, στιλάτος-η-ο

5.19 **loads of** (phr) /ˈləʊdz əv/ = a lot of sth. *You don't have to hurry. We have **loads of** time.*
αφθονία ή πλήθος από

5.20 **protect** (v) /prəˈtekt/ = to prevent sb or sth from being harmed or damaged. *laws to **protect** the environment*
➤ protection (n)
προστατεύω

5.21 **mate** (n) /meɪt/ = a friend. *I went out with my **mates**.*
φίλος-η

5.22 **shove** (v) /ʃʌv/ = to push sb or sth in a rough or careless way. *People were **shoving** to get into the crowded bus.*
➤ shove (n)
σπρώχνω

5 Extreme behaviour!

5.23 anyway (adv) /ˈeniweɪ/ = used when you are changing the subject of a conversation or returning to a previous subject. *Anyway, how are you these days?*
όπως και να έχει, εν πάσει περιπτώσει

5.24 expect (v) /ɪkˈspekt/ = to believe that sb must do sth because it is their duty. *My parents expect me to help with the housework.*
περιμένω
◆ expect sb to do sth

5.25 give up (phr v) /ˌɡɪv ˈʌp/ = to give sth that is yours to sb else. *They refused to give up their land.*
παραχωρώ

5.26 hand over (phr v) /ˌhænd ˈəʊvə/ = to give sth to sb with your hand, especially because they have asked for it or should have it. *The bullies ordered us to hand over our money.*
παραδίδω

5.27 march (v) /mɑːtʃ/ = to walk somewhere quickly, often because you are angry. *'I hate you!' she shouted and marched out of the room.*
κινούμαι με αποφασιστικό βήμα

5.28 demand (v) /dɪˈmɑːnd/ = to ask for sth in a very strong and determined way. *The head teacher demanded to know what was going on.* ➤ demand (n)
απαιτώ

5.29 get (v) /ɡet/ = to attack, hurt or catch sb. *The bully threatened to get him after school.*
εκδικούμαι

5.30 responsible (adj) /rɪˈspɒnsəbəl/ = being in charge of or looking after sb or sth. *The school is responsible for the safety of its students.* ➤ responsibility (n)
υπεύθυνος-η-ο
◆ responsible for. Opp: irresponsible

5.31 unfortunately (adv) /ʌnˈfɔːtʃənətli/ = used to say that you wish that sth had not happened or was not true. *Unfortunately, they cancelled the show.*
➤ unfortunate (adj)
δυστυχώς
Opp: fortunately

5.32 bang (v) /bæŋ/ = to hit part of your body against sth by accident. *I banged my knee on the corner of the bed.*
➤ bang (n)
κοπανώ, βροντοκτυπώ
◆ bang your knee/head, etc. on sth

5.33 revolting (adj) /rɪˈvəʊltɪŋ/ = very unpleasant. *The food was revolting and I couldn't eat it.*
αηδιαστικός-ή-ό

5.34 thump (n) /θʌmp/ = the sound or action of hitting sb or sth hard. *Paul gave him a thump on the back.*
➤ thump (v)
βρόντος, γδούπος

5.35 guilty (adj) /ˈɡɪlti/ = unhappy and ashamed because you have done sth wrong. *He felt guilty about stealing the DVD.* ➤ guilt (n)
ένοχος-η-ο
Opp: innocent

5.36 fight back (phr v) /ˌfaɪt ˈbæk/ = to fight or argue with sb who has attacked you or criticised you. *Kevin hit me, so I fought back.*
ανταποδίδω το χτύπημα, προβάλλω αντίσταση

5.37 disapprove (v) /ˌdɪsəˈpruːv/ = to think that sb or sth is bad or wrong. *Her parents disapprove of her friends.*
➤ disapproval (n)
αποδοκιμάζω
◆ disapprove of. Opp: approve

5.38 violence (n) /ˈvaɪələns/ = behaviour that is intended to hurt other people physically. *There's too much violence on TV these days.* ➤ violent (adj)
βία

5.39 get into trouble (phr) /ˌɡet ɪntə ˈtrʌbəl/ = if sb gets into trouble, they do sth wrong which they will be punished for. *He was always getting into trouble at school.*
μπλέκω σε μπελάδες

5.40 laugh at (phr v) /ˈlɑːf ət, æt/ = to make unkind or funny remarks about sb because you think they are stupid or look silly. *The other kids laughed at him when he made mistakes.*
γελώ (κοροϊδευτικά) σε βάρος

5.41 unless (conjunction) /ʌnˈles, ən-/ = used to say that sth will only happen if sth else happens. *The child won't go to sleep unless you tell her a story.*
εκτός αν

5.42 illegal (adj) /ɪˈliːɡəl/ = not allowed by law. *It is illegal to park your car here.*
παράνομος-η-ο
Opp: legal

5.43 law (n) /lɔː/ = the system of rules that people in a country or place must obey. *Passengers must wear seatbelts. It's the law.*
νόμος
◆ by law = σύμφωνα με το νόμο

5.44 insecure (adj) /ˌɪnsɪˈkjʊə/ = if you are insecure, you do not feel confident about yourself. *She's insecure about her appearance and thinks she's ugly.* ➤ insecurity (n)
ανασφαλής-ές
◆ insecure about. Opp: secure

5.45 call sb names (phr) /ˌkɔːl sʌmbədi ˈneɪmz/ = to insult sb by using unpleasant words to describe them. *They bullied me and called me names.*
βρίζω κάποιον-α

5.46 repeat (v) /rɪˈpiːt/ = to say or do sth again. *I didn't hear that. Please repeat it.* ➤ repetition (n)
επαναλαμβάνω

Extreme behaviour! 5

5.47 **bother** (v) /ˈbɒðə/ = to make sb feel slightly annoyed, worried or upset. *It was noisy but it didn't **bother** me.*
ενοχλώ

5.48 **class** (n) /klɑːs/ = the social group that you belong to, based on your job, income and education. *The children come from different social **classes**.*
κοινωνική τάξη

Vocabulary: Page 54

5.49 **mind** (v) /maɪnd/ = to feel annoyed or upset about sth. *It was raining but we didn't **mind**.*
με πειράζει, με νοιάζει

5.50 **seat** (n) /siːt/ = a place on a plane, train, etc. or a chair in a cinema, etc. that you pay to sit in. *I've booked two **seats** for the play.*
θέση

5.51 **logical** (adj) /ˈlɒdʒɪkəl/ = reasonable and sensible. *a **logical** answer* ➤ logic (n)
λογικός-ή-ό
Opp: illogical

5.52 **irregular** (adj) /ɪˈreɡjʊlə/ = not happening with the same amount of time or space between each thing and the next. *an **irregular** heartbeat*
ανώμαλος-η-ο, ακανόνιστος-η-ο
Opp: regular

5.53 **obey** (v) /əʊˈbeɪ, ə-/ = to do what a person, law or rule tells you to do. *She refused to **obey** the rules, so they punished her.* ➤ obedience (n), obedient (adj)
υπακούω
Opp: disobey

5.54 **legal** (adj) /ˈliːɡəl/ = allowed or done according to the law. *Is it **legal** to park here or will you get into trouble?*
νόμιμος-η-ο
Opp: illegal

5.55 **irresponsible** (adj) /ˌɪrəˈspɒnsəbəl/ = behaving in a careless way, without thinking of the bad results of what you do. *His **irresponsible** behaviour caused the accident.* ➤ irresponsibility (n)
ανεύθυνος-η-ο
Opp: responsible

5.56 **disagree** (v) /ˌdɪsəˈɡriː/ = to have a different opinion from sb else. *We **disagree** about most things.* ➤ disagreement (n)
διαφωνώ
◈ disagree with sb; disagree about sth. Opp: agree

5.57 **approve** (v) /əˈpruːv/ = to think that sb or sth is good, right or suitable. *My parents **approve** of my friends.*
εγκρίνω
◈ approve of

5.58 **right** (n) /raɪt/ = sth that you are legally or morally allowed to do. *the **right** to vote*
δικαίωμα

5.59 **seatbelt** (n) /ˈsiːtˌbelt/ = a strong belt that holds you safely in your seat in a car or plane. *Fasten your **seatbelt** when you get into the car.*
ζώνη ασφαλείας

5.60 **fasten** (v) /ˈfɑːsən/ = to join together the two sides of sth so that it is closed, or to become joined together. ***Fasten** your seatbelts.*
(προσ)δένω-ομαι
Opp: unfasten

5.61 **against the law** (phr) /əˌɡenst ðə ˈlɔː/ = illegal. *It is **against the law** to hit a child.*
παράνομος-η-ο

5.62 **fine** (n) /faɪn/ = money that you have to pay as a punishment for breaking a law or rule. *a parking **fine*** ➤ fine (v)
πρόστιμο, χρηματική ποινή

5.63 **undone** (adj) /ʌnˈdʌn/ = not tied or fastened. *Your shirt button is **undone**.* ➤ undo (v)
ξεκούμπωτος-η-ο, λυμένος-η-ο

5.64 **at least** (prep phr) /ət ˈliːst/ = not less than a particular number or amount. *There were **at least** a thousand people at the concert.*
τουλάχιστον

5.65 **tattoo** (n) /təˈtuː, tæˈtuː/ = a picture or design that is put permanently onto sb's skin using a needle and ink. *She has a **tattoo** of a butterfly on her arm.* ➤ tattoo (v)
τατουάζ

5.66 **body piercing** (n phr) /ˈbɒdi ˌpɪəsɪŋ/ = making a hole in a part of the body in order to fix a ring or other piece of jewellery to the body. *My parents got upset when I told them I wanted **body piercing**.*
τρύπα στο σώμα για σκουλαρίκι ή άλλο κόσμημα

5.67 **permission** (n) /pəˈmɪʃən/ = if you have permission to do sth, sb in authority allows you to do it. *The teacher gave us **permission** to leave early.* ➤ permit (v)
άδεια

5.68 **court** (n) /kɔːt/ = a place where a judge or a group of people decide whether sb is guilty of a crime. *If you do something illegal, you will have to go to **court**.*
δικαστήριο
◈ go to court

5.69 **judge** (n) /dʒʌdʒ/ = the person who controls a court of law and decides how criminals should be punished. *The **judge** sentenced him to one year in prison.* ➤ judge (v), judgement (n)
δικαστής

5.70 **prison** (n) /ˈprɪzən/ = a building where criminals are kept as a punishment. *Eddie broke the law and went to **prison**.* ➤ prisoner (n)
φυλακή

5.71 **licence** (n) /ˈlaɪsəns/ = an official document that gives you permission to do or own sth. *a driving **licence***
άδεια

5 Extreme behaviour!

5.72 bank account (n phr) /'bæŋk ə,kaʊnt/ = an arrangement that allows you to keep your money in a bank and take it out when you want to. *I have about 2,000 euros in my **bank account**.*
τραπεζικός λογαριασμός

5.73 vote (v) /vəʊt/ = to choose which person you want to elect or which plan you support by making a mark on a piece of paper or raising your hand. *Who are you going to **vote** for in the elections?* ➤ vote (n)
ψηφίζω

5.74 ID card (n phr) /ˌaɪ 'diː kɑːd/ = a card with your name, date of birth and photograph on it that proves who you are. *You need to show your **ID card** or they won't let you into the building.*
δελτίο ταυτότητας
Also: identity card

5.75 copy (n) /'kɒpi/ = sth that is made to look exactly like sth else. *Make a **copy** of this letter.* ➤ copy (v)
αντίγραφο

5.76 birth certificate (n phr) /'bɜːθ səˌtɪfɪkət/ = an official document that shows when and where you were born. *According to her **birth certificate**, she was born in 1967.*
πιστοποιητικό γέννησης

5.77 proof (n) /pruːf/ = sth that proves sth is true. *Have you got any **proof** that he is guilty?* ➤ prove (v)
απόδειξη, πειστήριο

Grammar: Page 55

5.78 argue (v) /'ɑːgjuː/ = to shout and say angry things to sb because you disagree with them. *They were **arguing** and looked very angry.* ➤ argument (n)
λογομαχώ, καυγαδίζω
◈ argue with sb; argue about sth

5.79 afterwards (adv) /'ɑːftəwədz/ = after an event or time that has been mentioned. *We'll go to the cinema and have coffee together **afterwards**.*
μετά, ύστερα

5.80 dye (v) /daɪ/ = to change the colour of sth using a dye. *She **dyed** her hair red.* ➤ dye (n)
βάφω

5.81 eyebrow (n) /'aɪbraʊ/ = the line of short hairs above your eye. *He raised his **eyebrows** in surprise.*
φρύδι

Listening: Page 56

5.82 go back (phr v) /gəʊ 'bæk/ = to have started at some time in the past. *a tradition that **goes back** 200 years*
χρονολογούμαι

5.83 henna (n) /'henə/ = a reddish-brown substance used to change the colour of hair or to dye the skin. *She dyed her hair reddish-brown using **henna**.*
χένvα

5.84 temporary (adj) /'tempərəri, -pəri/ = existing or happening only for a short time. *a **temporary** job*
προσωρινός-ή-ό
Opp: permanent

5.85 fade (v) /feɪd/ = if material fades or if sth fades it, it becomes less bright. *The sunlight **faded** the curtains.*
ξεθωριάζω

5.86 fashion statement (n phr) /'fæʃən ˌsteɪtmənt/ = sth that you own or wear that is considered new or different and that is intended to make other people notice you. *Her tattoo was a **fashion statement**.*
ρούχο, κόσμημα, κλπ. που είναι στη μόδα και που εντυπωσιάζει

5.87 cause (v) /kɔːz/ = to make sth happen. *The ice on the road **caused** the accident.* ➤ cause (n)
προκαλώ

5.88 long-term (adj) /ˌlɒŋ 'tɜːm/ = continuing for a long period of time into the future. *the **long-term** effects of smoking*
μακροπρόθεσμος-η-ο
Opp: short-term

5.89 influence (v) /'ɪnfluəns/ = to change how sth develops or how sb behaves. *Her advice **influenced** my decision.* ➤ influence (n), influential (adj)
επηρεάζω

5.90 confirm (v) /kən'fɜːm/ = to show or prove that sth is true or right. *Can you **confirm** what he is saying?* ➤ confirmation (n)
επιβεβαιώνω

Speaking: Page 57

5.91 dislike (v) /dɪs'laɪk/ = to not like sb or sth. *Why do you **dislike** her so much?* ➤ dislike (n)
αντιπαθώ
Opp: like

5.92 permanent (adj) /'pɜːmənənt/ = continuing to exist for a long time or for all future time. *a **permanent** job*
μόνιμος-η-ο
Opp: temporary

5.93 change your mind (phr) /ˌtʃeɪndʒ jə 'maɪnd/ = to change your decision or opinion about sth. *I've **changed my mind** about going out. I'm going to stay home.*
αλλάζω γνώμη

5.94 full stop (interjection) /ˌfʊl 'stɒp/ = used at the end of a sentence to emphasise that you do not want to say any more about a subject. *I don't want to discuss this any more. **Full stop**.*
τελεία και παύλα

Extreme behaviour! 5

5.95 **exactly** (adv) /ɪgˈzæktli/ = used to show that you agree completely with sb. 'We should have less homework.' '**Exactly**!' ➤ exact (adj)
ακριβώς

5.96 **personally** (adv) /ˈpɜːsənəli/ = used to emphasise that you are giving your own opinion. **Personally**, I think it's a bad idea. ➤ personal (adj), person (n)
προσωπικά

5.97 **harmful** (adj) /ˈhɑːmfəl/ = causing damage or hurt. a **harmful** drug ➤ harm (n, v), harmless (adj)
βλαβερός-ή-ό

5.98 **design** (n) /dɪˈzaɪn/ = a pattern used to decorate sth. curtains with a pretty **design** ➤ design (v), designer (n)
σχέδιο

5.99 **mark** (v) /mɑːk/ = to write or draw on sth for sb else to see. **Mark** the things you want with a tick. ➤ mark (n)
σημαδεύω

5.100 **support** (v) /səˈpɔːt/ = to help to show that sth is true. **Support** what you say by using examples. ➤ support (n)
επιβεβαιώνω, ενισχύω

5.101 **decorate** (v) /ˈdekəreɪt/ = to make sth look more attractive by putting sth pretty on it. Paintings **decorated** the walls. ➤ decoration (n)
διακοσμώ, στολίζω

Use your English: Pages 58–59

5.102 **point** (v) /pɔɪnt/ = to show sth to sb by holding up one of your fingers or a thin object towards it. 'That's my car,' she said, **pointing** at a white Ford.
δείχνω (με το δάκτυλο)
◆ point at/to

5.103 **blame** (v) /bleɪm/ = to say that sb or sth is responsible for sth bad. Marie **blames** me for the accident.
➤ blame (n)
κατηγορώ
◆ blame sb for sth

5.104 **judge** (v) /dʒʌdʒ/ = to form or give an opinion about sb or sth using the information you have. Never **judge** a person by their looks.
κρίνω

5.105 **latest** (adj) /ˈleɪtəst/ = the most recent or the newest. all the **latest** gossip ➤ late (adj)
ο/η/το τελευταίος-α-ο, ο/η/το πιο πρόσφατος-η-ο

5.106 **troublemaker** (n) /ˈtrʌbəlˌmeɪkə/ = sb who deliberately causes problems. The police took the **troublemakers** to the police station. ➤ trouble (n)
ταραξίας

5.107 **dress** (v) /dres/ = to wear a particular type of clothes. **dress** fashionably ➤ dress (n)
ντύνομαι

5.108 **express** (v) /ɪkˈspres/ = to show your thoughts or feelings by the way you look or your actions. **express** your feelings ➤ expression (n), expressive (adj)
εκφράζω

5.109 **individuality** (n) /ˌɪndɪvɪdʒuˈæləti/ = the quality that makes sb different from everybody else. work that allows children to express their **individuality**
➤ individual (n, adj)
ατομικότητα

5.110 **big** (adj) /bɪg/ = important and serious. a **big** decision
σημαντικός-ή-ό

5.111 **insult** (n) /ˈɪnsʌlt/ = a remark or action that is offensive or shows a lack of respect. That was an **insult** and I'll never forgive you! ➤ insult (v), insulting (adj)
βρισιά, προσβολή

5.112 **be out of order** (phr) /bi ˌaʊt əv ˈɔːdə/ = if sb's behaviour is out of order, it is unacceptable. I think what Katie said **was out of order**. She should apologise.
είμαι απαράδεκτος-η-ο

5.113 **totally** (adv) /ˈtəʊtl-i/ = completely. I agree with you **totally**. ➤ total (adj, n)
εντελώς, τελείως

5.114 **unacceptable** (adj) /ˌʌnəkˈseptəbəl/ = sth that is unacceptable is wrong or bad and should not be allowed to continue. **unacceptable** behaviour
απαράδεκτος-η-ο

5.115 **point of view** (n phr) /ˌpɔɪnt əv ˈvjuː/ = sb's personal opinion or attitude in a situation. Let me explain my **point of view**.
άποψη

5.116 **brave** (adj) /breɪv/ = behaving with courage in a frightening situation. It was **brave** of you to tell her the truth. ➤ bravery (n)
γενναίος-α-ο

5.117 **emphasise** (v) /ˈemfəsaɪz/ = if you emphasise sth you say or write, you give it special importance so that people will notice it. The teacher **emphasised** the importance of correct spelling. ➤ emphasis (n)
τονίζω, δίνω έμφαση

5.118 **weird** (adj) /wɪəd/ = unusual and strange. I had a **weird** dream.
αλλόκοτος-η-ο

5.119 **headache** (n) /ˈhedeɪk/ = a pain in your head. I must take an aspirin. I've got a **headache**.
πονοκέφαλο

5.120 **pierce** (v) /pɪəs/ = to make a hole in or through sth using an object with a sharp point. I'm getting my ears **pierced**.
(δια)τρυπώ

5.121 **fair** (n) /feə/ = a large outdoor event where you can buy things, get information, etc. an art **fair**
έκθεση

5 Extreme behaviour!

Writing: Pages 60–61

5.122 a pain (n phr) /ə 'peɪn/ = sb or sth that is very annoying. *It's **a pain** looking after my little brother.*
κακός μπελάς
Also: a pain in the neck

5.123 go through (phr v) /gəʊ 'θruː/ = to search a container or place. *Dave **went through** his pockets looking for the keys.*
ψάχνω

5.124 nick (v) /nɪk/ = to steal sth. *Somebody's **nicked** my purse!*
κλέβω, βουτώ

5.125 'coz (conjunction) /kəz, kɒz/ = (informal) because. *I got into trouble **'coz** I was late.*
επειδή, διότι

5.126 space (n) /speɪs/ = a place where a person can do what they like and enjoy their privacy. *Please don't come into my bedroom. I need my **space**.*
ο χώρος μου

5.127 pinch (v) /pɪntʃ/ = to steal sth. *Who **pinched** my mobile phone?*
κλέβω, βουτώ

5.128 change (n) /tʃeɪndʒ/ = sth that is interesting or enjoyable because it is different from what is usual. *Let's eat out for a **change**.*
αλλαγή
◆ for a change

5.129 diary (n) /'daɪəri/ = a book in which you write down things that have happened to you. *Tony writes everything that happens to him in his **diary**.*
ημερολόγιο

5.130 hidden (adj) /'hɪdn/ = difficult to see or find. **hidden** *cameras* ➤ hide (v)
κρυφός-ή-ό

5.131 be in the wrong (phr) /bi ɪn ðə 'rɒŋ/ = to make a mistake or deserve the blame for sth. *I **was in the wrong**, so I apologised.*
έχω άδικο

5.132 column (n) /'kɒləm/ = numbers or words written under each other down a page. *Add up the numbers in the **column**.*
στήλη

5.133 tidy up (phr v) /ˌtaɪdi 'ʌp/ = to make a place look tidy. ***Tidy up** after you've finished.*
συγυρίζω, τακτοποιώ

5.134 instruction (n) /ɪn'strʌkʃən/ = an order telling you what you must do. *They gave us strict **instructions** not to leave the building.* ➤ instruct (v)
οδηγία

5.135 jealous (adj) /'dʒeləs/ = feeling angry or unhappy because sb else has sth that you wish you had. *You're **jealous** of me because I got better marks.*
➤ jealousy (n)
ζηλιάρης
◆ jealous of

5.136 borrow (v) /'bɒrəʊ/ = to use sth that belongs to sb else and give it back to them later. *Can I **borrow** the car tonight, Dad?*
δανείζομαι

5.137 after all (phr) /ˌɑːftər 'ɔːl/ = used when you are saying sth that shows that what you have just said is right. *Don't shout at her. **After all**, the accident wasn't her fault.*
εξάλλου

5.138 lock (n) /lɒk/ = sth you use to fasten a door, drawer, etc. and that you usually open with a key. *I put the key in the **lock** and opened the door.* ➤ lock (v)
κλειδαριά

5.139 form (n) /fɔːm/ = a way of writing or saying a word that shows its number, tense, etc. *'Men' is the plural **form** of 'man'.* ➤ form (v)
γλωσσική μορφή

5.140 close (adj) /kləʊs/ = if people are close, they like or love each other very much. *We are **close** friends.*
στενός-ή-ό

5.141 in secret (prep phr) /ɪn 'siːkrət/ = without other people knowing. *The meeting was held **in secret**.*
μυστικά

5.142 hard (adj) /hɑːd/ = difficult to do or understand. *It's **hard** to say when Glenn will be back.*
δύσκολος-η-ο

5.143 join in (phr v) /dʒɔɪn 'ɪn/ = to begin to take part in sth that other people are doing. *The other children wouldn't let Sam **join in** their games.*
συμμετέχω

5.144 briefly (adv) /'briːfli/ = in as few words as possible. *Sonia described the film **briefly**.* ➤ brief (adj)
με συντομία

5.145 understanding (n) /ˌʌndə'stændɪŋ/ = sympathy and kindness that you show towards sb with problems or worries. *Harry thanked us for our **understanding**.*
➤ understand (v)
κατανόηση

5.146 entertaining (adj) /ˌentə'teɪnɪŋ/ = interesting and enjoyable. *an **entertaining** evening* ➤ entertain (v), entertainment (n), entertainer (n)
διασκεδαστικός-ή-ό

5.147 positive (adj) /'pɒzətɪv/ = hopeful and confident. *You should try and be more **positive**.*
θετικός-ή-ό
Opp: negative

Extreme behaviour! 5

5.148 note (n) /nəʊt/ = a feeling or quality. *She ended her speech on a personal note*.
τόνος
◆ on a positive/personal note

5.149 swap (v) /swɒp/ = to exchange sth you have for sth that sb else has. *Can I swap seats with you?*
ανταλλάσσω

WORDZONE SPECIAL

Get has many meanings. Here are some of them:

• to attack, hurt or catch sb.	*'I'll **get** you for this!'* he shouted.
• to change to a new state, feeling or situation; to become.	*It's **getting** cold.*
• to buy or obtain something.	*What shall I **get** you for your birthday?*
• to receive or be given something.	*I **got** an email from Bob today.*
• to move or arrive somewhere.	*How can I **get** to the station?*

Vocabulary and grammar practice

 1 Read the sentences 1–8. Choose the sentences a or b that have a similar meaning.

1 Unless you leave immediately, you won't be home by dark.
   a You'll be home by dark only if you leave immediately.
   b You'll be home by dark if you don't leave immediately.

2 Your comments were out of order.
   a You put things in the wrong order.
   b It was wrong of you to make those comments.

3 All this hard work is a pain.
   a All this hard work is hurting my back.
   b I dislike doing all this hard work.

4 She has at least five tattoos.
   a She has five tattoos or more.
   b She has fewer than five tattoos.

5 Stop calling him names.
   a Stop using his first name and his surname.
   b Stop insulting him.

6 The food was revolting.
   a I hated the food.
   b The food was different.

7 If he doesn't listen to us, we'll get him later.
   a If he doesn't listen to us, we'll punish him later.
   b If he doesn't listen to us, we'll make him understand later.

8 The kids in his class laugh at him.
   a He tells funny stories and the kids in his class laugh.
   b The kids in his class make fun of him.

5 Extreme behaviour!

2 Choose the correct word to complete the sentences.

1 My father *disapproves / disagrees* of tattoos. He thinks they're ugly.
2 Sara has a *long-term / temporary* job this summer at the local library.
3 Many teenagers feel *unfair / insecure* when they are with people they don't know well.
4 We stopped at the bakery *briefly / accidentally* to buy some bread.
5 When did you have your ears *pinched / pierced* ?
6 Have you got a copy of your birth *certificate / identity* ?
7 When you are eighteen, you will have the *right / permission* to vote.
8 The police caught the *bullies / troublemakers* and took them to the police station.
9 Please let's discuss the subject calmly and you can explain things from your point of *opinion / view*.
10 My parents don't approve *for / of* my boyfriend because he has body piercing.

3 Complete the sentences with the correct form of these phrasal verbs.

fall over   fight back   give up   go through   hand over   join in   sort out   tidy up

1 While she was running down the street, Meg .... something and broke her leg.
2 They .... my bag and found some personal letters.
3 The little girl .... her seat to the old man on the bus.
4 The school bullies forced the child to .... his money.
5 Your room's a mess! Please .... it ....
6 The teacher started laughing and the whole class ....
7 When are you going to .... the problem? You said you'd find a solution!
8 He hit me first, so I ....

4 Complete the sentences with the correct form of these verbs.

apologise   argue   bother   demand   dye   ignore   nick   react   shove   tease

1 How will Stephen .... when he hears the news?
2 They don't agree about anything and .... all the time.
3 It really .... me when people tell lies.
4 I was angry with the shop assistant and .... to speak to the manager.
5 Please .... my brother. He's just being silly.
6 Nadia has .... her hair black. I think she looks great!
7 I hate it when people push and .... each other to get on the bus.
8 I can't find my calculator. I think my sister's .... it!
9 We .... my little brother about his big ears but he doesn't mind. He just laughs.
10 She dropped my mobile phone and broke it but she .... and bought me a new one.

Extreme behaviour! 5

 Conditionals: zero, first, second
Complete the text with the correct form of the verbs in brackets.

Imagine this. What 1) ………………………… (you / do) if your best friend 2) ………………………… (ignore) you one day? How 3) ………………………… (you / react) if she suddenly 4) ………………………… (stop) hanging out with you and said she preferred the company of more popular kids? 5) ………………………… (you / be) upset but say nothing, or 6) ………………………… (you / ask) your friend to tell you what was wrong?

Sudden changes in behaviour are quite common, especially among teenagers. Research has shown that when teenagers are under pressure, their behaviour 7) ………………………… (may / become) strange or unpredictable. Hanging out with popular kids is one way to become more popular yourself.

If I 8) ………………………… (be) you, I 9) ………………………… (be) brave and face my friend. Unless you 10) ………………………… (do) this, you 11) ………………………… (never / know) what the matter is.

 so, such, such a, too, not … enough
Rewrite the sentences so that the meaning stays the same. Use the words in brackets.

1 They were such cool tattoo designs that I wanted to have one. (so)
   The tattoo designs ……………………………………………………………… .

2 Everybody likes Nicky because she has a great sense of humour. (such)
   Nicky ……………………………………………………………… .

3 The trousers were too short for me. (long)
   The trousers ……………………………………………………………… .

4 Martin is such a shy boy that he never speaks in class. (so)
   Martin is ……………………………………………………………… .

5 You aren't old enough to have a driving licence. (too)
   You're ……………………………………………………………… .

6 That's such a cool hair colour! (so)
   That hair colour ……………………………………………………………… !

7 This CD is so wonderful that I listen to it all the time. (such)
   This is ……………………………………………………………… .

8 The bullies were so horrible that we complained to the head teacher. (such)
   They were ……………………………………………………………… .

5 Extreme behaviour!

Test yourself!

Choose the word or phrase that best completes the conversation or sentence.

1 Natalie is …… good dancer that she came first in the competition.
   A such
   B so a
   C such a
   D so

2 Could we …… seats? I prefer to sit by the window.
   A bang
   B push
   C shove
   D swap

3 'I'm thinking of piercing my eyebrow.'
   'I …… do that if I were you.'
   A won't
   B don't
   C wouldn't
   D didn't

4 I don't …… staying at home on my own. Actually, I like it.
   A approve
   B bother
   C judge
   D mind

5 If people ignore me, I …… miserable.
   A am feeling
   B feel
   C would feel
   D felt

6 Kelly lives in a …… house in a rich neighbourhood.
   A posh
   B brave
   C jealous
   D positive

7 They're …… nice people that we like spending time with them.
   A so
   B so a
   C such
   D such a

8 'Do you like this colour on me?'
   'Well, to be honest, I think it's …… .'
   A enough bright
   B too bright enough
   C not bright enough
   D not enough bright

9 Dad got a …… for illegal parking yesterday.
   A fine
   B form
   C licence
   D column

10 People who don't …… the law often get into trouble with the police.
   A confirm
   B influence
   C obey
   D replace

11 'Aren't we going to wait for Molly?'
   'She's usually …… late that we rarely wait for her.'
   A so
   B so a
   C such
   D such a

12 It's your decision but …… , I don't think it's a good idea.
   A accidentally
   B afterwards
   C exactly
   D personally

13 Unless you …… , I'll never speak to you again.
   A apologise
   B apologised
   C will apologise
   D would apologise

14 It is important for young people to express their …… . After all, everybody is different.
   A permission
   B behaviour
   C understanding
   D individuality

6 Stay in or go out?

Reading: Pages 62–63

6.1 **stay in** (phr v) /ˌsteɪ ˈɪn/ = to stay in your home and not go out. *Let's **stay in** and watch TV.*
μένω στο σπίτι

6.2 **recognise** (v) /ˈrekəgnaɪz, ˈrekən-/ = to know sb or sth because you have seen them before and remember them. *He had changed and I didn't **recognise** him!*
➤ recognition (n)
αναγνωρίζω

6.3 **flex** (v) /fleks/ = to bend part of your body so that your muscles stretch and become tight. ***Flex** your muscles.*
(για άσκηση ή προετοιμασία για κίνηση) κάμπτω, λυγίζω

6.4 **make history** (phr) /ˌmeɪk ˈhɪstəri/ = to do sth important that will be recorded and remembered. *Columbus **made history** when he discovered the New World.*
γράφω ιστορία

6.5 **heading** (n) /ˈhedɪŋ/ = the title at the top of a piece of writing. *read the paragraph **headings***
επικεφαλίδα

6.6 **recommendation** (n) /ˌrekəmenˈdeɪʃən/ = a suggestion of what sb should do. *The report made some **recommendations** to improve schools.*
➤ recommend (v)
σύσταση

6.7 **review** (v) /rɪˈvjuː/ = to write a report about a new book, film, game or television show. *She **reviews** films for a newspaper.* ➤ review (n), reviewer (n)
γράφω κριτική, κρίνω

6.8 **background** (n) /ˈbækgraʊnd/ = the general situation in which sth happens. *The **background** of the story is the last war.*
φόντο

6.9 **detailed** (adj) /ˈdiːteɪld/ = including a lot of information. *a **detailed** description of the film* ➤ detail (n)
λεπτομερής-ές

6.10 **thrill** (n) /θrɪl/ = a strong feeling of excitement and pleasure. *the **thrill** of driving a fast car*
έξαψη, συναρπαγή

6.11 **surely** (adv) /ˈʃɔːli/ = used to show that you are surprised at sth. ***Surely** you don't believe her!*
μη μου πεις πως

6.12 **ingredient** (n) /ɪnˈgriːdiənt/ = one of the qualities that you need to achieve sth. *The film has all the **ingredients** necessary to win an Oscar.*
συστατικό

6.13 **hooked** (adj) /hʊkt/ = if you are hooked on sth, you like it a lot and want to continue doing it. *children who are **hooked** on computer games*
εθισμένος-η-ο
◆ hooked on

6.14 **best-selling** (adj) /ˌbest ˈselɪŋ/ = a best-selling product is sth which a lot of people buy. *a list of **best-selling** DVDs*
μεγάλης εμπορικής επιτυχίας

6.15 **none** (pronoun) /nʌn/ = not any of sth, or not one person or thing. *'Can I have some coffee?' 'Sorry, there's **none** left.'*
κανένας/καμία/κανένα, κανείς, ούτε ένας/μία/ένα

6.16 **put out** (phr v) /pʊt ˈaʊt/ = to take sth outside your house and leave it there. ***Put** the cat **out** before you go to bed.*
βγάζω έξω

6.17 **dull** (adj) /dʌl/ = not interesting or exciting. *It was a **dull** party, so we left early.*
βαρετός-ή-ό, πληκτικός-ή-ό

6.18 **in fact** (prep phr) /ɪn ˈfækt/ = used when you are adding sth, especially sth surprising, to emphasise what you have just said. *I know the Browns well. **In fact**, I had dinner with them last week.*
στην πραγματικότητα, εδώ που τα λέμε

6.19 **publisher** (n) /ˈpʌblɪʃə/ = a person or company that produces books, magazines, etc. and offers them for sale. *a **publisher** of magazines for young people*
➤ publish (v), publication (n)
εκδότης

6.20 **worldwide** (adv) /ˌwɜːldˈwaɪd/ = everywhere in the world. *The company employs 2,000 people **worldwide**.*
παγκοσμίως

6.21 **come out** (phr v) /kʌm ˈaʊt/ = if a book, CD, etc. comes out, it becomes available for people to buy. *When does his new book **come out**?*
δημοσιεύομαι, κυκλοφορώ, προβάλλομαι

6.22 **versatile** (adj) /ˈvɜːsətaɪl/ = having many different uses. ***versatile** clothes that you can wear everywhere*
πολλαπλών χρήσεων ή εφαρμογών

6.23 **online** (adv) /ˌɒnˈlaɪn/ = connected to or using a computer or network of computers. *Our school went **online** this year.*
συνδεδεμένος-η-ο στο Διαδίκτυο

6.24 **portable** (adj) /ˈpɔːtəbəl/ = easy to carry. *a **portable** television*
φορητός-ή-ό

6 Stay in or go out?

6.25 involve (v) /ɪnˈvɒlv/ = if an activity or situation involves sth, that thing is a part of it. *His job **involves** a lot of travelling.* ➤ involvement (n)
συνεπάγομαι

6.26 battle (n) /ˈbætl/ = a fight between two armies or groups, especially in a war. *the **battle** of Marathon*
μάχη

6.27 objective (n) /əbˈdʒektɪv/ = sth that you are working hard to achieve. *Our **objective** is to raise money.*
στόχος, επιδίωξη

6.28 opponent (n) /əˈpəʊnənt/ = sb who is competing against you in a sport or competition. *Her **opponent** was better than her, so she lost the match.*
αντίπαλος

6.29 reactions (n pl) /riˈækʃənz/ = your ability to move quickly when sth, usually dangerous, happens suddenly. *Athletes need to have quick **reactions**.* ➤ react (v)
αντιδράσεις

6.30 concentration (n) /ˌkɒnsənˈtreɪʃən/ = when you think very carefully about sth you are doing. *To do well in an exam, **concentration** is important.* ➤ concentrate (v)
αυτοσυγκέντρωση

6.31 interactive (adj) /ˌɪntərˈæktɪv/ = involving communication between a computer, television, etc. and the person using it. ***interactive** software*
διαδραστικός

6.32 respond (v) /rɪˈspɒnd/ = to behave in a particular way after sth has happened or sb has done sth. *How did they **respond** to the crisis?* ➤ response (n)
ανταποκρίνομαι
◆ respond to

6.33 input (n) /ˈɪnpʊt/ = information that is put into a computer. *respond to **input*** ➤ input (v)
εισαγωγή δεδομένων ή εντολών

6.34 action-packed (adj) /ˌækʃən ˈpækt/ = an action-packed film, book, etc. contains a lot of exciting events. *Most kids love **action-packed** holidays.*
γεμάτος-η-ο δράση

6.35 exist (v) /ɪgˈzɪst/ = to be real, present or alive. *Do UFOs really **exist**?* ➤ existence (n)
υπάρχω

6.36 evil (n) /ˈiːvəl/ = sth that is very bad and has a very cruel or harmful effect. *the **evils** of war* ➤ evil (adj)
κακό, δεινό

6.37 intelligent (adj) /ɪnˈtelɪdʒənt/ = good at understanding ideas and thinking clearly. *an **intelligent** student* ➤ intelligence (n)
νοήμων, έξυπνος-η-ο

6.38 bookworm (n) /ˈbʊkwɜːm/ = sb who likes reading very much. *My brother is a **bookworm** – he reads about five or six books a month.*
βιβλιοφάγος

6.39 eventually (adv) /ɪˈventʃuəli/ = after a long time. *She worked hard and **eventually** succeeded.* ➤ eventual (adj)
επιτέλους

6.40 lead (v) /liːd/ = to cause sth to happen, or to cause sb to do sth. *a decision that **led** to success*
έχω ως αποτέλεσμα, οδηγώ (σε)
◆ lead to. Irr v: lead–led–led

6.41 graphics (n pl) /ˈɡræfɪks/ = pictures or images, especially those produced on a computer. *The new version of the computer game has brilliant **graphics**.*
σχηματικά ηλεκτρονικού υπολογιστή

6.42 version (n) /ˈvɜːʃən/ = one form of sth that is slightly different from all other forms. *one **version** of the story*
εκδοχή

6.43 artificial intelligence (n phr) /ˌɑːtɪfɪʃəl ɪnˈtelɪdʒəns/ = the study of how to make computers do intelligent things that people do, such as think and make decisions. ***Artificial intelligence** will change our lives in the future.*
τεχνητή νοημοσύνη

6.44 programme (v) /ˈprəʊɡræm/ = to give a set of instructions to a machine to make it do sth. *I've **programmed** the video to record the film.* ➤ programme (n)
προγραμματίζω
Also: program (v)

6.45 criticism (n) /ˈkrɪtɪsɪzəm/ = when you say that a person or thing is bad in some way. *He disagreed with the teacher's **criticism** of his work.* ➤ criticise (v), critic (n)
κριτική

6.46 patience (n) /ˈpeɪʃəns/ = the ability to stay calm and not get angry when you are waiting for sth or doing sth difficult. *I don't have enough **patience** to be a teacher.* ➤ patient (adj)
υπομονή
Opp: impatience

6.47 feature (n) /ˈfiːtʃə/ = an important, interesting or typical part of sth. *an important **feature** of his music*
χαρακτηριστικό

6.48 range (n) /reɪndʒ/ = a group of things that are different but belong to the same general type. *You can choose from a wide **range** of colours.* ➤ range (n)
γκάμα

6.49 character (n) /ˈkærɪktə/ = a person in a book, play, film, etc. *a **character** in a book*
χαρακτήρας (διηγήματος, θεατρικού έργου, κλπ.)

6.50 percent (n) /pəˈsent/ = an amount equal to five, ten, etc. parts out of a total of a hundred parts. *Only fifty **percent** of the people voted.*
τοις εκατό

57

Stay in or go out? 6

6.51 speed (n) /spiːd/ = how fast sth moves. *What **speed** were you travelling at?*
ταχύτητα

6.52 predictable (adj) /prɪˈdɪktəbəl/ = behaving or happening in the way that you expect, and not different or interesting. *an entertaining but **predictable** film*
➤ predict (v), prediction (n)
προβλέψιμος-η-ο, αναμενόμενος-η-ο
Opp: unpredictable

6.53 majority (n) /məˈdʒɒrəti/ = most of the people or things in a group. *The **majority** of students passed. Only a few failed.*
πλειοψηφία
Opp: minority

6.54 male (adj) /meɪl/ = belonging to the sex that cannot have babies. *a **male** lion* ➤ male (n)
αρσενικός-ή-ό
Opp: female

6.55 purpose (n) /ˈpɜːpəs/ = the purpose of sth is what it is intended to achieve. *What is the **purpose** of your visit to England?*
σκοπός

6.56 communication (n) /kəˌmjuːnɪˈkeɪʃən/ = when people talk to each other or give each other information. ***communication** between teachers and parents*
➤ communicate (v)
επικοινωνία

6.57 extra (adj) /ˈekstrə/ = in addition to the usual things or amount. *We ordered a pizza with **extra** cheese.*
πρόσθετος-η-ο, επιπλέον

6.58 relate (v) /rɪˈleɪt/ = if one thing relates to another, it is connected with it in some way. *I collect anything that **relates** to the football team I support.* ➤ relation (n)
(συ)σχετίζω-ομαι
◆ relate to

Vocabulary: Page 64

6.59 connected (adj) /kəˈnektɪd/ = if two things are connected to each other, they are joined together. *My computer is **connected** to a printer.*
συνδεδεμένος-η-ο

6.60 device (n) /dɪˈvaɪs/ = a machine or tool used for a particular purpose. *a small electronic **device***
συσκευή

6.61 keyboard (n) /ˈkiːbɔːd/ = a set of keys on a computer, a piano, etc., which you press to produce letters or sounds. *I need a new **keyboard** for my computer.*
πληκτρολόγιο

6.62 laptop (n) /ˈlæptɒp/ = a small computer you can carry with you. *I use a **laptop** if I'm travelling by train.*
φορητός υπολογιστής

6.63 memory stick (n phr) /ˈmeməri stɪk/ = a small device or flat card that is used to store information electronically and which fits into computers, digital cameras, etc. *I have the information here on my **memory stick**.*
φορητός δίσκος μνήμης

6.64 mouse (n) /maʊs/ = a small object connected to a computer that you move with your hand to give instructions to the computer. *I need a new **mouse** for my computer.*
ποντίκι υπολογιστή

6.65 screen (n) /skriːn/ = the part of a television or computer where the picture or information appears. *a computer with an eighteen-inch **screen***
οθόνη

6.66 centimetre (n) /ˈsentɪˌmiːtə/ = a unit for measuring length. *There are 100 **centimetres** in a metre.*
εκατοστό (του μέτρου)

6.67 click (v) /klɪk/ = to press a button on a computer mouse to make the computer do sth. ***Click** on the icon.*
➤ click (n)
κάνω κλικ

6.68 well-known (adj) /ˌwel ˈnəʊn/ = known about by a lot of people. *She is a **well-known** artist.*
διάσημος-η-ο

6.69 numerical (adj) /njuːˈmerɪkəl/ = expressed in numbers or relating to numbers. *The pages should be in **numerical** order.* ➤ number (n)
αριθμητικός-ή-ό

6.70 operate (v) /ˈɒpəreɪt/ = to work or to make sth work. *The machine is **operating** smoothly.* ➤ operation (n)
λειτουργώ

6.71 complicated (adj) /ˈkɒmplɪkeɪtɪd/ = sth that is complicated has a lot of different parts and is difficult to understand or deal with. *The instructions are **complicated** and I can't understand them.*
➤ complicate (v)
περίπλοκος-η-ο

6.72 microchip (n) /ˈmaɪkrəʊtʃɪp/ = a very small piece of silicon containing electronic parts, used in computers and other machines. *a **microchip** in an electronic device*
μικροψηφίδα, μικροτσίπ

6.73 spread (v) /spred/ = to tell a lot of people about sth, or to become known by a lot of people. *He's **spreading** lies about me!*
διαδίδω
Irr v: spread–spread–spread

6.74 development (n) /dɪˈveləpmənt/ = the process of becoming bigger, better, more important, etc, or the result of this process. *important new **developments** in computer technology* ➤ develop (v)
εξέλιξη

6 Stay in or go out?

6.75 **sensitive** (adj) /ˈsensətɪv/ = reacting to very small changes in light, temperature, position, etc. *a **sensitive** thermometer* ➤ sensitivity (n)
ευαίσθητος-η-ο

6.76 **access** (n) /ˈækses/ = the right to enter a place, use sth, see sb, etc. *In some places people don't have **access** to clean water.* ➤ access (v)
πρόσβαση
◆ have access to

6.77 **structure** (n) /ˈstrʌktʃə/ = sth that has been built. *a large wooden **structure***
κατασκεύασμα

6.78 **download** (v) /ˌdaʊnˈləʊd, ˌdaʊnˈləʊd/ = to receive information or programs on a computer, especially using the Internet. *Peter often **downloads** games from the Internet.*
καταφορτώνω (μηχανογραφικά)
Opp: upload

6.79 **wherever** (adv) /weərˈevə/ = in any place. *Sit **wherever** you like.*
οπουδήποτε

6.80 **take it in turns** (phr) /ˌteɪk ɪt ɪn ˈtɜːnz/ = if a group of people take turns doing sth, first one person does it, then another. *They **took it in turns** to do the cooking.*
εναλλάσσομαι

6.81 **call out** (phr v) /ˌkɔːl ˈaʊt/ = to say sth loudly. *'Hello! Is anybody there?' I **called out**.*
καλώ, φωνάζω

Grammar: Page 65

6.82 **definite** (adj) /ˈdefənət/ = completely certain and not likely to be changed. *I can't give you a **definite** answer.*
εξακριβωμένος-η-ο, συγκεκριμένος-η-ο

6.83 **display** (v) /dɪˈspleɪ/ = if a computer displays information, it shows it. *The computer **displayed** an error message.* ➤ display (n)
εμφανίζω, δείχνω

6.84 **content** (n) /ˈkɒntent/ = the ideas or information in a book, programme, etc. *The **content** of this magazine is not suitable for young people.* ➤ contain (v)
περιεχόμενο

6.85 **rating** (n) /ˈreɪtɪŋ/ = a measurement of how popular, good, important, etc. sb or sth is. *The president's popularity **rating** has fallen.* ➤ rate (v)
αξιολόγηση

6.86 **guidelines** (n pl) /ˈɡaɪdlaɪnz/ = official advice about the way to do sth. ***guidelines*** *on writing essays*
καθοδηγητικές ή κατευθυντήριες γραμμές

6.87 **academically** (adv) /ˌækəˈdemɪkli/ = in a way that relates to education, especially in a college or university. ***Academically**, it was a good year for me and I passed all my exams.* ➤ academic (adj), academy (n)
ακαδημαϊκά

6.88 **challenging** (adj) /ˈtʃæləndʒɪŋ/ = difficult in an interesting or enjoyable way. *a **challenging** project* ➤ challenge (n, v)
δύσκολος-η-ο, αλλά και ενδιαφέρων-ουσα-ον

6.89 **attitude** (n) /ˈætɪtjuːd/ = what you think and feel about sth. *a strange **attitude** towards the subject*
στάση

Listening: Page 66

6.90 **awful** (adj) /ˈɔːfəl/ = very bad or unpleasant. *The weather was **awful**. It was cold and wet.*
απαίσιος-α-ο

6.91 **suggest** (v) /səˈdʒest/ = to tell sb your ideas about what should be done. *My doctor **suggested** that I should stay in bed for a few days.* ➤ suggestion (n)
προτείνω
◆ suggest sth; suggest (that) sb (should) do sth; suggest doing sth

6.92 **disappointed** (adj) /ˌdɪsəˈpɔɪntɪd/ = unhappy because sth you hoped for did not happen or was not as good as you expected. *We were **disappointed** when they said they couldn't come to our party.* ➤ disappoint (v), disappointment (n), disappointing (adj)
απογοητευμένος-η-ο
◆ disappointed at/about

6.93 **tone** (n) /təʊn/ = the way your voice sounds, which shows how you are feeling or what you mean. *The **tone** of her voice showed that she was angry.*
ύφος ή τόνος φωνής
◆ tone of voice

Speaking: Page 67

6.94 **findings** (n pl) /ˈfaɪndɪŋz/ = sth that has been learnt or decided as the result of an official study. *The scientists discussed their **findings**.*
ευρήματα, πόρισμα, διαπίστωση

6.95 **dress up** (phr v) /ˌdres ˈʌp/ = to wear clothes that are more formal than the ones you usually wear. *It's an formal party, so we have to **dress up**.*
ντύνομαι επίσημα

6.96 **stunning** (adj) /ˈstʌnɪŋ/ = extremely beautiful. *You look **stunning** in that dress!*
εκθαμβωτικός-ή-ό

Stay in or go out? 6

6.97 **note** (n) /nəʊt/ = sth that you write down in order to remember sth. *I'll make a **note** of your new address.*
σημείωση

6.98 **plenty** (pronoun) /ˈplenti/ = a large quantity that is enough or more than enough. *We don't need any more money. We have **plenty**.*
αφθονία, πληθώρα
◈ plenty of

Use your English: Pages 68–69

6.99 **dynamic** (adj) /daɪˈnæmɪk/ = full of energy and ideas. *Terence is a **dynamic** businessman.*
δυναμικός-ή-ό

6.100 **size** (n) /saɪz/ = how big or small sth is. *What **size** shoes do you wear?*
μέγεθος

6.101 **shape** (n) /ʃeɪp/ = the form that sth has, for example round, square, etc. *a card in the **shape** of a heart*
σχήμα

6.102 **material** (n) /məˈtɪəriəl/ = a solid substance that you can use to make things. *What **material** is the table made of: wood, metal or plastic?*
υλικό

6.103 **leather** (n) /ˈleðə/ = animal skin used for making shoes, bags, etc. *a **leather** belt*
δέρμα

6.104 **metal** (n) /ˈmetl/ = a hard, usually shiny, substance such as iron, gold or steel. *Is it made of **metal** or plastic?*
μέταλλο

6.105 **untidy** (adj) /ʌnˈtaɪdi/ = not neat. *Your room is **untidy**.*
➤ untidiness (n)
ακατάστατος-η-ο
Opp: tidy

6.106 **quad bike** (n phr) /kwɒd baɪk/ = a small vehicle similar to a motorcycle but with four wide wheels, usually ridden on rough paths or fields. *drive a **quad bike***
τετράτροχη μοτοσικλέτα

6.107 **neat** (adj) /niːt/ = arranged in a tidy and careful way. *Her room was **neat** and tidy.* ➤ neatness (n)
συγυρισμένος-η-ο

6.108 **elegant** (adj) /ˈelɪgənt/ = graceful and attractive. *an **elegant**, well-dressed woman* ➤ elegance (n)
κομψός-ή-ό

6.109 **mean** (adj) /miːn/ = cruel and not kind. *Don't be **mean** to your sister!* ➤ meanness (n)
ευτελής-ές, ποταπός-ή-ό

6.110 **cheerful** (adj) /ˈtʃɪəfəl/ = happy and showing this by your behaviour. *She always looks **cheerful**.*
χαρούμενος-η-ο

6.111 **freezing** (adj) /ˈfriːzɪŋ/ = extremely cold. *It's **freezing** here in winter!* ➤ freeze (v), frozen (adj)
παγωμένος-η-ο

6.112 **icy** (adj) /ˈaɪsi/ = covered in ice. ***icy** roads*
παγερός-ή-ό, παγωμένος-η-ο

6.113 **active** (adj) /ˈæktɪv/ = always doing things or moving around a lot. *He's eighty but he's very **active**.*
➤ action (n), activity (n)
δραστήριος-α-ο

6.114 **energetic** (adj) /ˌenəˈdʒetɪk/ = strong, active and working hard. *a young and **energetic** leader*
➤ energy (n)
δραστήριος-α-ο

6.115 **dramatic** (adj) /drəˈmætɪk/ = exciting and impressive. *She made a **dramatic** speech and everybody cheered.*
➤ drama (n)
συγκλονιστικός-ή-ό, δραματικός-ή-ό

6.116 **hi-tech** (adj) /ˌhaɪ ˈtek/ = using the most modern machines, equipment and methods. *a new **hi-tech** camera*
υψηλής τεχνολογίας
Also: high-tech

6.117 **everyday** (adj) /ˈevrideɪ/ = ordinary, usual or happening every day. *Accidents are part of **everyday** life.*
καθημερινός-ή-ό

6.118 **plain** (adj) /pleɪn/ = easy to understand or recognise. *It's **plain** to see that he doesn't like us.*
σαφής-ές, ξεκάθαρος-η-ο

6.119 **operation** (n) /ˌɒpəˈreɪʃən/ = when people work together in a planned way in order to do sth. *a rescue **operation***
οργανωμένη προσπάθεια, επιχείρηση

6.120 **plot** (n) /plɒt/ = the events that form the main story of a book, film or play. *The film has an exciting **plot**.*
πλοκή

6.121 **spy** (n) /spaɪ/ = sb whose job is to find out secret information about a country or organisation. *The film is about a **spy** who discovers an important secret.*
➤ spy (v)
κατάσκοπος

6.122 **villain** (n) /ˈvɪlən/ = the main bad character in a story, film, etc. *The hero fights the **villain** at the end of the film.*
κακούργος

6.123 **wire-framed** (adj) /ˌwaɪə ˈfreɪmd/ = having a frame of thin metal in the form of a thread. ***wire-framed** glasses*
με μεταλλικό σκελετό

6.124 **spectacles** (n pl) /ˈspektəkəlz/ = glasses. *I can't see without my **spectacles**.*
γυαλιά (όρασης)

6 Stay in or go out?

6.125 lightning bolt (n phr) /ˈlaɪtnɪŋ bəʊlt/ = lightning that appears as a white line in the sky. *The tree was struck by a **lightning bolt**.*
αστραπή
Also: bolt of lighting

6.126 switch on (phr v) /ˌswɪtʃ ˈɒn/ = to turn on a machine, light, etc. using a switch. *It's dark. **Switch on** the light.*
ανάβω ή ανοίγω (με διακόπτη)

6.127 power (n) /ˈpaʊə/ = force or physical strength. *The **power** of the explosion was enormous.*
➤ powerful (adj), powerless (adj)
δύναμη

6.128 contain (v) /kənˈteɪn/ = to include sth. *Does the film **contain** violence?* ➤ content (n)
έχω ως περιεχόμενο, (εμ)περιέχω

6.129 deadly (adj) /ˈdedli/ = very dangerous and likely to cause death. *a **deadly** poison*
θανάσιμος-η-ο

6.130 virus (n) /ˈvaɪərəs/ = a very small living thing that causes diseases. *Colds are caused by a **virus**.*
ιός

6.131 spoil (v) /spɔɪl/ = to make sth less good or enjoyable. *The rain **spoilt** our picnic.*
χαλώ, καταστρέφω
Irr v: spoil–spoilt–spoilt

6.132 individual (adj) /ˌɪndɪˈvɪdʒuəl/ = an individual person or thing is just one, considered separately from other people or things. *Each **individual** drawing is different.*
➤ individual (n), individuality (n)
ατομικός-ή-ό

6.133 mass (n) /mæs/ = a large amount or number of sth all together. *a **mass** of clouds*
μάζα

6.134 substance (n) /ˈsʌbstəns/ = any type of solid, liquid or gas. *The bag was covered with a sticky **substance**.*
ουσία

6.135 abstract (adj) /ˈæbstrækt/ = based on ideas rather than specific examples or real events. *Beauty is an **abstract** idea.*
αφηρημένος-η-ο

6.136 honesty (n) /ˈɒnəsti/ = the quality of being honest, i.e. not lying, cheating or stealing. *I admire him for his **honesty**.* ➤ honest (adj)
εντιμότητα, τιμιότητα
Opp: dishonesty

6.137 peace (n) /piːs/ = when there is no war or fighting or when everything is very calm and quiet. *the **peace** of the countryside* ➤ peaceful (adj)
ειρήνη

6.138 author (n) /ˈɔːθə/ = sb who has written a book. *Robert Louis Stevenson was the **author** of 'Treasure Island'.*
συγγραφέας

6.139 interviewer (n) /ˈɪntəvjuːə/ = the person who asks the questions in an interview (= a formal meeting in which someone is asked questions). *Nadia answered the **interviewer's** question.* ➤ interview (n, v)
το πρόσωπο που παίρνει συνέντευξη

6.140 tip (n) /tɪp/ = a simple but useful piece of advice about how to do sth. *some useful **tips** on how to study*
χρήσιμη πληροφορία

6.141 would-be (adj) /ˈwʊd biː/ = a would-be writer, actor, etc. is sb who wants to be a writer, actor, etc. *Joan is taking part in a competition for **would-be** singers.*
επίδοξος-η-ο

6.142 fairly (adv) /ˈfeəli/ = more than a little but much less than very. *She speaks English **fairly** well.*
αρκετά

6.143 give up (phr v) /gɪv ˈʌp/ = to stop trying to do sth. *You shouldn't **give up** so easily.*
παραιτούμαι

6.144 novel (n) /ˈnɒvəl/ = a long written story about characters and events that are not real. *He wrote his first **novel** when he was twenty-nine.* ➤ novelist (n)
μυθιστόρημα

6.145 ink (n) /ɪŋk/ = a coloured liquid used for writing, printing or drawing. *a message written in black **ink***
μελάνι

Writing: Pages 70–71

6.146 genre (n) /ˈʒɒnrə/ = a type of art, music, literature, etc. that has a particular style or feature. *Science fiction is a **genre** that I enjoy.*
θεματικό εκφραστικό ύφος ή τεχνοτροπία

6.147 non-fiction (n) /ˌnɒn ˈfɪkʃən/ = books about real facts or events. *Mary is looking for a book in the **non-fiction** section of the library.*
πεζογραφία που έχει ως θέμα πραγματικά πρόσωπα, γεγονότα, κλπ.

6.148 romance (n) /rəʊˈmæns, ˈrəʊmæns/ = a story about love between two people. *a beautiful **romance***
➤ romantic (adj)
ρομαντικό διήγημα

6.149 section (n) /ˈsekʃən/ = one of the parts that sth is divided into. *I always read the sports **section** of the newspaper.*
σελίδα εφημερίδας, περιοδικού, κλπ. αφιερωμένη σε κάποιο θέμα

6.150 strength (n) /streŋθ/ = your strengths are the good things about you or the things you are good at. *We have all got **strengths** and weaknesses.* ➤ strengthen (v), strong (adj)
ιδιαίτερη ικανότητα, φόρτε

Stay in or go out? 6

6.151 weakness (n) /ˈwiːknəs/ = a problem that makes sb or sth less likely to be successful or that can be easily attacked or criticised. *The soundtrack is not good. In fact, it is one of the film's main **weaknesses**.*
➤ weak (adj), weaken (v)
αδυναμία

6.152 relevant (adj) /ˈreləvənt/ = directly relating to the thing that is being discussed. *Please give me the **relevant** details only.* ➤ relevance (n)
σχετιζόμενος-η-ο, σχετικός-ή-ό
Opp: irrelevant

6.153 title (n) /ˈtaɪtl/ = the name given to a book, painting, play, etc. *the **title** of her novel*
τίτλος

6.154 series (n) /ˈsɪəriːz/ = a set of television or radio programmes with the same characters or on the same subject. *a new comedy **series***
σειρά
Plural: series

6.155 discover (v) /dɪsˈkʌvə/ = to learn sth that you did not know about before. *Who **discovered** Australia?*
➤ discovery (n)
ανακαλύπτω

6.156 series (n) /ˈsɪəriːz/ = several events or actions of the same kind that happen one after the other. *a **series** of accidents*
σειρά, αλληλουχία
Plural: series

6.157 event (n) /ɪˈvent/ = sth that happens, especially sth important, interesting or unusual. *the most important **events** of the year*
γεγονός, συμβάν

6.158 bring up (phr v) /ˌbrɪŋ ˈʌp/ = to look after children until they are adults. *Rachel was **brought up** by her grandmother.*
μεγαλώνω, ανατρέφω

6.159 actually (adv) /ˈæktʃuəli, -tʃəli/ = used to emphasise that sth is true, especially when it is a little surprising or unexpected. *'Are you disappointed?' 'No. **Actually**, I feel quite pleased.'* ➤ actual (adj)
στην πραγματικότητα

6.160 moreover (adv) /mɔːˈrəʊvə/ = used to introduce information which adds to or supports sth you have just said. *The new design is not very good. **Moreover**, it is expensive.*
επιπλέον, συν τοις άλλοις

6.161 desperately (adv) /ˈdespərətli/ = in a way that shows willingness to do anything to change a bad situation, even if it is dangerous or unpleasant. *The doctors tried **desperately** to save her life.*
➤ desperate (adj), despair (n, v)
απεγνωσμένα

6.162 circumstances (n pl) /ˈsɜːkəmstænsɪz, -stənsɪz/ = the facts or conditions that affect what happens in a situation. *the mysterious **circumstances** of his death*
συνθήκες
◈ under (these) circumstances

6.163 death (n) /deθ/ = the end of sb's life. *Einstein lived in the United States until his **death**.* ➤ dead (adj), die (v)
θάνατος

6.164 as a result (phr) /əz ə rɪˈzʌlt/ = because of sth. *It was freezing. **As a result**, the flowers died.*
ως αποτέλεσμα

6.165 MI6 (abbreviation) /ˌem aɪ ˈsɪks/ = Military Intelligence Section 6 of the British Secret Intelligence Service. *They are spies and work for **MI6**.*
βρετανικές μυστικές υπηρεσίες

6.166 take up (phr v) /ˌteɪk ˈʌp/ = to accept an invitation or suggestion. *Thanks for the offer. I think I'll **take** it **up**.*
(απο)δέχομαι

6.167 in spite of (phr) /ɪn ˈspaɪt əv, ɒv/ = although; despite. *We enjoyed ourselves **in spite of** the rain.*
παρά τον/την/το

6.168 headquarters (n pl) /ˌhedˈkwɔːtəz, ˈhedkwɔːtəz/ = the main office of a large company or organisation. *the **headquarters** of the organisation*
αρχηγείο

6.169 enemy (n) /ˈenəmi/ = sb who hates you and wants you to fail. *He made many **enemies**.*
εχθρός

6.170 strongly (adv) /ˈstrɒŋli/ = used to emphasise that sb should seriously consider what you are saying to them. *I **strongly** advise you to be careful.*
με έμφαση

6.171 recommend (v) /ˌrekəˈmend/ = to say that sb or sth is good. *Can you **recommend** a good restaurant?*
➤ recommendation (n)
συνιστώ

6.172 laureate (n) /ˈlɔːriət/ = sb who has been given an important prize or honour, especially the Nobel Prize. *Greece's Nobel **laureate**, George Seferis*
πρόσωπο στο οποίο απονεμήθηκε τιμητική διάκριση για το πνευματικό του έργο

6.173 encourage (v) /ɪnˈkʌrɪdʒ/ = to try to help sb succeed, for example by giving them confidence or determination. *My parents **encouraged** me to continue with my music studies.* ➤ encouragement (n), encouraging (adj)
ενθαρρύνω
Opp: discourage

6.174 optimistic (adj) /ˌɒptəˈmɪstɪk/ = believing that good things will happen in the future. *Tom's **optimistic** about finding a job.* ➤ optimism (n)
αισιόδοξος
Opp: pessimistic

6 Stay in or go out?

6.175 realistic (adj) /rɪəˈlɪstɪk/ = showing things as they really are. *a **realistic** TV drama* ➤ real (adj), reality (n)
ρεαλιστικός-ή-ό

6.176 summary (n) /ˈsʌməri/ = a short statement that gives the main information about sth. *Write a brief **summary** of the story.* ➤ summarise (v)
περίληψη

WORDZONE SPECIAL

Some words are easy to understand if you know Greek! For example:
- *dynamic* (from 'δυναμικός')
- *dramatic* (from 'δραματικός')
- *academic* (from 'ακαδημαϊκός')

Other words also come from the Greek. Look at these words that appeared in this unit.

character   criticism   energetic   graphics   history   metal   series

Vocabulary and grammar practice

1 Choose the correct word to complete the sentences.

1 Can you *encourage / recommend* a good restaurant in your area?
2 How does this machine *operate / programme*? Can you show me?
3 I disagree with the person who *reviewed / summarised* the film. I thought it was great.
4 She has changed a lot and you might not *relate / recognise* her.
5 The scientist's discovery *wrote / made* history.
6 Janet beat her *opponent / objective* in the match yesterday.
7 Shall we *have / take* it in turns to do the washing up?
8 Those plastic bags *contain / involve* some old clothes that I want to give away.

2 Match 1–6 with a–f and make compound adjectives and adverbs. Then complete the sentences.

1	action-	☐	a	known
2	best-	☐	b	line
3	hi-	☐	c	packed
4	on	☐	d	selling
5	well-	☐	e	tech
6	world	☐	f	wide

1 I watched the film on TV last night. It was a(n) .... thriller.
2 My mother bought the latest .... equipment for her business.
3 He is a(n) .... jazz musician and many people bought tickets for his concert.
4 Philip Pullman wrote a number of .... children's books.
5 That television series is very popular ....
6 I want to go .... and look for some information on the Internet.

Stay in or go out? 6

3 Complete the sentences with these nouns.

access bookworm content feature genre recommendations version weakness

1 The review said that the .... of the film is not suitable for children.
2 Unfortunately, they don't have Internet .... in their village.
3 Science fiction is not a(n) .... I like. I prefer comedies.
4 In the report she made several .... on how to improve the restaurant.
5 I love this .... of the song. It's really cool!
6 The costumes are a very important .... of the play.
7 I'm not a(n) .... but my sister is. She reads a lot!
8 Do you think that is the only .... of the novel or were there other things you didn't like?

4 Past simple and present perfect simple
Complete the letter with the correct form of the verbs in brackets. Use the past simple or present perfect simple.

Dear Rachel,

Guess what! I 1) .... (just / write) my first film review! I'm really excited because the local newspaper is going to publish it next week. The film I reviewed is called 'Lost in Love' and it 2) .... (come out) about a month ago. 3) .... (you / see) it yet? It's a romantic comedy with Bridget Farlow in the leading role. I 4) .... (watch) the film three times last week. In the end, I was quite bored but I 5) .... (not want) to miss any important details! Then, after watching the film, I 6) .... (make) a list of its strengths and weaknesses but it was hard to find any negative points. No wonder the film 7) .... (be) such a huge success!

Anyway, I 8) .... (always / want) to write for a newspaper, so you can imagine how pleased I am!

5 Countable and uncountable nouns; quantifiers
Complete the sentences with these words.

a few (x2) a little any (x2) many much plenty of

1 It's quiet tonight. There are only .... people in the restaurant.
2 We don't have to hurry. There's .... time. In fact, we can have a coffee before the film starts.
3 I can't buy the book now. I only have .... money with me.
4 How .... mobile phones have you got?
5 There isn't .... milk at all in the fridge.
6 I've decided to stay for .... more days. I'll leave next week.
7 We don't have .... milk but there's enough for two cups of coffee.
8 Is there .... reason why you don't read books?

6 Stay in or go out?

Test yourself!

Choose the word or phrase that best completes the conversation or sentence.

1 You will …… the fun if you tell us how the film ends!
   A display
   B spoil
   C relate
   D discover

2 I think Susan is …… on computer games. She plays all the time!
   A hooked
   B disappointed
   C involved
   D flexed

3 '…… my MP3 player? I can't find it.'
   'I think it's in the kitchen.'
   A Did you see
   B You saw
   C Have you seen
   D You have seen

4 Please don't speak to me in that …… of voice!
   A strength
   B structure
   C thrill
   D tone

5 I have wanted to be a photographer …… I was a teenager.
   A until
   B for
   C already
   D since

6 The book was quite good but it had a …… ending.
   A predict
   B prediction
   C predictable
   D predicting

7 'Has Jill left yet?'
   ' Yes, she …… yesterday.'
   A left
   B has left
   C did leave
   D was leaving

8 'How …… sugar did you put in the cake?'
   'One cup.'
   A many
   B much
   C a few
   D a little

9 I need a new …… to store my photographs on.
   A screen
   B memory stick
   C console
   D mouse

10 Press the button to …… the machine.
   A bring up
   B give up
   C come out
   D switch on

11 I …… MP3s from the Internet before.
   A never have downloaded
   B never downloaded
   C have never downloaded
   D have downloaded never

12 Laptops are …… , so you can carry them with you when you travel.
   A complicated
   B portable
   C dynamic
   D irresponsible

13 I've had this keyboard …… years.
   A for
   B since
   C already
   D yet

14 Leonard asked me for …… .
   A an advice
   B some advice
   C some advices
   D many advices

Time to revise 3 | Units 5–6

1 Match the adjectives 1–8 with their definitions a–h.

1. awful
2. energetic
3. guilty
4. jealous
5. optimistic
6. responsible
7. rude
8. versatile

a believing that good things will happen in the future
b speaking or behaving in a way that is not polite
c being in charge of or looking after sb or sth
d having many different uses
e strong and active
f very bad or unpleasant
g angry or unhappy because sb else has sth that you wish you had
h unhappy and ashamed because you have done sth wrong

2 Choose the correct word to complete the sentences.

1. We must obey the rules that *protect / test* us from danger.
2. Have you seen that new comedy *plot / series*? It's great!
3. The subject is challenging and requires *behaviour / concentration*.
4. Ben made some nasty *comments / judges* about my appearance.
5. Sylvia was *given up / brought* up by her grandmother.
6. The graphics on this website are *portable / stunning*. They're really beautiful!
7. I didn't know that Elaine had a driving *licence / right*.
8. Every year there are new *developments / situations* in computer technology.

3 Complete the sentences with the correct form of the words in capitals.

1. My mother didn't watch the film because she really hates .... **VIOLENT**
2. I think we should tell someone about the bullies but my friend .... **AGREE**
3. .... , there was a lot of traffic, so we missed the start of the film. **FORTUNE**
4. You must have a lot of .... if you want to be a good teacher. **PATIENT**
5. Jack is a .... child and he hates seeing other people suffering. **SENSE**
6. Were they very .... when their team lost the match? **DISAPPOINT**

4 Complete the second sentence so that it has a similar meaning to the first sentence, using the word given. Do not change the word given. You must use between two and five words, including the word given.

1. If I don't finish my work tonight, I won't go out. **UNLESS**
   I won't go out .... my work tonight.
2. The coffee pot is almost empty. **MUCH**
   There .... coffee in the pot.
3. Frank is too irresponsible to look after the children. **ENOUGH**
   Frank .... to look after the children.
4. My sister got her laptop in February. **SINCE**
   My sister .... February.
5. How long have you had this console? **BUY**
   When .... this console?

7 Horrible history

Reading: Pages 74–75

7.1 **historical** (adj) /hɪˈstɒrɪkəl/ = relating to people or things that happened or existed in the past. *a mixture of **historical** facts and fiction* ➤ history (n), historian (n)
που ανήκει ή αναφέρεται στο παρελθόν, ιστορικός-ή-ό

7.2 **century** (n) /ˈsentʃəri/ = a period of 100 years, used especially in dates. *The church was built in the thirteenth **century**.*
αιώνας

7.3 **filmmaker** (n) /ˈfɪlmˌmeɪkə/ = sb who makes films for the cinema or television. *Have you heard of the **filmmaker** Michael Moore?* ➤ film (n, v)
σκηνοθέτης ταινιών

7.4 **clearly** (adv) /ˈklɪəli/ = without any doubt. ***Clearly**, the situation was serious.* ➤ clear (adj)
ολοφάνερα

7.5 **not at all** (phr) /ˌnɒt ət ˈɔːl/ = used to say that sth is not even slightly true, or to ask if sth is even slightly true. *That's **not at all** true. It's a lie!*
καθόλου

7.6 **robber** (n) /ˈrɒbə/ = sb who steals money or other things from a bank, shop, etc. *The police caught the **robbers** as they were coming out of the bank.* ➤ rob (v), robbery (n)
ληστής
◈ bank robber

7.7 **murderer** (n) /ˈmɜːdərə/ = sb who kills another person. *He is a thief and a **murderer**.* ➤ murder (n, v)
δολοφόνος

7.8 **attack** (v) /əˈtæk/ = to try to hurt or kill sb. *Somebody **attacked** her while she was walking home.* ➤ attack (n)
επιτίθεμαι

7.9 **valuable** (adj) /ˈvæljuəbəl, -jəbəl/ = worth a lot of money. *It's a **valuable** ring. It cost a lot of money.* ➤ value (n)
πολύτιμος-η-ο

7.10 **it's no good** (phr) /ɪts ˌnəʊ ˈɡʊd/ = used to say that an action will not achieve what you want. ***It's no good** telling him – he won't listen.*
δεν ωφελεί να
◈ it's no good doing sth

7.11 **treasure** (n) /ˈtreʒə/ = a group of valuable things such as gold, silver, jewels, etc. *The pirates stole the **treasure**.*
θησαυρός

7.12 **port** (n) /pɔːt/ = a place where ships arrive and leave from. *There were many ships in the **port**.*
λιμάνι

7.13 **jewel** (n) /ˈdʒuːəl/ = a valuable stone such as a diamond. *The queen has many beautiful precious **jewels**.*
➤ jeweller (n), jewellery (n)
πολύτιμο πετράδι

7.14 **perhaps** (adv) /pəˈhæps/ = used to say that sth may happen or may be true but you are not sure. *They're late – **perhaps** they missed the train.*
ίσως
Syn: maybe

7.15 **at times** (prep phr) /ət ˈtaɪmz/ = sometimes. *I like school but I get bored **at times**.*
ενίοτε, μερικές φορές

7.16 **certainly** (adv) /ˈsɜːtnli/ = without any doubt. *You **certainly** look nice in your new clothes.* ➤ certain (adj), certainty (n)
ασφαλώς, βεβαίως

7.17 **luxury** (n) /ˈlʌkʃəri/ = great comfort and pleasure, especially from beautiful or expensive things. *Enjoy the **luxury** of your own private swimming pool.*
➤ luxurious (adj)
πολυτέλεια

7.18 **cruise ship** (n phr) /ˈkruːz ʃɪp/ = a large ship with bars, restaurants, etc. that people have holidays on. *We spent our holiday on a **cruise ship**.*
κρουαζιερόπλοιο

7.19 **nowadays** (adv) /ˈnaʊədeɪz/ = now, compared to what happened in the past. *People live longer **nowadays**.*
στις μέρες μας

7.20 **Caribbean** (n) /ˌkærɪˈbiːən/ = the sea between Central America, South America and the Caribbean islands, west of the Atlantic Ocean. *a holiday in the **Caribbean***
Καραϊβική

7.21 **filthy** (adj) /ˈfɪlθi/ = extremely dirty. *Wash those jeans. They're **filthy**!* ➤ filth (n)
βρομερός-ή-ό

7.22 **cramped** (adj) /kræmpt/ = a cramped room or building does not have enough space for the people or things in it. *Six people lived in a tiny, **cramped** flat.*
στριμωγμένος-η-ο

7.23 **human** (adj) /ˈhjuːmən/ = belonging to or relating to people. ***human** weaknesses* ➤ human (n)
ανθρώπινος-η-ο

7.24 **sweat** (n) /swet/ = liquid that comes out through your skin, especially when you are hot or nervous. *He wiped the **sweat** from his hands.* ➤ sweat (v), sweaty (adj)
ιδρώτας

Horrible history 7

7.25 **on board** (prep phr) /ɒn ˈbɔːd/ = on a ship, plane or spacecraft. *There were about 1,000 passengers on board the ship.*
επί του πλοίου ή μεταφορικού μέσου

7.26 **unimaginable** (adj) /ˌʌnɪˈmædʒɪnəbəl/ = very difficult to imagine. *unimaginable beauty*
αδιανόητος-η-ο
Opp: imaginable

7.27 **privacy** (n) /ˈprɪvəsi, ˈpraɪ-/ = when you are alone and not seen or heard by other people. *Teenagers need privacy sometimes.* ➤ private (adj)
απομόνωση, προσωπική ζωή

7.28 **stomach** (n) /ˈstʌmək/ = the part of your body where food is digested. *I ate too much and my stomach hurt.*
στομάχι

7.29 **stomachache** (n) /ˈstʌməkeɪk/ = a pain in your stomach. *She went to the doctor because she had a stomachache.*
στομαχόπονο

7.30 **because of sb/sth** (phr) /bɪˈkɒz əv ˌsʌmbədi, ˌsʌmθɪŋ/ = as a result of sth or sb. *They cancelled the match because of the rain.*
εξαιτίας

7.31 **dry** (adj) /draɪ/ = having no water or other liquid inside or on the surface. *The bread is hard and dry.* ➤ dry (v)
ξηρός-ή-ό

7.32 **tasteless** (adj) /ˈteɪstləs/ = tasteless food is unpleasant because it does not have a strong taste. *The soup was tasteless because it didn't have any salt.* ➤ taste (v, n), tasty (adj),
άγευστος-η-ο

7.33 **rotten** (adj) /ˈrɒtn/ = rotten food or wood is in bad condition because it is old. *Throw away the rotten apples.* ➤ rot (v, n)
σάπιος-α-ο

7.34 **menu** (n) /ˈmenjuː/ = a list of all the food that is available for a meal in a restaurant. *Waiter, could we have the menu, please?*
μενού

7.35 **rat** (n) /ræt/ = an animal like a large mouse with a long tail. *We could hear the rats in the dark cellar.*
αρουραίος

7.36 **companion** (n) /kəmˈpænjən/ = sb you spend a lot of time with or who travels somewhere with you. *One of her travelling companions became ill.* ➤ company (n)
συνταξιδιώτης, σύντροφος
◈ travelling companion

7.37 **tropical** (adj) /ˈtrɒpɪkəl/ = in or from the hottest parts of the world. *tropical fruit* ➤ tropics (n pl)
τροπικός-ή-ό

7.38 **poisonous** (adj) /ˈpɔɪzənəs/ = containing a substance that can kill or harm you if you eat it, drink it, etc., or producing that substance. *Those chemicals are poisonous, so don't touch them.* ➤ poison (n, v)
δηλητηριώδης-ες

7.39 **flea** (n) /fliː/ = a very small jumping insect that bites animals and drinks their blood. *Our dog has fleas.*
ψύλλος

7.40 **satellite** (n) /ˈsætəlaɪt/ = a machine that has been sent into space to receive and send radio or television signals. *a satellite in space*
δορυφόρος

7.41 **navigation** (n) /ˌnævɪˈɡeɪʃən/ = when you decide which direction your car or ship should go. *Navigation is difficult without a compass.* ➤ navigate (v), navigator (n)
ναυσιπλοΐα, πλοήγηση
◈ satellite navigation = πλοήγηση μέσω δορυφόρου

7.42 **route** (n) /ruːt/ = the roads, paths, etc. that you follow to get from one place to another. *What's the quickest route to the station?*
διαδρομή

7.43 **voyage** (n) /ˈvɔɪ-ɪdʒ/ = a long trip, especially in a ship. *The voyage from England to India used to take months.*
ταξίδι (σε θάλασσα)

7.44 **sit around** (phr v) /ˌsɪt əˈraʊnd/ = to sit and not do very much. *Magda sits around watching TV all day.*
κάθομαι χωρίς να ασχολούμαι με κάτι ουσιαστικό

7.45 **sew** (v) /səʊ/ = to use a needle and thread to make or repair clothes. *My mother taught me to sew my own clothes.* ➤ sewing (n)
ράβω

7.46 **exotic** (adj) /ɪɡˈzɒtɪk/ = sth that is exotic seems unusual and exciting because it is from a foreign country. *the exotic music of the East*
εξωτικός-ή-ό

7.47 **land** (n) /lænd/ = the solid dry part of the Earth's surface. *The pirates could see land in the distance.*
στεριά
◈ on land

7.48 **AD** (abbreviation) /ˌeɪ ˈdiː/ = used to show that a date is a particular number of years after the birth of Christ. *Constantinople fell in 1453 AD.*
μετά Χριστού
◈ AD = Anno Domini. 'Anno Domini' is Latin and means 'in the year of our Lord'.

7.49 **historian** (n) /hɪˈstɔːriən/ = sb who studies history. *Philip is an art historian.* ➤ history (n), historical (adj)
ιστορικός ερευνητής

7.50 **illegally** (adv) /ɪˈliːɡəli/ = in a way that is not allowed by law. *She parked here illegally.* ➤ illegal (adj)
παράνομα
Opp: legally

7 Horrible history

7.51 **maritime** (adj) /ˈmærɪtaɪm/ = near the sea or relating to it. *a **maritime** museum*
παράκτιος-α-ο, παραθαλάσσιος-α-ο, θαλασσινός-ή-ό

7.52 **speedboat** (n) /ˈspiːdbəʊt/ = a small fast boat with a powerful engine. *They went for a ride in a **speedboat**.*
ταχύπλοο σκάφος

7.53 **on your way** (prep phr) /ˌɒn jɔː ˈweɪ/ = while you are going somewhere. *I bought some milk **on my way** home from school.*
καθ' οδόν

7.54 **during** (prep) /ˈdjʊərɪŋ/ = all through a period of time. *It rained **during** the night.*
κατά τη διάρκεια

7.55 **stay** (n) /steɪ/ = a short period of time that you spend somewhere. *We hope you enjoy your **stay** at our hotel.*
➤ stay (v)
διαμονή, παραμονή

7.56 **escape** (v) /ɪˈskeɪp/ = to get away from a dangerous place or unpleasant situation. *He **escaped** from prison.*
➤ escape (n)
δραπετεύω
◆ escape from

7.57 **stone** (n) /stəʊn/ = a jewel. *a necklace with precious **stones***
πολύτιμο πετράδι

7.58 **liquid** (n) /ˈlɪkwɪd/ = a substance that is not solid or a gas, such as water or milk. *Add a little **liquid** to the sauce.*
υγρό

7.59 **condition** (n) /kənˈdɪʃən/ = the state that sth or sb is in. *the terrible **condition** of the roads*
κατάσταση

7.60 **produce** (v) /prəˈdjuːs/ = to grow or make sth. *Greece **produces** very good wine.* ➤ producer (n), production (n), product (n)
παράγω

7.61 **needle** (n) /ˈniːdl/ = a small thin piece of metal that you use for sewing, with a point at one end and a hole at the other end. *She found a **needle** and some thread and sewed the button on the shirt.*
βελόνα

7.62 **thread** (n) /θred/ = a long thin string of cotton, silk, etc., used to sew cloth. *a needle and **thread***
κλωστή

7.63 **legend** (n) /ˈledʒənd/ = an old well-known story about adventures or magical events. *He told the children the **legend** of Robin Hood.* ➤ legendary (adj)
θρύλος

Vocabulary: Page 76

7.64 **decade** (n) /ˈdekeɪd/ = a period of ten years. *The building is four **decades** old.*
δεκαετία

7.65 **BC** (abbreviation) /ˌbiː ˈsiː/ = before Christ – used after a date. *Socrates died in 399 **BC**.*
προ Χριστού

7.66 **millennium** (n) /mɪˈleniəm/ = a period of 1000 years, or the time when a new 1000-year period begins. *How did they celebrate the **millennium**?*
χιλιετία

7.67 **fortnight** (n) /ˈfɔːtnaɪt/ = two weeks. *The meetings take place once a **fortnight**.*
δεκαπενθήμερο

7.68 **ordinal number** (n phr) /ˈɔːdɪnəl ˌnʌmbə/ = a number such as first, second or third. *Do you know the **ordinal numbers** in English?*
τακτικό αριθμητικό

7.69 **Middle Ages** (n phr) /ˌmɪdl ˈeɪdʒɪz/ = the period in European history between about 1100 and 1500 AD. *Life in the **Middle Ages** was difficult for most people.*
Μεσαίωνας (12ος-15ος αιώνας)

7.70 **sail** (v) /seɪl/ = to travel across water in a boat or ship. *We **sailed** along the coast of Rhodes.* ➤ sail (n), sailor (n)
αρμενίζω, αποπλέω

7.71 **control** (v) /kənˈtrəʊl/ = to have the power to decide what will happen in an organisation or place. *She **controls** a large business.* ➤ control (n)
κυβερνώ, ιθύνω, ελέγχω

7.72 **date from** (phr v) /ˈdeɪt frəm, frɒm/ = to have existed since a particular time. *The church **dates from** the thirteenth century.*
χρονολογώ-ούμαι

7.73 **mid** (prefix) /mɪd/ = middle. *She's in her **mid**-twenties.*
μεσο-

7.74 **advantage** (n) /ədˈvɑːntɪdʒ/ = a good or useful quality or condition that sth has. *Good public transport is one of the **advantages** of living in a big city.*
πλεονέκτημα
Opp: disadvantage

7.75 **medicine** (n) /ˈmedsən/ = the treatment and study of illnesses and injuries. *Sarah wants to be a doctor and she's going to study **medicine** at the University of Reading.* ➤ medical (adj)
ιατρική

7.76 **scientific** (adj) /ˌsaɪənˈtɪfɪk/ = relating to science. *an important **scientific** discovery* ➤ science (n), scientist (n)
επιστημονικός-ή-ό

Horrible history 7

7.77 **method** (n) /ˈmeθəd/ = a way of doing sth. *This is a **method** of measuring the temperature.*
μέθοδος

7.78 **calculate** (v) /ˈkælkjʊleɪt/ = to find out how much sth will cost, how long sth will take, etc., by using numbers. *I'm trying to **calculate** how much paint we need.*
➤ calculator (n), calculation (n)
υπολογίζω

7.79 **distance** (n) /ˈdɪstəns/ = the amount of space between two places or things. *What's the **distance** from Athens to Thessaloniki?* ➤ distant (adj)
απόσταση

7.80 **injured** (adj) /ˈɪndʒəd/ = an injured person or animal has been hurt. *The **injured** passengers were taken to hospital.* ➤ injure (v), injury (n)
τραυματισμένος-η-ο, πληγωμένος-η-ο

7.81 **force** (v) /fɔːs/ = to make sb do sth they do not want to do. *I **forced** her to tell me the truth.* ➤ force (n)
(εξ)αναγκάζω, υποχρεώνω
◆ force sb to do sth

Grammar: Page 77

7.82 **recruit** (v) /rɪˈkruːt/ = to find new people to work in a company, join an organisation, do a job, etc. *It's not easy to **recruit** people to do this job.* ➤ recruit (n)
προσελκύω, προσεταιρίζομαι

7.83 **harbour** (n) /ˈhɑːbə/ = an area of water next to the land where ships can stay safely. *The ships sailed into the **harbour**.*
λιμάνι

7.84 **inspect** (v) /ɪnˈspekt/ = to visit a building or organisation officially in order to make sure everything is satisfactory and rules are being obeyed. *After the earthquake they **inspected** the school to make sure it was safe.*
➤ inspector (n), inspection (n)
επιθεωρώ

7.85 **sausage** (n) /ˈsɒsɪdʒ/ = a mixture of meat and spices that is put into a small tube of skin and cooked. *We're having **sausages** for dinner.*
λουκάνικο

7.86 **bowl** (n) /bəʊl/ = a round container that is open at the top, used to hold food or liquids. *Put the soup into a **bowl**.*
γαβάθα

7.87 **sauce** (n) /sɔːs/ = a thick cooked liquid that is served with food. *spaghetti with tomato **sauce***
σάλτσα

7.88 **get on** (phr v) /get ˈɒn/ = get inside a vehicle like a bus or train. *She **got on** the bus at Clark Street.*
επιβιβάζομαι
Opp: get off

Listening: Page 78

7.89 **object** (n) /ˈɒbdʒɪkt/ = a thing that you can see, hold or touch. *a small silver **object***
αντικείμενο

7.90 **bone** (n) /bəʊn/ = one of the hard parts that form the frame of the body. *Sam broke a **bone** in his foot.*
κόκαλο

7.91 **coin** (n) /kɔɪn/ = a round piece of money made of metal. *a pound **coin***
κέρμα

7.92 **pottery** (n) /ˈpɒtəri/ = pots, dishes, etc. made out of baked clay. ***pottery** made in Ancient Greece* ➤ pot (n), potter (n)
κεραμικά

7.93 **jewellery** (n) /ˈdʒuːəlri/ = small things that you wear for decoration, such as rings and necklaces. *a piece of gold **jewellery***
κόσμημα-τα

7.94 **skull** (n) /skʌl/ = the bones of a person's or animal's head. *the **skull** of a dead animal*
κρανίο

7.95 **tool** (n) /tuːl/ = sth such as a hammer or a screwdriver which you use to make or repair things. *I need my **tools** to make a wooden box.*
εργαλείο

7.96 **weapon** (n) /ˈwepən/ = sth that is used to attack people or to fight against people. *They attacked us with knives and other **weapons**.*
όπλο

7.97 **arrow** (n) /ˈærəʊ/ = a thin straight weapon with a point at one end that you shoot from a bow. *a bow and **arrow***
βέλος

7.98 **northern** (adj) /ˈnɔːðən/ = in or from the north of a country or area. *The man had a **northern** accent.*
➤ north (n)
βόρειος-α-ο

7.99 **New England** (n phr) /njuː ˈɪŋglənd/ = the states of the northeastern United States. *They come from **New England**.*
Νέα Αγγλία

7.100 **archaeology** (n) /ˌɑːkiˈɒlədʒi/ = the study of ancient societies by examining the remains of their buildings, their tools, the places where they were buried, etc. *Does Helen teach **archaeology** at university?*
➤ archaeologist (n), archaeological (adj)
αρχαιολογία

7.101 **powerfully** (adv) /ˈpaʊəfəli/ = with a lot of physical power, strength or force. *He sang **powerfully** and we could hear him from a distance.* ➤ powerful (adj), power (n)
δυνατά

7 Horrible history

7.102 fort (n) /fɔːt/ = a strong building used by soldiers for defending a place. *The soldiers inside the **fort** waited for their enemies to come closer.*
φρούριο, οχυρό

7.103 Roman (n) /ˈrəʊmən/ = a citizen of the ancient empire or city of Rome. *The **Romans** were good architects.*
➤ Roman (adj), Rome (n)
Ρωμαίος-α

7.104 around (adv) /əˈraʊnd/ = used when you do not know an exact number to give a number that is close to it. *There were **around** 10,000 people in the stadium.*
περίπου
Also: about

7.105 site (n) /saɪt/ = a place where sth important or interesting happened. *the **site** of the battle*
τοποθεσία

7.106 deserted (adj) /dɪˈzɜːtɪd/ = a deserted place is empty and quiet. *At night the streets are **deserted**.*
➤ desert (v)
εγκαταλελειμμένος-η-ο, έρημος-η-ο

7.107 abbreviation (n) /əˌbriːviˈeɪʃən/ = a shorter form of a word. *'Dr' is the **abbreviation** for 'Doctor'.*
➤ abbreviate (v)
βραχυγραφία

Speaking: Page 79

7.108 gallery (n) /ˈgæləri/ = a room or building where you can look at famous paintings and other types of art. *We visited several art **galleries** in Florence.*
γκαλερί

7.109 statue (n) /ˈstætʃuː/ = a large image of a person or animal made of stone, wood or metal. *a **statue** of Apollo*
άγαλμα

7.110 make out (phr v) /meɪk ˈaʊt/ = to be able to hear, see or understand sth. *She could **make out** a dark shape in the distance.*
διακρίνω

Use your English: Pages 80–81

7.111 at the time (prep phr) /ət ðə ˈtaɪm/ = at a time in the past when sth happened. *'Where were you when James was born?' 'I was living in Mexico **at the time**.'*
εκείνη την περίοδο

7.112 by the time (prep phr) /baɪ ðə ˈtaɪm/ = when. ***By the time** I arrived, he had left.*
ήδη μέχρι τότε

7.113 process (n) /ˈprəʊses/ = a series of events or changes that happen naturally. *the natural **process** of change*
διαδικασία, πορεία

7.114 from time to time (prep phr) /frəm ˌtaɪm tə ˈtaɪm/ = sometimes but not often. *We see each other **from time to time**.*
κατά καιρούς, κάθε τόσο

7.115 most of the time (phr) /ˈməʊst əv ðə ˌtaɪm/ = very often or almost always. *I feel happy **most of the time** but occasionally I feel sad.*
τον περισσότερο χρόνο

7.116 on time (prep phr) /ɒn ˈtaɪm/ = at the correct time or the time that was arranged. *You must get to school **on time**.*
στην ώρα

7.117 prisoner (n) /ˈprɪzənə/ = sb who is kept in a prison as a punishment. *The **prisoners** sleep in cells with small windows.* ➤ prison (n)
κρατούμενος-η

7.118 guard (n) /gɑːd/ = sb whose job is to protect a person or place or to make sure that a person does not escape. *Bill works as a security **guard**.* ➤ guard (v)
φρουρός, φύλακας

7.119 physical (adj) /ˈfɪzɪkəl/ = relating to your body rather than your mind. ***physical** strength*
σωματικός-ή-ό

7.120 palm tree (n phr) /ˈpɑːm triː/ = a tall tree with large pointed leaves at the top that grows near beaches or in deserts. *The hotel had a lovely garden with **palm trees**.*
φοινικιά

7.121 perfect (adj) /ˈpɜːfɪkt/ = not having any mistakes, faults or damage. *Her Spanish is **perfect**.* ➤ perfection (n)
τέλειος-α-ο

7.122 destination (n) /ˌdestɪˈneɪʃən/ = the place that you are travelling to. *We reached our **destination** late at night.*
προορισμός

7.123 surround (v) /səˈraʊnd/ = to be or go all around sb or sth. *The lake was **surrounded** by trees.*
➤ surrounding (adj), surroundings (n pl)
περιτριγυρίζω

7.124 climate (n) /ˈklaɪmət/ = the typical weather conditions in an area. *a dry **climate***
κλίμα

7.125 humid (adj) /ˈhjuːmɪd/ = humid air, weather, etc. feels hot and wet. *the **humid** heat of a tropical forest*
➤ humidity (n)
υγρός-ή-ό

7.126 emperor (n) /ˈempərə/ = a man who rules a group of countries. *Nero was a Roman **Emperor**.* ➤ empress (n), empire (n)
αυτοκράτορας

7.127 remote (adj) /rɪˈməʊt/ = far away. *They lived in a **remote** village in the mountains.*
απόμερος-η-ο

Horrible history 7

7.128 location (n) /ləʊˈkeɪʃən/ = a particular place or position. *Please show me the **location** of the town on the map.* ➤ locate (v)
τοποθεσία

7.129 criminal (n) /ˈkrɪmɪnəl/ = sb who is proved guilty of a crime. *The **criminal** was punished.* ➤ criminal (adj), crime (n)
εγκληματίας

7.130 in contrast (prep phr) /ɪn ˈkɒntrɑːst/ = used when comparing two people, things, etc. that are very different from each other. *It is sunny in Greece. **In contrast**, it's cloudy in Britain.*
σε αντίθεση
◆ in contrast to

7.131 director (n) /dɪˈrektə, daɪ-/ = sb who controls or manages an organisation or company. *Tom is the new **director** of the art gallery.* ➤ direct (v)
διευθυντής-ρια

7.132 breeze (n) /briːz/ = a gentle wind. *A light **breeze** blew from the sea.*
αεράκι

7.133 survive (v) /səˈvaɪv/ = to continue to live after an accident, war, illness, etc. *She **survived** the war.* ➤ survivor (n), survival (n)
διασώζομαι, επιζώ

7.134 thrilling (adj) /ˈθrɪlɪŋ/ = interesting and exciting. *It was a **thrilling** game.* ➤ thrill (n, v), thrilled (adj)
συναρπαστικός-ή-ό

7.135 guide (n) /gaɪd/ = a book that has information and advice on a particular subject. *I always take a good travel **guide** with me when I go on holiday.* ➤ guide (v)
οδηγός
◆ travel guide

7.136 remainder (n) /rɪˈmeɪndə/ = the part of sth that is left after everything else has gone. *John and Rita left the party early but the **remainder** of our guests left after midnight.* ➤ remain (v)
υπόλοιπο
◆ the remainder of

7.137 ache (v) /eɪk/ = if part of your body aches, you feel a continuous pain there. *My back **aches** from lifting those heavy boxes.* ➤ ache (n)
πονώ

7.138 speak up (phr v) /ˌspiːk ˈʌp/ = used to ask sb to speak more loudly. ***Speak up**, please. We can't hear you.*
μιλώ πιο δυνατά

7.139 join (v) /dʒɔɪn/ = to become a member of an organisation, society or group. *Barbara **joined** the company in 2002.*
προσχωρώ σε

7.140 prompt (n) /prɒmpt/ = a word or picture to help you or remind you what to say. *Look at the **prompts** and then talk to your partner.* ➤ prompt (v)
παρακίνηση προς ομιλητή, κλπ. να πει ή να πράξει κάτι, υποβολή

7.141 fluently (adv) /ˈfluːəntli/ = when you speak a language fluently, you speak it very well, without stopping or making mistakes. *She speaks Greek **fluently**.* ➤ fluent (adj), fluency (n)
με μεγάλη ευχέρεια λόγου

Writing: Pages 82–83

7.142 fascinate (v) /ˈfæsəneɪt/ = to interest you very much. *The story **fascinated** him.* ➤ fascination (n), fascinating (adj), fascinated (adj)
γοητεύω

7.143 move (v) /muːv/ = to go to a new place to live or work. *Marcos was born here but he **moved** to Volos when he was twenty.* ➤ move (n)
μετακομίζω

7.144 trumpet (n) /ˈtrʌmpɪt/ = a metal musical instrument that you blow into, with three buttons that you press to change the notes. *Fay plays the **trumpet** in the band.*
τρομπέτα

7.145 busk (v) /bʌsk/ = to play music in a public place to earn money. *John started his career in music by **busking** in the streets of London.* ➤ busker (n)
παίζω μουσικό όργανο σε δημόσιο χώρο (για να εισπράξω χρήματα)

7.146 divide (v) /dɪˈvaɪd/ = if sth divides or if you divide it, it separates into two or more parts. *The teacher **divided** the class into groups.* ➤ division (n)
διαιρώ-ούμαι, χωρίζω-ομαι
◆ divide sth into sth

7 Horrible history

WORDZONE SPECIAL

Easily confused words: jewel, jewellery

jewel, (precious) stone

A jewel is a valuable stone such as a diamond, ruby or emerald. *Jewel* is countable. We can also say *precious stone*.
The precious **jewels** shone in the light.
She wore a necklace of **precious stones**. I think they were rubies.

jewellery

Jewellery is the small things that you wear for decoration, such as rings and necklaces. *Jewellery* is uncountable.
My mother's expensive **jewellery** is at the bank.

Vocabulary and grammar practice

1 Complete the sentences with these adjectives.

cramped   deserted   exotic   filthy   humid   physical   remote

1 You need more .... exercise to get fit and lose weight.
2 Leave your shoes outside. They're .... and I've just washed the floor.
3 Let's have our meeting in a bigger room. This one is ....
4 The old house was .... and nobody had lived in it for ages.
5 On this tropical island you can find all sorts of .... flowers.
6 It was very .... weather and we were sweating.
7 Gary lives on a(n) .... farm miles from the nearest city.

2 Choose the correct word to complete the sentences.

1 Let's *calculate / divide* the cake into eight pieces.
2 The thieves *forced / attacked* us to hand over our money.
3 According to legend, Robin Hood lived in the *Mid / Middle* Ages.
4 When we finally reached our holiday *destination / site*, we were very tired.
5 In many countries, fresh water is a *luxury / privacy*.
6 The *route / voyage* from Ireland to America took several weeks.
7 The *historical / historian* wrote a book about the pirates of the Mediterranean.
8 Life was hard during the war and many people didn't *survive / surround*.

3 Complete the sentences with the correct form of the words in capitals.

1 The fish is .... and it smells horrible! **ROT**
2 That spider is .... , so please be careful. **POISON**
3 He gave her some .... diamond earrings for her birthday. **VALUE**
4 It snowed heavily in the .... parts of the country. **NORTH**
5 There isn't any .... proof that the drug works. **SCIENCE**
6 They say the film is based on .... events. **HISTORY**

Horrible history 7

4 **Complete the sentences with these words.**

at the time   by the time   centuries   decades   fortnight
from time to time   millennium   on time

1 Please hurry up or we won't get to the airport .... !
2 In the seventeenth and eighteenth .... , there were many pirates in the Caribbean.
3 .... the guards arrived, the prisoners had escaped.
4 We're going away on holiday for a(n) ....
5 We weren't living here when my sister was born. .... , we were living in a small cottage in the countryside.
6 The year 2000 was the start of the new ....
7 I like going for a long walk in the mountains ....
8 Julie was born three .... ago, so she is thirty years old.

5 **Past perfect simple and past perfect continuous**
Complete the text with the correct form of the verbs in brackets. Use the past perfect simple or past perfect continuous.

Joe 1) .... (sail) for most of the afternoon and he was feeling sleepy. He 2) .... (just / fall) asleep when he heard somebody shouting. Looking around, he saw a young woman in the water not far from his boat. She told him she 3) .... (swim) for hours and was very tired.

As soon as Joe 4) .... (pull) her on board, she told him her story. She said that pirates 5) .... (steal) her boat. They 6) .... (also / want) to kill her but she managed to escape.

Joe contacted the coastguards and they rushed to the scene of the crime. But by the time they got there, the pirates 7) .... (disappear) and nobody saw the woman's boat again.

6 ***can, could, be able to***
Choose the correct words to complete the sentences.

1 Jenny is only twelve but she *can / could* sew her own clothes.
2 We *can't / couldn't* continue our journey because the car had broken down.
3 The door was stuck but I pushed hard and in the end, I *could / was able to* open it.
4 *Will you be able / Can you* to finish the work tomorrow?
5 They *aren't / won't be* able to find the place unless they take a map with them.
6 In the nineteenth century most young girls *can / could* cook and sew.
7 Eagles *can / are able* see very well.
8 I want to *can / be able to* buy a boat one day.

7 Horrible history

Test yourself!

Choose the word or phrase that best completes the conversation or sentence.

1. Archaeologists found the …… of a man who lived around 400 BC.
   - A skull
   - B site
   - C fort
   - D object

2. I …… for hours, so I decided to stop for a cup of coffee.
   - A drove
   - B have been driving
   - C had driven
   - D had been driving

3. The jelly will turn into …… if you leave it outside the fridge.
   - A sweat
   - B port
   - C liquid
   - D thread

4. '…… to get here on time?'
   'Don't worry. Melanie is never late.'
   - A Will she be able
   - B Can she
   - C Was she able
   - D Could she

5. The prisons were often …… by the director.
   - A escaped
   - B surrounded
   - C produced
   - D inspected

6. They ……, so we couldn't talk to them.
   - A just left
   - B had just left
   - C had just been leaving
   - D just were leaving

7. The pirates occasionally ate fresh food but …… they didn't.
   - A at the time
   - B most of the time
   - C by the time
   - D from time to time

8. Lena was very tired as she …… articles all day.
   - A wrote
   - B was writing
   - C had written
   - D had been writing

9. Blackbeard was a famous pirate who lived in the ……. .
   - A eighteen decade
   - B eighteenth decade
   - C eighteenth century
   - D eighteen century

10. 'Why didn't Mary come to the cinema with us?'
    'She …… the film.'
    - A already saw
    - B was already seeing
    - C had already seen
    - D had already been seeing

11. At the beginning of the century many people …… from the countryside to the city.
    - A calculated
    - B moved
    - C forced
    - D recruited

12. Fortunately, we …… swim to the coast when our boat sank.
    - A can
    - B could
    - C are able to
    - D were able to

13. These snakes are dangerous because they …… a deadly poison.
    - A produce
    - B attack
    - C control
    - D force

14. They wanted to …… sew their own clothes.
    - A can
    - B could
    - C were able to
    - D be able to

8 Communication breakdown

Reading: Pages 84–85

8.1 **breakdown** (n) /ˈbreɪkdaʊn/ = the failure of a relationship or system. *He moved to another town after the **breakdown** of his marriage.*
διακοπή λειτουργίας, αποτυχία

8.2 **kick** (v) /kɪk/ = to hit or move sth with your foot. *Billy **kicked** the ball and scored a goal.* ➤ kick (n)
κλωτσώ

8.3 **sensor** (n) /ˈsensə/ = a piece of equipment that is used to find light, heat, movement, etc, even in very small amounts. *This device has small **sensors** to detect sound.*
αισθητήρας

8.4 **chip** (n) /tʃɪp/ = a small piece of silicon with electronic parts on it, that is used in computers. *This factory makes **chips** for computers.*
μικροτσίπ
Also: microchip

8.5 **design** (v) /dɪˈzaɪn/ = to make sth for a particular purpose or person. *The chair was **designed** for people with back trouble.* ➤ design (n), designer (n)
σχεδιάζω

8.6 **tool** (n) /tuːl/ = sth that can be used for a particular purpose. *Computers can be used as a **tool** for learning.*
μέσο, εργαλείο

8.7 **attract** (v) /əˈtrækt/ = to make sb like sth or feel interested in it. *The chance to travel **attracted** me to the job.* ➤ attraction (n), attractive (adj)
ελκύω, προσελκύω

8.8 **program** (n) /ˈprəʊɡræm/ = a set of instructions given to a computer to make it do sth. *a computer **program*** ➤ program (v)
πρόγραμμα ηλεκτρονικού υπολογιστή

8.9 **enter** (v) /ˈentə/ = to arrange to take part in a competition, race or examination, or to arrange for sb to do this. *He **entered** the competition but lost.* ➤ entry (n)
δηλώνω συμμετοχή

8.10 **develop** (v) /dɪˈveləp/ = to make a new product or idea over a period of time. *Scientists are **developing** new drugs to fight Aids.* ➤ development (n)
αναπτύσσω-ομαι

8.11 **competition** (n) /ˌkɒmpəˈtɪʃən/ = an organised event in which people or teams compete against each other. *Who won the **competition**?* ➤ competitor (n), compete (v), competitive (adj)
αγώνισμα

8.12 **essential** (adj) /ɪˈsenʃəl/ = important and necessary. *A balanced diet is **essential** for good health.*
απαραίτητος-η-ο

8.13 **produce** (v) /prəˈdjuːs/ = to make sth using a particular process or skill. *The factory **produces** cars.* ➤ producer (n), product (n), production (n), productive (adj)
παράγω

8.14 **urgently** (adv) /ˈɜːdʒəntli/ = in a way that shows that sth is very important and needs to be dealt with immediately. *We need help **urgently**.* ➤ urgent (adj)
επειγόντως

8.15 **programmable** (adj) /ˈprəʊɡræməbəl/ = able to be controlled by a computer or electronic program. *a **programmable** heating system*
που μπορεί να προγραμματιστεί

8.16 **humanoid** (adj) /ˈhjuːmənɔɪd/ = having a human shape and qualities. *The robot had a **humanoid** appearance.* ➤ humanoid (n)
ανθρωποειδής-ές

8.17 **commercial** (adj) /kəˈmɜːʃəl/ = relating to the buying and selling of things and with making money. *The film was a **commercial** success.* ➤ commerce (n)
εμπορικός-ή-ό

8.18 **radar** (n) /ˈreɪdɑː/ = equipment that can find the position of things such as planes and ships using radio waves. *We could see the planes on the **radar** screen.*
ραντάρ

8.19 **vision** (n) /ˈvɪʒən/ = the ability to see. *Will the operation improve my **vision**?* ➤ visible (adj), visual (adj)
όραση

8.20 **detect** (v) /dɪˈtekt/ = to notice sth that is not easy to see, hear, etc. *The planes were **detected** by the radar.* ➤ detective (n), detection (n)
εντοπίζω, ανιχνεύω

8.21 **powerful** (adj) /ˈpaʊəfəl/ = having a lot of physical power, strength or force. *This car has a **powerful** engine.* ➤ power (n), powerless (adj)
δυνατός-ή-ό

8.22 **penalty** (n) /ˈpenəlti/ = a chance to kick the ball into the goal in a game of football, given because the other team has not obeyed a rule. *Townsend kicked a **penalty** in the last minute.*
πέναλτι

8 Communication breakdown

8.23 replace (v) /rɪˈpleɪs/ = to start using a different person or thing instead of the one you use now. *Their computer is very old. They should **replace** it.* ➤ replacement (n)
αντικαθιστώ
❖ replace sb/sth with sb/sth

8.24 remote-controlled (adj) /rɪˌməʊt kənˈtrəʊld/ = using radio waves to control sth such as a television from a distance. *They gave him a **remote-controlled** model plane for his birthday.* ➤ remote control (n)
τηλεκατευθυνόμενος-η-ο

8.25 robotic (adj) /rəʊˈbɒtɪk/ = controlled by a computer and able to move and do jobs that humans usually do. *Sony made a famous **robotic** dog called Aibo.* ➤ robotics (n), robot (n)
ρομποτικός-ή-ό

8.26 alive (adj) /əˈlaɪv/ = living and not dead. *She isn't dead! She's **alive**!* ➤ live (v), life (n)
ζωντανός-ή-ό

8.27 aggressive (adj) /əˈɡresɪv/ = behaving in an angry or violent way towards sb. ***aggressive** behaviour* ➤ aggression (n)
επιθετικός-ή-ό

8.28 joypad (n) /ˈdʒɔɪpæd/ = a device for computer games that has buttons to control images on the screen. *a mini **joypad** with modern features*
χειριστήριο κονσόλας παιχνιδιών

8.29 be fitted with sth (phr) /bɪ ˈfɪtɪd wɪð ˌsʌmθɪŋ/ = to have sth as a permanent part. *My car **is fitted with** an alarm.*
είναι εξοπλισμένος-η-ο με

8.30 environment (n) /ɪnˈvaɪrənmənt/ = the conditions in which you live and work that affect your life. *a safe **environment** for children* ➤ environmental (adj)
περιβάλλον

8.31 touch (n) /tʌtʃ/ = the sense that you use in order to feel things, especially by putting your finger, hand, etc. on sth. *The snake's skin was dry to the **touch**.* ➤ touch (v)
άγγιγμα

8.32 sonic (adj) /ˈsɒnɪk/ = relating to sound. *His new hi-fi system offers **sonic** perfection.*
ηχητικός-ή-ό

8.33 direction (n) /dɪˈrekʃən, daɪ-/ = the place or point that you are moving, facing or pointing towards. *We walked in the **direction** of the hotel.* ➤ direct (v)
κατεύθυνση

8.34 jaw (n) /dʒɔː/ = one of the two bones in your face that contain your teeth. *She broke her **jaw** in the accident.*
σαγόνι

8.35 limit (v) /ˈlɪmɪt/ = to stop sth from increasing beyond a particular point. *Try to **limit** the amount of salt you eat.* ➤ limit (n)
περιορίζω

8.36 own goal (n phr) /ˌəʊn ˈɡəʊl/ = a goal that you accidentally score against your own team without intending to in a game of football, hockey, etc. *The player scored an **own goal** and his team lost the match.*
αυτογκόλ

8.37 once (adv) /wʌns/ = in the past but not now. *They were **once** close friends.*
κάποτε

8.38 shaped (adj) /ʃeɪpt/ = having a particular shape. *The alien's head was **shaped** like an egg.* ➤ shape (n, v)
με σχήμα

8.39 brick (n) /brɪk/ = a hard block of baked clay used for building walls, houses, etc. *a house made of **bricks***
τούβλο

8.40 leap (v) /liːp/ = to jump high into the air or over sth. *She **leapt** over the wall.* ➤ leap (n)
πηδώ
Irr v: leap–leapt–leapt

8.41 straight (adv) /streɪt/ = in a line that is not bent or curved. *The car was coming **straight** towards me.*
σε ευθεία γραμμή

8.42 website (n) /ˈwebsaɪt/ = a place on the internet where you can go to find out information about a company, person, subject, etc. *You will find more information on their **website**.*
ιστοσελίδα

8.43 experiment (n) /ɪkˈsperɪmənt/ = a scientific test to find out or prove sth. *The scientists did a number of **experiments**.* ➤ experiment (v)
πείραμα

8.44 researcher (n) /rɪˈsɜːtʃə/ = a person who studies a subject in detail so they can discover new facts about it. *The **researcher** discovered some interesting facts.* ➤ research (n, v)
ερευνητής

8.45 beat (v) /biːt/ = to get more points, votes, etc. than other people in a game or competition. *Spain **beat** Italy 3–1.*
νικώ

8.46 whichever (determiner) /wɪtʃˈevə/ = any of a group of things or people. *Choose **whichever** one you like.*
οποιοσδήποτε/οποιαδήποτε/οποιοδήποτε

8.47 replacement (n) /rɪˈpleɪsmənt/ = sb or sth that replaces another person or thing. *This battery is dead – I must get a **replacement**.*
αντικατάσταση

8.48 robotics (n) /rəʊˈbɒtɪks/ = the study of how robots are made and used. *Andrew wants to study **robotics**.*
ρομποτική μηχανική

8.49 life-size (adj) /ˈlaɪf saɪz/ = a life-size picture, model, etc. of sth or sb is the same size as they really are. *She painted a **life-size** picture of her dog.*
φυσικού μεγέθους

Communication breakdown 8

8.50 **specially** (adv) /ˈspeʃəli/ = for one particular purpose or person. *a chair that was **specially** designed for people with back problems* ➤ special (adj)
ειδικά

8.51 **act** (v) /ækt/ = to behave in a particular way. *Stop **acting** like a baby!*
συμπεριφέρομαι

8.52 **rectangular** (adj) /rekˈtæŋɡjʊlə/ = shaped with four straight sides and four angles of ninety degrees. *a **rectangular** room* ➤ rectangle (n)
ορθογώνιος-α-ο

8.53 **block** (n) /blɒk/ = a piece of a solid material with straight sides. *The child played with her wooden **blocks**.*
τεμάχιο στερεής ύλης

8.54 **absolutely** (adv) /ˌæbsəˈluːtli/ = completely or totally. *Are you **absolutely** sure?* ➤ absolute (adj)
απόλυτα

8.55 **necessary** (adj) /ˈnesəsəri/ = if sth is necessary, you need it in order to have sth or do sth. *'Do I have to wake up early?' 'No, that won't be **necessary**.'* ➤ necessity (n)
απαραίτητος-η-ο
Opp: unnecessary

8.56 **for sale** (prep phr) /fə ˈseɪl/ = available to be bought. *Is this table **for sale**?*
προς πώληση

8.57 **use** (n) /juːs/ = a purpose for which sth can be used. *The drug has many **uses**.* ➤ use (v), useful (adj), useless (adj)
χρήση

Vocabulary: Page 86

8.58 **properly** (adv) /ˈprɒpəli/ = correctly or in a way that is considered right. *I can't see **properly** without my glasses.* ➤ proper (adj)
σωστά, καλά

8.59 **scissors** (n pl) /ˈsɪzəz/ = a small tool with two blades that you use for cutting paper, hair or material. *Cut the paper with the **scissors**.*
ψαλίδι

8.60 **signal** (n) /ˈsɪɡnəl/ = a series of light waves, sound waves, etc. that carry information to a radio, television, etc. *send a **signal*** ➤ signal (v)
σήμα

8.61 **remote control** (n phr) /rɪˌməʊt kənˈtrəʊl/ = a piece of equipment that you use to control sth such as a television from a distance. *We've lost the **remote control** for the television.*
τηλεχειριστήριο

8.62 **audible** (n) /ˈɔːdəbəl/ = loud enough to be heard. *Her voice was not **audible** at the back of the room.*
ικανός-ή-ό να ακουστεί
Opp: inaudible

8.63 **hearing** (n) /ˈhɪərɪŋ/ = the sense that you use to hear sounds. *My grandfather's **hearing** is not as good as it used to be.* ➤ hear (v)
ακοή

8.64 **scent** (n) /sent/ = a pleasant smell. *the **scent** of roses*
μυρωδιά

8.65 **tongue** (n) /tʌŋ/ = the soft moveable part in your mouth that you use for tasting and speaking. *I bit my **tongue**.*
γλώσσα

8.66 **visual** (adj) /ˈvɪʒuəl/ = relating to seeing. *The movie has a strong **visual** impact.*
οπτικός-ή-ό

8.67 **sight** (n) /saɪt/ = the ability to see. *She's blind. She lost her **sight** when she was a child.* ➤ see (v)
όραση

8.68 **smell** (n) /smel/ = the ability to notice or recognise smells. *I have a very good sense of **smell**.* ➤ smell (v), smelly (adj)
όσφρηση

8.69 **taste** (n) /teɪst/ = the feeling that sth you eat or drink produces in your mouth. *the **taste** of chocolate* ➤ taste (v), tasty (adj), tasteless (adj)
γεύση

8.70 **sense** (n) /sens/ = one of the five physical abilities of sight, hearing, touch, taste and smell. *Dogs have a good **sense** of smell.* ➤ sense (v), sensitive (adj)
αίσθηση

8.71 **sensitive** (adj) /ˈsensətɪv/ = easily affected by physical things. *a **sensitive** skin*
ευαίσθητος-η-ο

8.72 **explore** (v) /ɪkˈsplɔː/ = to travel around an area to find out what it is like. *They spent a week **exploring** the island.* ➤ explorer (n), exploration (n)
εξερευνώ

8.73 **mountaineer** (n) /ˌmaʊntəˈnɪə/ = sb who climbs mountains as a sport. *The **mountaineers** climbed to the top of the mountain.* ➤ mountain (n)
αλπινιστής, ορειβάτης

8.74 **engine** (n) /ˈendʒɪn/ = the part of a vehicle that produces the power that makes it move. *Luke stopped the car and turned off the **engine**.* ➤ engineer (n)
κινητήρας

8.75 **own** (v) /əʊn/ = to legally have sth because you bought it or have been given it. *They **own** two cars.* ➤ owner (n)
κατέχω, έχω την κυριότητα

8 Communication breakdown

8.76 **manufacture** (v) /ˌmænjʊˈfæktʃə/ = to use machines to make goods, usually in large numbers or amounts. *The company **manufactures** clothes.* ➤ manufacture (n), manufacturer (n)
κατασκευάζω, παράγω

8.77 **electronics** (n) /ˌelɪkˈtrɒnɪks/ = the science of making electronic equipment, such as computers or televisions. *She's studying **electronics** at university.*
➤ electronic (adj)
ηλεκτρονική

8.78 **astronomer** (n) /əˈstrɒnəmə/ = a scientist who studies the stars and planets. *the **astronomer** who discovered the new comet* ➤ astronomy (n)
αστρονόμος

8.79 **mind** (n) /maɪnd/ = your thoughts or your ability to think, feel and imagine things. *Relaxation is good for your **mind** and body.*
νους, μυαλό

Grammar: Page 87

8.80 **female** (adj) /ˈfiːmeɪl/ = belonging to the sex that can have babies or produce eggs. *a **female** elephant and her baby* ➤ female (n)
θηλυκός-ή-ό
Opp: male

8.81 **inventor** (n) /ɪnˈventə/ = sb who has invented sth. *Who was the **inventor** of the computer?* ➤ invent (v), invention (n)
εφευρέτης

8.82 **interact** (v) /ˌɪntərˈækt/ = to talk to people and do things with them. *The computer has been programmed to **interact** with people.* ➤ interaction (n)
αλληλεπιδρώ

8.83 **thoroughly** (adv) /ˈθʌrəli/ = carefully and completely. *We cleaned the house **thoroughly**.* ➤ thorough (adj)
παντελώς, πέρα για πέρα

8.84 **dialect** (n) /ˈdaɪəlekt/ = a form of a language that is spoken in one part of a country. *We couldn't understand the local **dialect**.*
διάλεκτος

8.85 **display** (n) /dɪˈspleɪ/ = an arrangement of objects for people to look at. *a **display** of African masks*
➤ display (v)
έκθεση, έκθεμα

8.86 **case** (n) /keɪs/ = a container for storing or protecting sth. *a **case** for my tools*
θήκη, προθήκη
◆ display case

8.87 **receptionist** (n) /rɪˈsepʃənɪst/ = sb whose job is to welcome and help people when they arrive at a hotel, office building, etc. *The hotel **receptionist** welcomed the guests.* ➤ reception (n)
υπάλληλος της υποδοχής, ρεσεψιονίστας

8.88 **tour** (n) /tʊə/ = a journey in which you visit several different places in a country, area etc. *a **tour** of Athens*
➤ tour (v), tourist (n)
γύρος, περιήγηση

8.89 **guide** (n) /ɡaɪd/ = sb whose job is to show a place to tourists. *Diana works as a **guide** in the summer.*
➤ guide (v)
ξεναγός
◆ tour guide

8.90 **customer** (n) /ˈkʌstəmə/ = sb who buys things from a shop or company. *There was only one **customer** in the shop.*
πελάτης-ισσα

8.91 **outlet** (n) /ˈaʊtlət/ = a shop that sells a company's products. *We buy our clothes from an **outlet** at the shopping mall.*
κατάστημα (αποκλειστικής) λιανικής πώλησης

8.92 **battery** (n) /ˈbætəri/ = an object that provides the electrical power for a toy, machine, car, etc. *I need a new **battery** for my mobile phone.*
μπαταρία

8.93 **contact** (v) /ˈkɒntækt/ = to telephone or write to sb. *Who can we **contact** in an emergency?* ➤ contact (n)
έρχομαι σε επαφή, επικοινωνώ (με)

Listening: Page 88

8.94 **passage** (n) /ˈpæsɪdʒ/ = a small part of a book, poem, speech, piece of music, etc. *He read a short **passage** from the book.*
απόσπασμα

8.95 **identify** (v) /aɪˈdentɪfaɪ/ = to recognise sb or sth and say correctly who or what they are. *She was able to **identify** her attacker.* ➤ identification (n)
αναγνωρίζω, προσδιορίζω ταυτότητα

8.96 **extract** (n) /ˈekstrækt/ = a small part of a story, poem, song, etc. *Let's watch an **extract** from the film.*
➤ extract (v)
απόσπασμα

Speaking: Page 89

8.97 **awareness** (n) /əˈweənəs/ = knowledge or understanding of a particular subject or situation. *Do you have any **awareness** of the dangers?* ➤ aware (adj)
επίγνωση, συναίσθηση
◆ awareness of

Communication breakdown 8

8.98 **foreign** (adj) /ˈfɒrən/ = from or relating to a country that is not your own. *She spoke with a **foreign** accent.* ➤ foreigner (n)
ξένος-η-ο

8.99 **head** (n) /hed/ = the leader or most important person in a group or organisation. *the **head** of the organisation*
αρχηγός

8.100 **appeal** (v) /əˈpiːl/ = if sth appeals to you, you think it is attractive or interesting. *That idea doesn't **appeal** to me at all.* ➤ appeal (n)
ελκύω, θέλγω
◆ appeal to

8.101 **cotton** (n) /ˈkɒtn/ = cloth or thread made from the cotton plant. *a **cotton** shirt*
βαμβάκι

8.102 **silk** (n) /sɪlk/ = soft cloth made from the threads produced by a silkworm. *a **silk** dress*
μετάξι

8.103 **card** (n) /kɑːd/ = thick stiff paper. *Write your name on a piece of **card**.*
χαρτόνι

8.104 **plain** (adj) /pleɪn/ = without anything added or without decoration. *a **plain** card with no pictures on it*
απλός-ή-ό, μονόχρωμος-η-ο

Use your English: Pages 90–91

8.105 **media** (n pl) /ˈmiːdiə/ = television, radio and newspapers. *The **media** reported the news.*
μέσα μαζικής ενημέρωσης

8.106 **fall apart** (phr v) /ˌfɔːl əˈpɑːt/ = to break into many pieces, especially because of being old. *When I opened the old book, it **fell apart**.*
διαλύομαι

8.107 **break up** (phr v) /ˌbreɪk ˈʌp/ = to end a relationship with a husband, wife, boyfriend, etc. *Troy is sad because he **broke up** with Marcia last month.*
διακόπτω σχέσεις με, χωρίζω

8.108 **cut off** (phr v) /ˌkʌt ˈɒf/ = to stop supplying electricity, gas, water, etc. to sb. *They **cut off** the electricity because I had forgotten to pay the bill.*
κόβω την παροχή

8.109 **turn up** (phr v) /ˌtɜːn ˈʌp/ = to make a television, radio, heater, etc. produce more sound, heat, etc. *I can't hear what they're saying. Please **turn up** the television.*
δυναμώνω την ένταση

8.110 **turn down** (phr v) /ˌtɜːn ˈdaʊn/ = to make a machine such as a television, heater, etc. produce less sound, heat, etc. *Can you **turn down** the heater? It's very hot in here.*
μειώνω την ένταση

8.111 **connection** (n) /kəˈnekʃən/ = when two or more machines or telephones are joined together or joined to a larger system, using an electrical connection. *a free Internet **connection*** ➤ connect (v)
σύνδεση

8.112 **raise your voice** (phr) /ˌreɪz jə ˈvɔɪs/ = to speak loudly or shout because you are angry. *He was angry and **raised his voice**.*
υψώνω τη φωνή μου

8.113 **relationship** (n) /rɪˈleɪʃənʃɪp/ = a situation in which two people have romantic feelings for each other. *My grandparents had a loving **relationship**.*
σχέση

8.114 **increase** (v) /ɪnˈkriːs/ = if you increase sth, or if it increases, it becomes bigger in amount, number or degree. *The number of prisoners has **increased** dramatically.* ➤ increase (n)
αυξάνω-ομαι

8.115 **decrease** (v) /dɪˈkriːs/ = to become less, or to make sth do this. *Crime **decreased** by thirty percent last year.* ➤ decrease (n)
μειώνω-ομαι, ελαττώνω-ομαι

8.116 **avoid** (v) /əˈvɔɪd/ = to prevent sth bad from happening. *She **avoided** trouble by keeping quiet.* ➤ avoidance (n)
αποφεύγω

8.117 **face-to-face** (adj) /ˌfeɪs tə ˈfeɪs/ = a face-to-face meeting, conversation, etc. is one where you are with another person. *Do you want to talk about the problem over the phone or would you prefer a **face-to-face** discussion?*
πρόσωπο με πρόσωπο

8.118 **line** (n) /laɪn/ = a telephone wire or connection. *I'm sorry, the **line** is busy. Please try again later.*
τηλεφωνική σύνδεση

8.119 **speech** (n) /spiːtʃ/ = when sb speaks, or the way that they speak. *Her **speech** was clear and they understood everything she said.* ➤ speak (v)
ικανότητα του λόγου ή της ομιλίας, ομιλία

8.120 **immediate** (adj) /ɪˈmiːdiət/ = happening or done now, with no delay. *The drug has **immediate** results.*
άμεσος-η-ο

8.121 **accessible** (adj) /əkˈsesəbəl/ = easy to reach, find or use. *The castle is not **accessible** by road.* ➤ access (n, v)
προσπελάσιμος-η-ο
Opp: inaccessible

8.122 **flirt** (v) /flɜːt/ = to behave as if you are sexually attracted to sb, but not in a very serious way. *He **flirts** with the women in the office.* ➤ flirt (n)
ερωτοτροπώ, φλερτάρω

8 Communication breakdown

8.123 third (n) /θɜːd/ = one of three equal parts into which sth can be divided. *I've finished about a **third** of the work.*
(ένα) τρίτο

8.124 quarter (n) /ˈkwɔːtə/ = one of four equal parts into which sth can be divided. *Cut the cake into **quarters**.*
(ένα) τέταρτο

8.125 social (adj) /ˈsəʊʃəl/ = having the ability or opportunity to behave and speak properly with other people. *He has no **social** skills.*
κοινωνικός-ή-ό

8.126 affirmative (adj) /əˈfɜːmətɪv/ = an affirmative answer or action means 'yes' or shows agreement. *an **affirmative** reply*
καταφατικός-ή-ό
Opp: negative

Writing: Pages 92–93

8.127 thunderstorm (n) /ˈθʌndəstɔːm/ = a storm with thunder and lightning. *There was a **thunderstorm** last night and this morning everything was wet.*
καταιγίδα

8.128 wire (n) /waɪə/ = a piece of metal like a thick thread, used for carrying electricity. *Have you connected all the **wires**?*
σύρμα
◆ telephone wire

8.129 dead (adj) /ded/ = an engine, telephone, etc. that is dead is not working because there is no power. *Suddenly, the phone went **dead** and we were cut off.*
εκτός λειτουργίας
◆ go dead

8.130 recharge (v) /ˌriːˈtʃɑːdʒ/ = to put a new supply of electricity into a battery. *I need to **recharge** the battery of my mobile phone.* ➤ charge (v)
ξαναφορτίζω

8.131 set up (phr v) /ˌset ˈʌp/ = to get equipment ready to be used. *He **set up** a computer in the classroom.*
προετοιμάζω για λειτουργία

8.132 broadband (n) /ˈbrɔːdbænd/ = a system of connecting computers to the internet and moving information at a very high speed. *Are you on **broadband** yet?*
ευρυζωνική σύνδεση

8.133 volume (n) /ˈvɒljuːm/ = the amount of sound produced by a television, radio, etc. *Can you turn down the **volume** on the TV?*
ένταση ήχου

8.134 complaint (n) /kəmˈpleɪnt/ = sth that you say or write when you are annoyed or unhappy about sth. ***complaints** about the poor service in the shop* ➤ complain (v)
παράπονο
◆ make a complaint

8.135 helpline (n) /ˈhelplaɪn/ = a telephone number that you can ring if you need advice or information. *Call the **helpline** if you've got a problem.*
γραμμή εξυπηρέτησης

8.136 in connection with (prep phr) /ɪn kəˈnekʃən wɪð, wɪθ/ = concerning sth. *Police are questioning a man **in connection with** the crime.*
σε σχέση με

8.137 cover (v) /ˈkʌvə/ = if an insurance agreement or guarantee covers sb or sth, it promises to pay money if they are injured, damaged, stolen, etc. *This guarantee **covers** the machine for a year.*
καλύπτω

8.138 guarantee (n) /ˌɡærənˈtiː/ = a formal written promise by a company to repair or replace a product if it breaks. *a two-year **guarantee*** ➤ guarantee (v)
εγγύηση

8.139 repair (v) /rɪˈpeə/ = to make sth that is broken or damaged satisfactory again. *How much will it cost to **repair** the car?* ➤ repair (n)
επισκευάζω

8.140 forward (v) /ˈfɔːwəd/ = to send letters, packages or email messages to sb at another address. *If there are any letters for you, I'll **forward** them to your new address.*
προωθώ

8.141 service (n) /ˈsɜːvɪs/ = help or work that a business provides for customers, rather than goods produced by a business. *We offer a free information **service**.*
εξυπηρέτηση

8.142 cross (adj) /krɒs/ = annoyed. *She's **cross** about losing the money.*
φουρκισμένος-η-ο
◆ cross about

8.143 useless (adj) /ˈjuːsləs/ = not useful or effective at all. *I'm afraid that information is **useless** to me.*
άχρηστος-η-ο
Opp: useful

8.144 refund (n) /ˈriːfʌnd/ = an amount of money you have paid that is given back to you. *If you're not satisfied with the camera, we'll give you a **refund**.* ➤ refund (v)
επιστροφή χρημάτων

8.145 sign up (phr v) /ˌsaɪn ˈʌp/ = to put your name on a list because you want to do sth. *Ten people **signed up** for the trip to Paris.*
εγγράφομαι (σε όμιλο, κλπ.)

8.146 package (n) /ˈpækɪdʒ/ = a set of products sold or offered together. *a new software **package***
πακέτο

8.147 top (adj) /tɒp/ = best or most successful. *He is a **top** doctor.*
άριστος-η-ο, κορυφαίος-α-ο

Communication breakdown 8

8.148 quality (n) /ˈkwɒləti/ = how good or bad sth is. *bad **quality** material*
ποιότητα

8.149 keypad (n) /ˈkiːpæd/ = a small box with buttons on it that you press to put information into a computer, telephone, etc. *a phone **keypad***
πληκτρολόγιο τηλεφώνου, τηλεχειριστηρίου, κλπ.

8.150 top up (phr v) /ˌtɒp ˈʌp/ = to fill sth that is partly empty. *Let me **top up** your glass.*
(ξανα)γεμίζω

8.151 charge (v) /tʃɑːdʒ/ = to ask sb to pay a particular amount of money for sth. *They **charged** me fifty euros to repair my bicycle.*
χρεώνω

8.152 state (v) /steɪt/ = to say sth publicly or officially. *Please **state** your name and address.* ➤ statement (n)
δηλώνω, ανακοινώνω

8.153 furthermore (adv) /ˌfɜːðəˈmɔː/ = in addition to what has already been said. *He is clever and hard-working. **Furthermore**, he is reliable.*
επιπροσθέτως, συνάμα

8.154 take action (phr) /teɪk ˈækʃən/ = to do sth to deal with a problem. *We must **take action** to save our planet now.*
αναλαμβάνω δράση

WORDZONE SPECIAL

Easily confused words: programme, program

programme
A programme is a show on television or radio.
*Let's watch the **programme** on television.*
If you programme a machine, you give it a set of instructions to make it do sth.
*Can you **programme** the video recorder to record the film tonight?*

program
A program is a set of instructions given to a computer to make it do sth.
*He wrote a new computer **program**.*
If you program a computer, you give it a set of instructions to make it do sth.
*I don't know how to **program** a computer.*

Note: programme (British English) = program (American English)

Vocabulary and grammar practice

 Choose the correct word to complete the sentences.

1 The comedy we saw last night was a huge *commercial / social* success.
2 Sean is very *cross / aggressive* when he plays football.
3 Scientists are working to *develop / attract* robots that can play football really well.
4 She made a(n) *life-size / alive* statue of a horse.
5 The hotel is *programmable / accessible* by car and train.
6 Warm clothes are *essential / powerful* in a cold climate.
7 My trainers are too small for me. I must *repair / replace* them.
8 I saw some great cotton shirts for *sell / sale*.
9 What *tools / engines* do you need to fix the bicycle?
10 She spoke in such a soft voice that she wasn't *visible / audible* from the back of the hall.

8 Communication breakdown

2 Complete the sentences with these nouns.

customers   dialect   experiments   goal   guarantee   jaws
media   passage   refund   scent   vision   volume

1 I love the .... of fresh flowers.
2 Crocodiles have very powerful ....
3 The .... waited in a queue to pay for their things.
4 They speak a strange .... in that part of the country.
5 The scientists were in the lab doing some ....
6 You must have excellent .... to be a pilot.
7 This joypad is not working properly. I'm going to take it back to the shop and ask for a ....
8 Our new television is covered by a one-year ....
9 Our English teacher asked us to learn a short .... from the book by heart.
10 Ian's team mates were cross with him when he scored an own ....
11 I can't hear the news. Please turn up the .... on the radio.
12 The details of the scandal were reported in the ....

3 Match 1–8 and a–h to make sentences.

1 I recharge
2 She leapt
3 They're acting
4 They manufacture
5 These sensors detect
6 We explored
7 The idea appealed
8 They charged

a high-tech electronic equipment.
b me a lot of money to repair my car.
c the battery of my mobile phone every night.
d over the wall and ran away.
e sound.
f the beautiful countryside.
g to him.
h very immaturely!

4 Complete the text with these words.

absolutely   face-to-face   once   replace   service   signing   websites

1) .... it was 2) .... unimaginable to think of education without classrooms and teachers. Nowadays, however, you can find many 3) .... on the internet that offer courses in all sorts of subjects. More and more people are 4) .... up to do courses online. Instead of 5) .... contact with a teacher, students have access to a special 6) .... that tells them how well they are doing. Does this mean that computers will soon 7) .... teachers?

Communication breakdown 8

5 The passive
Rewrite the sentences in the passive.

1 People design new websites every day.
....
2 A young boy from China designed this robot.
....
3 They have already read this magazine twice.
....
4 They are using a robot to do the job.
....
5 They had sent many text messages.
....
6 The inventor will demonstrate the new model tomorrow.
....
7 They recharged these batteries an hour ago.
....
8 People speak four different dialects.
....
9 They are building a sports centre opposite the park.
....
10 Many people read the newspaper article about robotics.
....
11 They will repair the roof and then they will paint the walls.
....
12 Somebody has stolen my laptop!
....

6 Question tags
Complete the sentences with a question tag.

1 He borrowed your iPod again, ... ?
2 She isn't going to do the work, ... ?
3 They should have been here by now, ... ?
4 The line won't be fixed today, ... ?
5 The DVD player works better now, ... ?
6 You can't take pictures with this mobile phone, ... ?
7 We will get a refund, ... ?
8 You don't know how to repair this, ... ?
9 He isn't playing that computer game again, ... ?
10 The children have finished their homework, ... ?
11 She cooks very well, ... ?
12 It hadn't been raining all night, ... ?

8 Communication breakdown

Test yourself!

Choose the word or phrase that best completes the conversation or sentence.

1. The scientists did a(n) …… in the lab.
   - A tool
   - B direction
   - C experiment
   - D vision

2. Are you still …… with me? I told you I was sorry!
   - A aggressive
   - B cross
   - C straight
   - D thorough

3. The housework …… by robots in the future.
   - A is done
   - B is being done
   - C will do
   - D will be done

4. 'You haven't been reading my text messages, …… ?'
   'Of course not!'
   - A have you
   - B have I
   - C do you
   - D were you

5. Cats have a very good …… of hearing.
   - A sight
   - B sensor
   - C sense
   - D scent

6. 'Is the printer back yet?'
   'No it …… at the shop.
   - A is still repairing
   - B is still being repaired
   - C was still repaired
   - D will still be repaired

7. Please hurry! We need help …… !
   - A specially
   - B absolutely
   - C properly
   - D urgently

8. People need to …… with each other or they become sad and lonely.
   - A attract
   - B produce
   - C act
   - D interact

9. You will forgive me, …… ?
   - A don't you
   - B will you
   - C won't you
   - D wouldn't you

10. 'Did you send the email?'
    'Yes, but it ……. The address was wrong.'
    - A wasn't delivered
    - B won't deliver
    - C wasn't being delivered
    - D isn't delivering

11. I tried to call Jane but the line kept …… .
    - A falling apart
    - B topping up
    - C breaking up
    - D setting up

12. Unfortunately, the joypad …… covered by the guarantee and I had to buy a new one.
    - A wasn't
    - B hasn't been
    - C isn't being
    - D wasn't being

13. The price of laptops is …… and they are cheaper than they used to be.
    - A beating
    - B kicking
    - C increasing
    - D decreasing

14. Dinner …… at seven every day.
    - A serves
    - B is served
    - C will be serving
    - D served

Time to revise 4 | Units 7–8

   Complete the sentences with these nouns.

guide   harbour   needle   objects   route   site   voyage

1 The tour .... showed us around the old part of the city.
2 Let's take the quick .... home tonight, shall we?
3 The ship sailed into the .... and the sailors were happy to be back on dry land.
4 The archaeologist found some strange .... but she doesn't know what they are.
5 The .... lasted many weeks but eventually, the ship reached Australia.
6 I've torn my shirt and I need a(n) .... and some thread to mend it.
7 This is the .... of a famous battle.

   Choose the correct word to complete the sentences.

1 We enjoyed our *destination / stay* in London very much.
2 I was talking to my sister on the phone when the line *went dead / fell apart*.
3 I don't think that robots will ever *replace / replacement* people in my job.
4 She created a very clever computer *programme / program*.
5 It's no *help / good* waiting for him. He won't come.
6 Please don't *raise / increase* your voice! The accident wasn't my fault.
7 Can I have some *privacy / luxury*, please? I want to make a phone call.

3 **Choose the correct answer, A, B, C or D.**

A sense of taste

Do you know why your favourite food tastes so good? Well, have a look at your tongue in the mirror. Can you 1) ...... those small 'bumps' on its surface? In those bumps there are tiny 2) ...... that allow us to experience and enjoy the different flavours of food. These tiny organs 3) ...... taste buds and they work by sending 4) ...... , or messages, to the brain.

5) ...... has shown that our sense of taste changes as we get older. It is strongest in babies but 6) ...... people are fifty, it is much less sensitive. 7) ...... , it seems that girls have more taste buds than boys. Logically, they should be able to taste better, 8) ...... ?

1 **A** break up	**B** make out	**C** set up	**D** top up
2 **A** scissors	**B** coins	**C** sensors	**D** senses
3 **A** are called	**B** are being called	**C** called	**D** calling
4 **A** signals	**B** scents	**C** tools	**D** arrows
5 **A** Condition	**B** Decade	**C** Method	**D** Research
6 **A** at the time	**B** by the time	**C** most of the time	**D** from time to time
7 **A** Furthermore	**B** Specially	**C** In contrast	**D** In connection with
8 **A** isn't it	**B** don't they	**C** shouldn't they	**D** doesn't it

9 Getting on

Reading: Pages 96–97

9.1 **get on** (phr v) /ˌget ˈɒn/ = to have a friendly relationship with sb. *I **get on** with all my brothers and sisters.*
έχω καλή σχέση
◆ get on with sb

9.2 **sociable** (adj) /ˈsəʊʃəbəl/ = sb who is sociable is friendly and enjoys being with other people. *They are a **sociable** couple who have many friends.* ➤ social (adj), society (n)
κοινωνικός-ή-ό

9.3 **uncomfortable** (adj) /ʌnˈkʌmfətəbəl/ = embarrassed or worried. *She felt **uncomfortable** about being photographed.*
αμήχανος-η-ο
Opp: comfortable

9.4 **teen** (adj) /tiːn/ = relating to or used by teenagers. *a **teen** magazine* ➤ teen (n), teenage (adj), teenager (n)
εφηβικός-ή-ό

9.5 **nightmare** (n) /ˈnaɪtmeə/ = a very unpleasant or difficult experience. *The weather was bad and the voyage was a **nightmare**.*
εφιάλτης

9.6 **lifetime** (n) /ˈlaɪftaɪm/ = the period of time during which sb is alive. *I realised the job was the chance of a **lifetime**.*
ζωή, διάρκεια ζωής
◆ the chance of a lifetime = the best opportunity that you will ever have.

9.7 **housemate** (n) /ˈhaʊsmeɪt/ = a person who you share a house with but who is not a member of your family. *Two of my **housemates** are moving out.*
συγκάτοικος

9.8 **get to know** (phr) /ˌget tə ˈnəʊ/ = to gradually begin to know, like, etc. sb or sth. *When you **get to know** him, I'm sure you'll like him.*
γνωρίζω

9.9 **come from** (phr v) /ˈkʌm frəm, frɒm/ = to be born, obtained from or made somewhere. *She **came from** Rome but lived in London.*
προέρχομαι από, κατάγομαι από

9.10 **background** (n) /ˈbækgraʊnd/ = the type of education, experience and family that sb has. *The students at this college come from different **backgrounds**.*
καταγωγή, παρελθόν

9.11 **culture** (n) /ˈkʌltʃə/ = the art, beliefs, behaviour, ideas, etc. of a particular society or group of people. *I want to learn about British **culture**.* ➤ cultural (adj)
κουλτούρα, πολιτισμός

9.12 **have sth in common** (phr) /hæv ˌsʌmθɪŋ ɪn ˈkɒmən/ = to be similar in some way. *Italy and Greece **have** many things **in common**.*
έχω κάτι από κοινού

9.13 **eye contact** (n phr) /ˈaɪ ˌkɒntækt/ = when you look directly at sb the same time as they are looking at you. *People who are lying tend to avoid **eye contact**.*
οπτική επαφή

9.14 **(on the one hand …) on the other hand** (phr) /ɒn ðə ˈwʌn hænd, ɒn ðɪ ˈʌðə hænd/ = used when you are comparing two different facts or ideas. *On the one hand, they work slowly but **on the other hand**, they always do a good job.*
(αφ' ενός …) αφ' ετέρου

9.15 **likeable** (adj) /ˈlaɪkəbəl/ = likeable people are nice and easy to like. *Jo's a very **likeable** girl.* ➤ like (v)
αξιαγάπητος-η-ο, συμπαθής-ές

9.16 **scared** (adj) /skeəd/ = frightened or nervous about sth. *We were **scared** that something terrible might happen.* ➤ scare (v, n), scary (adj)
τρομαγμένος-η-ο

9.17 **burst** (v) /bɜːst/ = to move quickly and suddenly. *Dave **burst** into the room.*
εισβάλλω
◆ burst into. Irr v: burst–burst–brust

9.18 **appear** (v) /əˈpɪə/ = to seem. *Helen **appeared** to be nervous before her exam.* ➤ appearance (n)
φαίνομαι
◆ appear to do

9.19 **arrogant** (adj) /ˈærəgənt/ = behaving in an unpleasant or rude way because you think you are more important than other people. *He was an **arrogant** and selfish man.* ➤ arrogance (n)
αλαζονικός-ή-ό

9.20 **approach** (v) /əˈprəʊtʃ/ = to speak to sb for the first time. *They did not know how to **approach** her because she looked so angry.* ➤ approach (n), approachable (adj)
πλησιάζω, προσεγγίζω

9.21 **course** (n) /kɔːs/ = a period of time or a process during which sth happens. *Over the **course** of the summer, I got to know them well.*
πορεία, ροή
◆ over the course of (a few days/four weeks, etc.)

Getting on ... 9

9.22 various (adj) /ˈveəriəs/ = several different. *We had **various** things to do, so we didn't get bored.* ➤ vary (v), variety (n), varied (adj)
ποικίλος-η-ο

9.23 vary (v) /ˈveəri/ = if things of the same type vary, they are all different from each other. *The colour of the flowers **varied** from white to dark red.*
ποικίλλω

9.24 unblock (v) /ʌnˈblɒk/ = if you unblock a pipe, toilet, etc., you remove sth that is blocking it. *Use these chemicals to **unblock** the toilet and pipes.*
ξεβουλώνω
Opp: block

9.25 simulated (adj) /ˈsɪmjʊleɪtɪd/ = not real but made to look, sound or feel real. *a **simulated** flight in an aeroplane*
➤ simulate (v), simulator (n)
με προσομοίωση

9.26 the outside world (phr) /ði ˌaʊtsaɪd ˈwɜːld/ = the rest of the world. *The village was cut off from **the outside world** by snow.*
ο έξω κόσμος

9.27 except (prep) /ɪkˈsept/ = not including a particular thing, person or fact. *The shops are open every day **except** Sunday.* ➤ exception (n)
εκτός από

9.28 reflect (v) /rɪˈflekt/ = to show or be a sign of sth. *Does your bedroom **reflect** your personality?* ➤ reflection (n)
αντικατοπτρίζω-ομαι

9.29 strip sb of sth (phr v) /ˈstrɪp sʌmbədi əv ˌsʌmθɪŋ/ = to take sth important away from sb, especially their possessions, rank or property. *The thieves **stripped** us **of** all our money.*
αποστερώ, ξηλώνω

9.30 rule (n) /ruːl/ = an official instruction about what is allowed, especially in a game, organisation or job. *One of the **rules** in my house is that we all have to help with the housework.* ➤ rule (v), ruler (n)
κανόνας, κανονισμός

9.31 add (v) /æd/ = to say more about sth when you are speaking. *Dad asked me to help him and **added** that he wasn't feeling well.* ➤ addition (n)
προσθέτω
◆ add that

9.32 difficulty (n) /ˈdɪfɪkəlti/ = when sth is not easy to do. *Did you have **difficulty** finding our house?*
➤ difficult (adj)
δυσκολία
◆ have difficulty (in) doing sth

9.33 hold on to (phr v) /ˈhəʊld ˈɒn tə, tʊ/ = to keep sth and not give it to anybody. *I think I'll **hold on to** these CDs.*
κρατώ

9.34 remain (v) /rɪˈmeɪn/ = to continue to do sth. *Young children can't **remain** quiet for long.*
εξακολουθώ, παραμένω

9.35 over (adj) /ˈəʊvə/ = finished. *The programme is **over**. Let's go to bed now.*
τελειωμένος-η-ο

9.36 do without (phr v) /ˌduː wɪðˈaʊt/ = to not have sth. *There's no more butter and the shops are closed. We'll have to **do without**.*
κάνω χωρίς

9.37 directly (adv) /dɪˈrektli, daɪ-/ = exactly in a particular position or direction. *Lucas sat **directly** behind us.*
➤ direct (adj), direction (n), direct (v)
απευθείας, κατ' ευθείαν

9.38 accept (v) /əkˈsept/ = to take sth that sb offers you, or agree to sth sb suggests. *They offered me the job and I **accepted**.* ➤ acceptance (n)
δέχομαι

Vocabulary: Page 98

9.39 ambitious (adj) /æmˈbɪʃəs/ = determined to be successful or powerful. *He is **ambitious** and I'm sure he will succeed.* ➤ ambition (n)
φιλόδοξος-η-ο

9.40 competitive (adj) /kəmˈpetətɪv/ = determined to be more successful than other people. *Henrietta is very **competitive** and always wants to be the best at everything.* ➤ compete (v), competition (n), competitor (n)
ανταγωνιστικός-ή-ό

9.41 bossy (adj) /ˈbɒsi/ = always telling other people what to do in a way that is annoying. *My brother is **bossy** and keeps telling us what to do.* ➤ boss (n, v)
αυταρχικός-ή-ό

9.42 extrovert (n) /ˈekstrəvɜːt/ = sb who is confident and likes being with people. *She is an **extrovert** and loves acting in plays.* ➤ extroverted (adj)
εξωστρεφές άτομο
Opp: introvert

9.43 show off (phr v) /ˌʃəʊ ˈɒf/ = to do things to try to make people think you are clever, attractive, funny, etc. *Nick was **showing off** because Eve was there.*
➤ show-off (n)
προσπαθώ να κάνω φιγούρα

9.44 cheeky (adj) /ˈtʃiːki/ = rude or showing no respect, sometimes in an amusing way. *Don't be so **cheeky**!*
➤ cheek (n)
αυθάδης-ες

9.45 humorous (adj) /ˈhjuːmərəs/ = funny and enjoyable. *a **humorous** story* ➤ humour (n)
χιουμοριστικός-ή-ό, αστείος-α-ο

9 Getting on ...

9.46 sensitive (adj) /ˈsensətɪv/ = (1) able to understand other people's feelings and problems. (2) easily offended or hurt by the things that other people do or say. *Don't be unkind to Chris. He's very **sensitive**.* ➤ sensitivity (n)
ευαίσθητος-η-ο
Opp: insensitive

9.47 be into (v phr) /bi ˈɪntə ˌsʌmθɪŋ/ = to like and be interested in sth. *Diana **is** really **into** music.*
ενδιαφέρομαι για κάτι

9.48 assertive (adj) /əˈsɜːtɪv/ = behaving confidently to make people listen to you. *She is an **assertive** young woman with a strong personality.* ➤ assertiveness (n)
δυναμικός-ή-ό

9.49 talkative (adj) /ˈtɔːkətɪv/ = a talkative person talks a lot. *a **talkative** person* ➤ talk (v, n)
ομιλητικός-ή-ό, φλύαρος-η-ο

9.50 drive sb mad (phr) /ˌdraɪv ˈsʌmbədi ˈmæd/ = to make sb very angry. *That awful noise is **driving** me **mad**!*
τρελαίνω κάποιον-α

9.51 can't help (v phr) /kɑːnt ˈhelp/ = to be unable to stop yourself from doing sth. *The film was so sad that I **couldn't help** crying.*
δεν μπορώ παρά να
◆ can't help doing sth

9.52 think up (phr v) /ˌθɪŋk ˈʌp/ = to produce a new idea. *It's a great idea. Who **thought** it **up**?*
επινοώ, σκαρφίζομαι

9.53 insensitive (adj) /ɪnˈsensətɪv/ = sb who is insensitive does not notice other people's feelings and often does or says things that upset them. *He is **insensitive** sometimes and upsets people.* ➤ insensitivity (n)
στερούμενος-η-ο ευαισθησιών, αναίσθητος-η-ο

9.54 timid (adj) /ˈtɪmɪd/ = shy and not showing courage or confidence. *She is **timid** and is afraid of the school bullies.* ➤ timidity (n)
δειλός-ή-ό, συνεσταλμένος-η-ο

9.55 hard-working (adj) /ˌhɑːd ˈwɜːkɪŋ/ = working with a lot of effort. *a **hard-working** student*
εργατικός-ή-ό

9.56 unattractive (adj) /ˌʌnəˈtræktɪv/ = sb who is unattractive is not good-looking, especially in a way that puts you off. *His unpleasant personality makes him **unattractive**.*
άχαρος-η-ο
Opp: attractive

9.57 big-head (n) /ˈbɪɡ hed/ = sb who thinks they are very important, clever, etc. *Pat is such a **big-head**. No wonder nobody likes her!*
αλαζόνας

9.58 gossip (n) /ˈɡɒsɪp/ = sb who likes talking about other people's private lives. *Don't tell Rick anything. He's a terrible **gossip**.* ➤ gossip (v)
κουτσομπόλης-α

9.59 snob (n) /snɒb/ = sb who thinks they are better than people from a lower social position. *She doesn't talk to people who are not rich. She's a **snob**.* ➤ snobbish (adj)
σνομπ

Grammar: Page 99

9.60 go out with (phr v) /ɡəʊ ˈaʊt wɪð, wɪθ/ = to have a romantic relationship with sb. *Lisa used to **go out with** Todd.*
διατηρώ αισθηματικό δεσμό με

9.61 ironing (n) /ˈaɪənɪŋ/ = the activity of making clothes smooth with an iron. *I hate doing the **ironing**.*
➤ iron (v, n)
σιδέρωμα (ρούχων, κλπ.)

9.62 exhausted (adj) /ɪɡˈzɔːstɪd/ = extremely tired. *I was **exhausted** after the race.* ➤ exhaust (v), exhausting (adj), exhaustion (n)
εξουθενωμένος-η-ο

Listening: Page 100

9.63 stupid (adj) /ˈstjuːpɪd/ = not very clever or intelligent. *Of course they understand – they aren't **stupid**.*
➤ stupidity (n)
χαζός-ή-ό, κουτός-ή-ό

9.64 take place (v phr) /teɪk ˈpleɪs/ = to happen. *When did the robbery **take place**?*
συμβαίνω

Speaking: Page 101

9.65 be a laugh (phr) /bi ə ˈlɑːf/ = to be amusing. *I like being with Jen – she**'s a laugh**.*
είμαι αστείος-α-ο

9.66 stay out (phr v) /ˌsteɪ ˈaʊt/ = to remain away from home during the evening or night. *They **stayed out** till midnight.*
βγαίνω για να διασκεδάσω

9.67 suppose (v) /səˈpəʊz/ = used when agreeing to let sb do sth, especially when you do not want to. *'Can I borrow your computer?' 'I **suppose** so, but be careful with it.'*
υποθέτω

9.68 pardon (interjection) /ˈpɑːdn/ = used when you want sb to repeat sth because you did not hear it. *'Hurry up, Jonathan!' '**Pardon**?' 'I said hurry up!'*

9.69 as far as I'm concerned (phr) /əz ˌfɑːr əz ˈaɪm kənˌsɜːnd/ = to the degree that matters to me. *You can stay out until midnight **as far as I'm concerned**.*
όσον με αφορά

Getting on ... 9

9.70 act out (phr v) /ˌækt ˈaʊt/ = to show how sth happened by performing it like a play. *The children read the story and then **acted** it **out**.*
αναπαριστάνω

9.71 it's time (phr) /ɪts ˈtaɪm/ = used to say that sth should happen now. ***It's time** to go home. It's getting late.*
είναι ώρα να

Use your English: Pages 102–103

9.72 vowel (n) /ˈvaʊəl/ = one of the sounds shown in English by the letters a, e, i, o or u and sometimes y. *How many **vowels** are there in 'individual'?*
φωνήεν

9.73 soap opera (n phr) /ˈsəʊp ˌɒpərə/ = a television or radio story about the ordinary lives of the same group of people, which is broadcast very frequently. *I watched my favourite **soap opera** on TV.*
σαπουνόπερα
Also: soap

9.74 skateboard (n) /ˈskeɪtbɔːd/ = a short board with wheels that you stand and ride on. *Take your **skateboard** with you to the park.* ➤ skateboard (v)
τροχοσανίδα

9.75 independence (n) /ˌɪndɪˈpendəns/ = the freedom and ability to make your own decisions in life without having to ask other people for permission, help or money. *Having a job gives you financial **independence**.*
➤ independent (adj)
ανεξαρτησία
Opp: dependence

9.76 twin (n) /twɪn/ = one of two children born of the same mother at the same time. *Meet my **twin** sister, Nora.*
δίδυμος αδελφός, δίδυμη αδελφή

9.77 up to (sth) (phr) /ˈʌp tə ˌsʌmθɪŋ/ = doing sth secret or doing sth that you should not be doing. *The children are very quiet. What are they **up to**?*
be up to sth = σκαρώνω κάτι

9.78 on the whole (phr) /ɒn ðə ˈhəʊl/ = generally or usually. ***On the whole**, life was quieter after the children left.*
γενικώς

9.79 tell a joke (phr) /ˌtel ə ˈdʒəʊk/ = tell a funny story. *John is great at **telling jokes**.*
λέω ανέκδοτο

9.80 disadvantage (n) /ˌdɪsədˈvɑːntɪdʒ/ = sth that makes things more difficult to do or less pleasant for you. *the **disadvantages** of living in a city*
μειονέκτημα
Opp: advantage

Writing: Pages 104–105

9.81 well-dressed (adj) /ˌwel ˈdrest/ = wearing good clothes. *a **well-dressed** TV presenter*
καλοντυμένος-η-ο

9.82 creative (adj) /kriˈeɪtɪv/ = a creative person is good at thinking of new ideas. *He's a talented and **creative** film director.* ➤ create (v), creativity (n)
δημιουργικός-ή-ό

9.83 freaky (adj) /ˈfriːki/ = strange or unusual and a bit frightening. *a **freaky** accident* ➤ freak (n)
αλλόκοτος-η-ο

9.84 magically (adv) /ˈmædʒɪkli/ = in a way that involves using magic or mysterious powers. *At the end of the film, the witch **magically** disappeared.* ➤ magical (adj), magic (n), magician (n)
δια μαγείας

9.85 wake up (phr v) /ˌweɪk ˈʌp/ = to stop sleeping, or to make sb stop sleeping. *I **woke up** at five this morning.*
ξυπνώ

9.86 slim (adj) /slɪm/ = sb who is slim is thin in an attractive way. *You look **slimmer**. Have you lost weight?*
λεπτός-ή-ό

9.87 sensible (adj) /ˈsensəbəl/ = suitable for a particular purpose, especially a practical one. *Please wear **sensible** shoes when you go walking.*
άνετος-η-ο, κατάλληλος-η-ο

9.88 end up (phr v) /ˌend ˈʌp/ = to finally be in a particular place, situation or state without intending to. *She wanted to study for her test but she **ended up** talking to her friend on the phone.*
καταλήγω
◈ end up doing sth

9.89 get on like a house on fire (phr) /ˌget ɒn laɪk ə ˌhaʊs ɒn ˈfaɪə/ = to quickly have a very friendly relationship. *As soon as we met, we **got on like a house on fire**.*
τα πηγαίνω πολύ καλά με κάποιον-α

9.90 understanding (adj) /ˌʌndəˈstændɪŋ/ = showing sympathy towards sb who has problems. *I'm lucky to have such **understanding** parents.*
➤ understanding (n), understand (v)
συμπονετικός-ή-ό, που δείχνει κατανόηση

9.91 organised (adj) /ˈɔːɡənaɪzd/ = planned and arranged well. *a tidy and **organised** desk* ➤ organise (v) organisation (n)
οργανωμένος-η-ο

9.92 stressed (adj) /strest/ = so worried and tired that you cannot relax. *I've got an important exam and I feel **stressed**.* ➤ stress (v, n)
αγχομένος-η-ο

9 Getting on ...

9.93 get up (phr v) /ˌɡet ˈʌp/ = to get out of your bed after sleeping. *I woke up at seven but I only **got up** at eight.*
σηκώνομαι

9.94 baggy (adj) /ˈbæɡi/ = baggy clothes are big and loose. *Joan always wears **baggy** trousers.*
φαρδύς-ιά-ύ

9.95 trendy (adj) /ˈtrendi/ = modern and fashionable. *a **trendy** restaurant* ➤ trend (n)
μοντέρνος-α-ο

9.96 outspoken (adj) /aʊtˈspəʊkən/ = sb who is outspoken says what they think even though it may shock or offend people. *She is **outspoken** and sometimes upsets people.*
ευθαρσής-ές, σταράτος-η-ο

9.97 argument (n) /ˈɑːɡjʊmənt/ = a disagreement, especially one in which people talk loudly and angrily. *My friend and I had an **argument** but it wasn't serious.*
➤ argue (v)
διαφωνία, καυγάς
◈ have an argument

9.98 ruin (v) /ˈruːɪn/ = to spoil or destroy sth completely. *The accident **ruined** everything.* ➤ ruin (n), ruined (adj)
καταστρέφω

9.199 cousin (n) /ˈkʌzən/ = a child of your aunt or uncle. *Jane and I are **cousins**.*
εξάδελφος, εξαδέλφη

9.100 announcement (n) /əˈnaʊnsmənt/ = an important official statement about sth that has happened or will happen. *Listen! I have an important **announcement** to make.* ➤ announce (v)
ανακοίνωση
◈ make an announcement

WORDZONE SPECIAL

Easily confused words: wake up, get up

wake up
If you wake up, you stop sleeping but you don't necessarily get out of bed.
*I **woke up** when my alarm went off but I didn't want to get out of bed.*

get up
If you get up, you get out of your bed after sleeping.
*I woke up at seven but I only **got up** at eight.*

Vocabulary and grammar practice

 1 Complete the sentences with these adjectives.

ambitious   arrogant   bossy   cheeky   likeable   sociable   timid   uncomfortable

1 I'm not a(n) .... person and I prefer to be alone most of the time.
2 Rachel was a(n) .... girl, so she never spoke much in class.
3 I felt .... when I noticed a strange man staring at me.
4 He's very .... He thinks he's better than us because his parents are rich!
5 The contestants were .... young people who wanted to succeed.
6 You're a(n) .... little boy! Apologise now or I'll tell your parents!
7 They're .... people and they're popular with their neighbours.
8 Caitlin is so .... ! She's always telling her sisters what to do!

Getting on ... 9

2 **Complete the sentences with these prepositions.**

from   off   on   out (x2)   up (x3)

1 You should hold .... to those papers. You might need them one day.
2 Who thought .... the idea for this game show? It's great!
3 We stayed .... until midnight celebrating Gwen's birthday.
4 All the participants come .... different social backgrounds.
5 We usually get .... late on Sundays, so don't call me before eleven.
6 How long have you been going .... with him?
7 He always shows .... if there's a pretty girl at the party.
8 We didn't like each other at first but we ended .... being good friends.

3 **Rewrite the sentences with these words. Make any other necessary changes.**

appear   baggy   exhausted   housemate   nightmare   outspoken   ruined   trendy

1 Olivia is the person I share my house with.
   ....
2 What a horrible experience! I'll never do that again!
   ....
3 His behaviour completely spoilt our day.
   ....
4 Sophie was wearing a large, loose T-shirt.
   ....
5 You look extremely tired. Have you been working hard?
   ....
6 They seem to be happy together.
   ....
7 My brother always says what he thinks.
   ....
8 I like wearing fashionable clothes.
   ....

4 **Complete the sentences with these verbs.**

did   drove   got (x2)   had   stripped   told   took

1 They were poor, so they .... without new cothes.
2 The children .... their parents mad.
3 The meetings .... place in her office.
4 Brian and Pete .... on like a house on fire.
5 The twins .... me a very funny joke.
6 They .... him of all his possessions.
7 They .... to know each other very well.
8 Valerie and Thelma .... many interests in common.

9 Getting on ...

5 Reported speech
Rewrite the sentences in reported speech. Use the correct tenses and pronouns.

1 'Why don't you go out with him?' Sally asked Tina.
Sally asked Tina ....

2 'They have already left,' Justin said.
Justin said ....

3 'Tidy your room,' Mum told us
Mum told us ....

4 'I may be one of the finalists,' Frank said.
Frank said ....

5 'We aren't going to accept their offer,' they said.
They said ....

6 'Have you been reading my messages again?' Anne asked me.
Anne asked me ....

7 'Lisa is sleeping and I can't wake her,' Joe said.
Joe said ....

8 'You must try harder if you want to stay on *Big Brother*,' she said.
She said ....

6 -ing form and to- infinitive
Choose the correct words to complete the text.

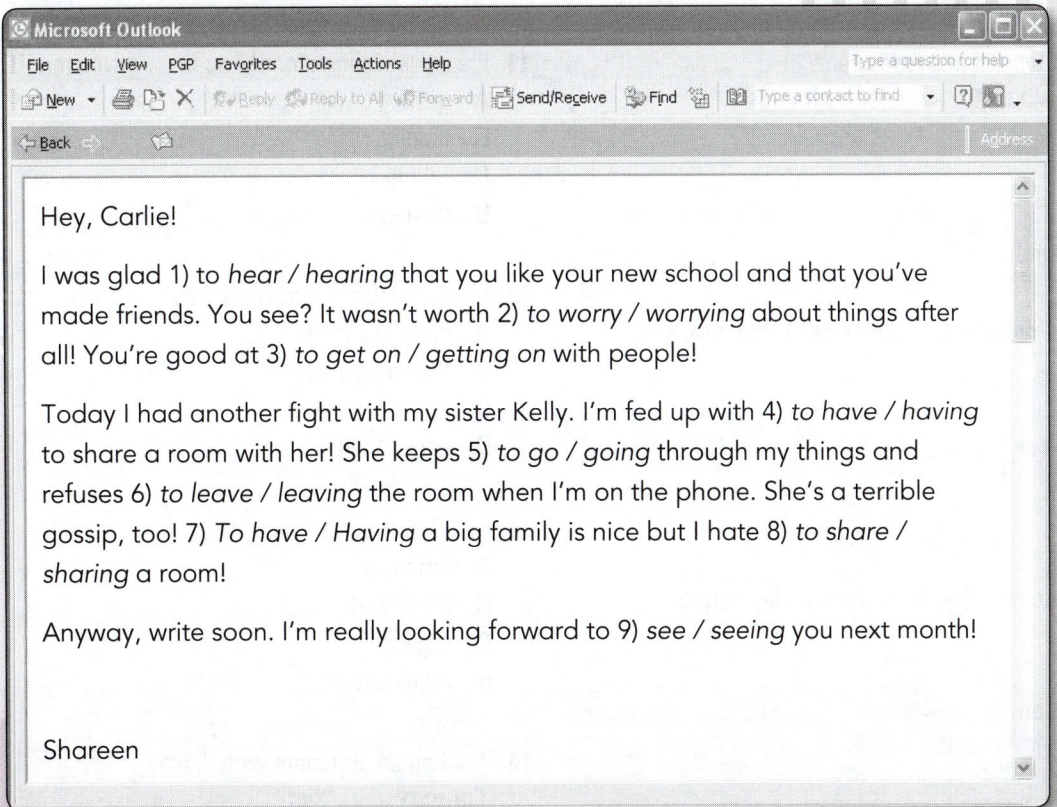

Hey, Carlie!

I was glad 1) *to hear / hearing* that you like your new school and that you've made friends. You see? It wasn't worth 2) *to worry / worrying* about things after all! You're good at 3) *to get on / getting on* with people!

Today I had another fight with my sister Kelly. I'm fed up with 4) *to have / having* to share a room with her! She keeps 5) *to go / going* through my things and refuses 6) *to leave / leaving* the room when I'm on the phone. She's a terrible gossip, too! 7) *To have / Having* a big family is nice but I hate 8) *to share / sharing* a room!

Anyway, write soon. I'm really looking forward to 9) *see / seeing* you next month!

Shareen

Getting on ... 9

Test yourself!

Choose the word or phrase that best completes the conversation or sentence.

1. Doug is too ...... sometimes. He hurt Jill's feelings yesterday.
   - **A** assertive
   - **B** outspoken
   - **C** talkative
   - **D** extrovert

2. Joel asked ...... us.
   - **A** if he can join
   - **B** can he join
   - **C** if could he join
   - **D** if he could join

3. I believe that our clothes ...... our personality.
   - **A** reflect
   - **B** accept
   - **C** approach
   - **D** suppose

4. 'Why don't we eat at a restaurant?'
   'Don't worry. I enjoy ...... for my friends.'
   - **A** cook
   - **B** to cook
   - **C** cooking
   - **D** to cooking

5. You have a guilty look on your face! What have you been ...... ?
   - **A** into
   - **B** on to
   - **C** up to
   - **D** out of

6. They told me that they ...... her the day before.
   - **A** see
   - **B** saw
   - **C** have seen
   - **D** had seen

7. Mike is a .... He really believes we all admire him!
   - **A** gossip
   - **B** big-head
   - **C** teen
   - **D** twin

8. 'Is Suzy still sleeping?'
   'Yes. She asked me ...... her.'
   - **A** don't wake
   - **B** didn't wake
   - **C** to not wake
   - **D** not to wake

9. Sylvio promised ...... more careful in future.
   - **A** to be
   - **B** being
   - **C** he is being
   - **D** will be

10. Tanya is really ...... acting.
    - **A** into
    - **B** out of
    - **C** from
    - **D** on to

11. Please leave me alone! You're ...... me mad!
    - **A** getting
    - **B** holding
    - **C** telling
    - **D** driving

12. My friend wanted to know why ...... her.
    - **A** hadn't I called
    - **B** I hadn't called
    - **C** didn't I call
    - **D** I not called

13. I work better if my desk is ....
    - **A** organise
    - **B** organised
    - **C** organiser
    - **D** organisation

14. 'Pat had an argument with Jimmy.'
    'I'm sorry ...... that.
    - **A** to hear
    - **B** hear
    - **C** hearing
    - **D** I'm hearing

10 Planet Earth

Reading: Pages 106–107

10.1 **planet** (n) /ˈplænɪt/ = a very large round object in space that moves around the sun or another star. *Mercury is the smallest **planet**.*
πλανήτης

10.2 **environment** (n) /ɪnˈvaɪrənmənt/ = the natural features of a place, for example its weather, the type of land it has and the type of plants that grow in it. *a forest **environment*** ➤ environmental (adj), environmentalist (n)
περιβάλλον

10.3 **serious** (adj) /ˈsɪəriəs/ = sth that is serious is important and should not be laughed at. *This is a very **serious** matter.*
σοβαρός-ή-ό

10.4 **Arctic** (n) /ˈɑːktɪk/ = the very cold area around the North Pole. *Polar bears live in the **Arctic**.* ➤ Arctic (adj)
Αρκτική

10.5 **accommodation** (n) /əˌkɒməˈdeɪʃən/ = a place to live, stay or work. *The college provides **accommodation** for all new students.* ➤ accommodate (v)
στέγαση, κατάλυμμα

10.6 **ice** (n) /aɪs/ = water that has frozen and become solid. *It was winter and there was **ice** on the roads.*
➤ icy (adj)
πάγος

10.7 **blizzard** (n) /ˈblɪzəd/ = a storm with a lot of wind and snow. *We got stuck in a **blizzard**.*
χιονοθύελλα

10.8 **glacier** (n) /ˈglæsiə/ = a large mass of ice that moves slowly down a mountain valley. *The **glacier** moved slowly down the mountain.*
παγετώνας

10.9 **effect** (n) /ɪˈfekt/ = a change or result that happens because of an event or action. *What will be the **effect** on the environment?* ➤ effective (adj)
επίπτωση
◆ effect on

10.10 **global warming** (n phr) /ˌgləʊbəl ˈwɔːmɪŋ/ = an increase in world temperatures caused by an increase in the amount of carbon dioxide in the atmosphere. *The warmer weather is a result of **global warming**.*
αύξηση της παγκόσμιας θερμοκρασίας

10.11 **highlight** (n) /ˈhaɪlaɪt/ = the most important, interesting or enjoyable part of sth. *One of the **highlights** of the holiday was the boat trip.* ➤ highlight (v)
εντυπωσιακό στιγμιότυπο, αποκορύφωμα

10.12 **sledge** (n) /sledʒ/ = a vehicle used for travelling on snow. *Grandpa made us a traditional wooden **sledge**.*
έλκηθρο

10.13 **pull** (v) /pʊl/ = to make sth move in a particular direction, especially towards you, by holding it and using force in that direction. *They **pulled** the child out of the water.*
έλκω, τραβώ

10.14 **husky** (n) /ˈhʌski/ = a dog with thick hair, often used for pulling sledges over snow. *A team of **huskies** pulled the sledge.*
χάσκι (ράτσα σκύλου)

10.15 **roller coaster** (n phr) /ˈrəʊlə ˌkəʊstə/ = a small railway which carries people up and down a steep track very fast for fun. *The children went for a ride on the **roller coaster**.*
ρώσικα βουνά (στο λούνα παρκ)

10.16 **temperature** (n) /ˈtempərətʃə/ = how hot or cold sth is. *Check the **temperature** of the water.*
θερμοκρασία

10.17 **survival** (n) /səˈvaɪvəl/ = the fact of continuing to live or exist. *Their chances of **survival** in those conditions are not great.* ➤ survive (v), survivor (n)
επιβίωση

10.18 **technique** (n) /tekˈniːk/ = a special skill or way of doing sth. *If you want to learn how to paint, you should learn some **techniques** first.* ➤ technical (adj), technician (n)
τεχνική

10.19 **clothing** (n) /ˈkləʊðɪŋ/ = clothes. *We put on warm **clothing** because it was cold.* ➤ clothes (n pl)
ιματισμός, ρούχα

10.20 **frostbite** (n) /ˈfrɒstbaɪt/ = a condition in which your fingers, toes, etc. become frozen and are badly damaged. *The Arctic explorers suffered from **frostbite**.* ➤ frost (n), frosty (adj)
κρυοπάγημα

10.21 **means** (n) /miːnz/ = a way of doing sth. *I think email is the best **means** of communication.*
μέσον
Plural: means

Planet Earth 10

10.22 transport (n) /ˈtrænspɔːt/ = a kind of vehicle or a system of buses, trains, etc, that you use for going from one place to another. *Buses are the best form of public **transport**.* ➤ transport (v)
μεταφορά
◆ means of transport

10.23 canoe (v) /kəˈnuː/ = to travel with a long light narrow boat that is pointed at both ends, which you move using a paddle. *They **canoed** down the river.* ➤ canoe (n)
κωπηλατώ, κάνω κανό

10.24 celebration (n) /ˌseləˈbreɪʃən/ = when you celebrate sth special, or an occasion or party when you celebrate sth. *Christmas is a time of joy and **celebration**.* ➤ celebrate (v)
εορτασμός

10.25 tribal (adj) /ˈtraɪbəl/ = connected with a group of people with the same language and customs who live together in the same area. *They want to study **tribal** art and customs.* ➤ tribe (n)
φυλετικός-ή-ό, της φυλής

10.26 rainforest (n) /ˈreɪnˌfɒrəst/ = a tropical forest with tall trees that are very close together, growing in an area where it rains a lot. *the **rainforests** that grow in tropical areas*
τροπικό δάσος, ομβρικό δάσος

10.27 destroy (v) /dɪˈstrɔɪ/ = to damage sth very badly so that it cannot be repaired. *A fire **destroyed** the building.* ➤ destruction (n), destructive (adj)
καταστρέφω

10.28 net (n) /net/ = a piece of material made of pieces of string, wire, etc., which are joined together with spaces between them, and that is used for catching fish, etc. *The fishermen caught many fish in their **nets**.*
δίκτυ
◆ fishing net

10.29 in the wild (prep phr) /ɪn ðə ˈwaɪld/ = in an area outside a farm or a zoo, where animals can live freely and naturally. *There are very few pandas living **in the wild** now.*
στην άγρια φύση

10.30 in danger (prep phr) /ɪn ˈdeɪndʒə/ = in a dangerous situation. *They believe their lives are **in danger**.*
σε κίνδυνο

10.31 hunter (n) /ˈhʌntə/ = sb who chases animals in order to catch and kill them. *The **hunter** killed a deer.* ➤ hunt (v, n)
κυνηγός

10.32 enclosure (n) /ɪnˈkləʊʒə/ = an area surrounded by a wall or fence. *You must not enter the lion **enclosure**.* ➤ enclose (v)
περίφραξη

10.33 proud (adj) /praʊd/ = feeling pleased because you think that sth you have achieved or are connected with is very good. *Her parents are **proud** of her.* ➤ pride (n)
υπερήφανος-η-ο
◆ proud of

10.34 brilliant (adj) /ˈbrɪljənt/ = extremely nice or enjoyable. *'How was your holiday?' 'It was **brilliant**!'*
υπέροχος-η-ο

10.35 desert (n) /ˈdezət/ = very hot dry land where few plants grow. *the Sahara **desert***
έρημος

10.36 hut (n) /hʌt/ = a small simple building with only one or two rooms. *They live in a wooden **hut** in the forest.*
καλύβα

10.37 dung (n) /dʌŋ/ = solid waste from animals, especially large animals. *There was a lot of cow **dung** in the field.*
περιττώματα ζώου, κοπριά

10.38 on foot (prep phr) /ɒn ˈfʊt/ = if you go somewhere on foot, you walk there. *They went to school **on foot**.*
με τα πόδια

10.39 track (v) /træk/ = to follow sb or sth by looking for signs of their movement. *The hunter **tracked** the animal through the forest.* ➤ track (n)
ακολουθώ τα ίχνη

10.40 endanger (v) /ɪnˈdeɪndʒə/ = to put sb or sth in a dangerous or harmful situation. *Smoking **endangers** your health.* ➤ endangered (adj)
εκθέτω σε κίνδυνο
◆ endangered species = απειλούμενο είδος

10.41 rhino (n) /ˈraɪnəʊ/ = a large heavy animal with thick skin and a horn on its nose. *It is illegal to hunt **rhinos**.*
ρινόκερος
Also: rhinoceros

10.42 Namibian (adj) /nəˈmɪbiən/ = belonging to or referring to Namibia, a large desert country in south-western Africa. ***Namibian** lions*
της Ναμίμπιας

10.43 boiling (adj) /ˈbɔɪlɪŋ/ = extremely hot. *It's **boiling** in here. Open a window.* ➤ boil (v)
it's boiling = κάνει πάρα πολύ ζέστη, βράζει
Also: boiling hot

10.44 cross (v) /krɒs/ = to go from one side of a road, river, room, etc. to the other. *Take care when you **cross** the road.*
διασχίζω

10.45 sand (n) /sænd/ = the substance that forms deserts and beaches, which consists of many small grains of rocks or minerals. *The children built castles in the **sand** on the beach.* ➤ sandy (adj)
άμμος

10 Planet Earth

10.46 rare (adj) /reə/ = not happening often, or not common. *He was excited to see such a **rare** bird.* ➤ rarity (n)
σπάνιος-α-ο

10.47 smelly (adj) /'smeli/ = having a strong unpleasant smell. *Those dirty socks are **smelly**.* ➤ smell (n, v)
δύσοσμος-η-ο

10.48 luggage (n) /'lʌgɪdʒ/ = the bags, etc. that you carry when you are travelling. *We put our **luggage** in the car and left for our holiday.*
αποσκευή, αποσκευές

10.49 Ecuador (n) /'ekwədɔː/ = a country in South America. ***Ecuador** must be a beautiful country.*
Ισημερινός, Εκουαδόρ

10.50 on horseback (prep phr) /ɒn 'hɔːsbæk/ = riding a horse. *They made the journey **on horseback**.*
be on horseback = βαίνω έφιππος

10.51 marking (n) /'mɑːkɪŋ/ = a coloured shape or pattern on sth. *The young birds have red **markings** on their wings.* ➤ mark (n, v)
σημάδι, σχέδιο

10.52 cage (n) /keɪdʒ/ = a structure made of wires or bars in which birds or animals can be kept. *a bird in a **cage***
κλουβί

10.53 habitat (n) /'hæbɪtæt/ = the natural home of a plant or animal. *It was great to see monkeys in their natural **habitat**.*
φυσική κατοικία (ζώου), φυσικό περιβάλλον (φυτού)
◆ natural habitat

10.54 go free (v phr) /gəʊ 'friː/ = to leave a cage and go where you want. *The adult animals can **go free** when they can survive on their own.*
αφήνομαι ελεύθερος-η-ο

10.55 volcano (n) /vɒl'keɪnəʊ/ = a mountain that sometimes explodes, sending out fire and hot rocks. *The island has an active **volcano**.* ➤ volcanic (adj)
ηφαίστειο

10.56 freezing (adj) /'friːzɪŋ/ = very cold. *It's **freezing** outside!* ➤ freeze (v), frozen (adj)
it's freezing = έχει παγωνιά
Also: freezing cold

10.57 mist (n) /mɪst/ = a layer of cloud close to the ground that makes it difficult for you to see very far. *The **mist** was starting to disappear.* ➤ misty (adj)
ομίχλη, καταχνιά

10.58 tough (adj) /tʌf/ = difficult or involving problems. *It was a **tough** job.*
ζόρικος-η-ο, δύσκολος-η-ο

10.59 expedition (n) /ˌekspə'dɪʃən/ = a long and carefully organised journey. *an **expedition** to the North Pole*
εξερευνητική αποστολή

10.60 conservation (n) /ˌkɒnsə'veɪʃən/ = the protection of natural things such as animals, plants, forests, etc. ***conservation** of the countryside* ➤ conserve (v), conservationist (n)
διατήρηση, συντήρηση

10.61 species (n) /'spiːʃiːz/ = a group of animals or plants of the same kind. *Many different **species** of monkeys live in the rainforest.*
είδος
Plural: species

10.62 sheet (n) /ʃiːt/ = a large flat area of sth such as ice or water spread over a surface. *A **sheet** of ice covered the lake.*
επίστρωμα, στρώμα
◆ sheet of ice

10.63 mountainous (adj) /'maʊntənəs/ = a mountainous area has a lot of mountains. *We visited the **mountainous** coast of Wales.*
ορεινός-ή-ό

10.64 frozen (adj) /'frəʊzən/ = feeling very cold. *I must put on warm boots. My feet are **frozen**.*
παγωμένος-η-ο

10.65 wildlife (n) /'waɪldlaɪf/ = animals and plants living in natural conditions. *We must protect the area's **wildlife**.*
άγρια πανίδα και χλωρίδα, άγρια φύση

10.66 increase (n) /'ɪnkriːs/ = a rise in amount or level. *an **increase** in temperature* ➤ increase (v)
αύξηση
◆ increase in. Opp: decrease

10.67 cope (v) /kəʊp/ = to succeed in dealing with everything you have to do, especially when it is very difficult. *How does she **cope** with six kids?*
τα καταφέρνω, αντεπεξέρχομαι
◆ cope with

Vocabulary: Page 108

10.68 drought (n) /draʊt/ = a long period of dry weather when there is not enough water. *The country has had two years of **drought**.*
ανομβρία, ξηρασία

10.69 flood (n) /flʌd/ = a very large amount of water that covers an area that is usually dry. *Their homes were destroyed by the **floods**.* ➤ flood (v)
πλημμύρα

10.70 heat wave (n phr) /'hiːt weɪv/ = a period of unusually hot weather. *During the **heat wave** it was impossible to work outside.*
κύμα καύσωνος

10.71 hurricane (n) /'hʌrɪkən/ = a violent storm with very strong fast winds. *Many villages were destroyed by the **hurricane**.*
τυφώνας

Planet Earth 10

10.72 lightning (n) /ˈlaɪtnɪŋ/ = a bright flash of electrical light in the sky during a storm. *There was a storm with thunder and **lightning**.*
αστραπή

10.73 period (n) /ˈpɪəriəd/ = a length of time. *We stayed there during the holiday **period**.*
περίοδος

10.74 dry (adj) /draɪ/ = dry weather does not have rain. *The weather tomorrow will be hot and **dry**.* ➤ dry (v)
ξηρός-ή-ό

10.75 flash (n) /flæʃ/ = a sudden quick bright light. *a **flash** of lightning*
ακαριαία λάμψη

10.76 electricity (n) /ˌelɪkˈtrɪsəti/ = the power that is carried by wires and used to make lights and machines work. *The cooker works with **electricity**.* ➤ electrical (adj), electric (adj), electrician (n)
ηλεκτρισμός, ηλεκτρική ενέργεια

10.77 pour (v) /pɔː/ = to rain heavily. *Take an umbrella with you. It's **pouring**.*
βρέχει καταρρακτωδώς
◆ pour with rain

10.78 soaking (adj) /ˈsəʊkɪŋ/ = completely wet. *a **soaking** towel* ➤ soak (v)
καταμουσκεμένος-η-ο
Also: soaking wet

10.79 sticky (adj) /ˈstɪki/ = weather that is sticky makes you feel uncomfortably hot, wet and dirty. *It was a hot and **sticky** day.* ➤ stick (v)
ζεστός-ή-ό και υγρός-ή-ό

10.80 mow (v) /məʊ/ = to cut grass with a machine. *Dan **mowed** the lawn.* ➤ mower (n)
κόβω (γρασίδι, κλπ.) με χλοοκοπτική μηχανή

10.81 lawn (n) /lɔːn/ = an area of grass that is kept cut short. *The children played on the **lawn**.*
χλοοτάπητας

10.82 strike (v) /straɪk/ = to hit sb or sth. *The church tower was **struck** by lightning.*
κτυπώ

10.83 knock (v) /nɒk/ = to hit sb or sth so that they move or fall down. *I accidentally **knocked** the glass off the table.* ➤ knock (n)
κτυπώ

10.84 melt (v) /melt/ = to change from solid to liquid, or to make sth do this by heating it. *The sun came out and the snow **melted**.*
λιώνω

10.85 suffer (v) /ˈsʌfə/ = to experience and be badly affected by sth. *He **suffered** brain damage.*
υφίσταμαι (ζημιά, κλπ.)

10.86 severe (adj) /sɪˈvɪə/ = very bad. *I have a **severe** headache.*
σοβαρός-ή-ό

10.87 damage (n) /ˈdæmɪdʒ/ = physical harm done to sth so that it is broken or spoiled. *The earthquake caused a lot of **damage** to houses.* ➤ damage (v)
ζημιά

10.88 fortunately (adv) /ˈfɔːtʃənətli/ = happening because of good luck. ***Fortunately**, the weather was excellent.* ➤ fortunate (adj), fortune (n)
ευτυχώς, κατά καλή τύχη
Opp: unfortunately

10.89 recover (v) /rɪˈkʌvə/ = to get better after an illness, injury, shock, etc. *My uncle is **recovering** from a bad cold.* ➤ recovery (n)
αναρρώνω
◆ recover from

Grammar: Page 109

10.90 camp (n) /kæmp/ = a place where people stay in tents for a short time. *After exploring the jungle all morning, we returned to **camp**.* ➤ camp (v)
καταυλισμός, κατασκήνωση

Listening: Page 110

10.91 cockroach (n) /ˈkɒkrəʊtʃ/ = a large insect that sometimes lives in places where there is food. *There were **cockroaches** in the dirty kitchen.*
κατσαρίδα

10.92 worm (n) /wɜːm/ = a small long thin creature without bones or legs that lives in soil. *There are **worms** in the soil.*
σκουλήκι

10.93 porridge (n) /ˈpɒrɪdʒ/ = oats that are cooked in milk or water and eaten hot for breakfast. ***Porridge** is made with oats and milk.*
χυλός βρώμης

10.94 provide (v) /prəˈvaɪd/ = to give sb sth they need. *They will **provide** milk and biscuits.* ➤ provision (n)
προσφέρω, παρέχω

10.95 regret (v) /rɪˈgret/ = to feel sorry about sth you have done and wish you had not done it. *We **regretted** selling our car.* ➤ regret (n)
μετανοιώνω
◆ regret sth/doing sth

10 Planet Earth

Speaking: Page 111

10.96 miss (v) /mɪs/ = to feel sad because you cannot be with sb that you like, cannot do sth that you enjoy, etc. *He **missed** his friend when he moved to another town.*
μου λείπει

10.97 shower (n) /ʃaʊə/ = the act of washing the body by standing under running water. *I have a **shower** every morning before breakfast.* ➤ shower (v)
ντους
◆ have a shower

10.98 mosquito (n) /məˈskiːtəʊ/ = a small flying insect that sucks the blood of people and animals. ***Mosquitoes** bit me last night.*
κουνούπι

10.99 bit (n) /bɪt/ = a small piece of sth. *There were **bits** of broken glass everywhere.*
μικρό τεμάχιο

10.100 panther (n) /ˈpænθə/ = a large black wild animal that is a type of cat. *We saw a **panther** in the forest.*
πάνθηρας

10.101 no way! (phr) /nəʊ ˈweɪ/ = used to say that you will definitely not do or allow sth. *'Mum, can I borrow the car?' '**No way!**'*
σε καμία περίπτωση!

10.102 sleeping bag (n phr) /ˈsliːpɪŋ bæɡ/ = a large warm bag for sleeping in. *We're going camping, so we'll need our **sleeping bags**.*
υπνόσακος

10.103 five-star (adj) /faɪv ˈstɑː/ = used to show how good the quality of sth is, especially a hotel or restaurant. *They are rich, so they stayed in a **five-star** hotel.*
πέντε αστέρων

10.104 heavy (adj) /ˈhevi/ = large in amount. *There was **heavy** snow last night.*
δυνατός-ή-ό, έντονος-η-ο, πολύ
◆ heavy rain/snow/traffic

10.105 tarantula (n) /təˈræntjʊlə/ = a large poisonous spider. *He was bitten by a **tarantula**.*
ταραντούλα (είδος αράχνης)

10.106 mile (n) /maɪl/ = a unit for measuring distance, equal to 1,609 metres. *My house is about five **miles** from here.*
μίλι

10.107 straight (adv) /streɪt/ = immediately; without delay. *I went home **straight** after school.*
κατευθείαν
Also: straight away

10.108 member (n) /ˈmembə/ = sb who belongs to a group or organisation. *She's a **member** of the tennis club.*
➤ membership (n)
μέλος

Use your English: Pages 112–113

10.109 reuse (v) /ˌriːˈjuːz/ = to use sth again. *The bottles can be **reused** many times.* ➤ reusable (adj)
ξαναχρησιμοποιώ

10.110 careless (adj) /ˈkeələs/ = not taking enough care. *She was **careless** and made mistakes.* ➤ carelessness (n), care (n, v)
απρόσεκτος-η-ο
Opp: careful

10.111 carefree (adj) /ˈkeəfriː/ = having no worries or problems. *They had a happy and **carefree** childhood.*
ανέμελος-η-ο, ξένοιαστος-η-ο

10.112 chlorine (n) /ˈklɔːriːn/ = a yellow-green gas that is used to keep swimming pools clean. *The pool smelled of **chlorine**.*
χλώριο
◆ chlorine-free = without chlorine

10.113 harmless (adj) /ˈhɑːmləs/ = unable or unlikely to cause harm. *Don't worry. That snake is **harmless**.*
➤ harm (n, v)
άκακος-η-ο, ακίνδυνος-η-ο
Opp: harmful

10.114 recycle (v) /ˌriːˈsaɪkəl/ = to put glass, paper, etc. through a special process so that it can be used again. *Glass bottles can be **recycled**.* ➤ recyclable (adj)
ανακυκλώνω

10.115 supply (n) /səˈplaɪ/ = an amount of sth that can be used. *a week's **supply** of fresh meat* ➤ supply (v)
παροχή, (αν)εφοδιασμός

10.116 attention (n) /əˈtenʃən/ = the act of fixing your mind on sth. *I want your **attention**, please. This is important!*
προσοχή
◆ pay attention = δίνω προσοχή

10.117 unlikely (adj) /ʌnˈlaɪkli/ = not expected; improbable. *I won't take an umbrella. It's **unlikely** to rain.*
απίθανος-η-ο
Opp: likely

10.118 throw away (phr v) /θrəʊ əˈweɪ/ = to get rid of sth that you do not want or need. *Can I **throw** those boxes **away**?*
πετώ

10.119 litter (n) /ˈlɪtə/ = paper, bottles, cans, etc. that people do not want and have left on the ground in a public place. *Throw the **litter** in the bin, not on the street.*
➤ litter (v)
σκουπίδια

10.120 light bulb (n phr) /ˈlaɪt bʌlb/ = the glass part of an electric light, where the light shines from. *Sue changed the **light bulb**.*
ηλεκτρική λάμπα

Planet Earth 10

10.121 energy-saving (adj) /ˈenədʒi ˌseɪvɪŋ/ = using less energy so as not to waste any. **energy-saving** tips
που εξοικονομεί ενέργεια

10.122 environmentally-friendy (adj) /ɪnˌvaɪrənmentl-i ˈfrendli/ = not harmful to the environment. **environmentally-friendly** products
φιλικός-ή-ό προς το περιβάλλον

10.123 mercury (n) /ˈmɜːkjəri/ = a silver-coloured liquid metal used in thermometers. **Mercury** is used in old-fashioned thermometers.
υδράργυρος

10.124 wind-up (adj) /waɪnd ʌp/ = relating to a machine or toy that you turn part of several times in order to make it move or start working. an old **wind-up** toy
➤ wind up (phr v)
κουρδιστός-ή-ό

10.125 torch (n) /tɔːtʃ/ = a small electric lamp that you carry in your hand. He shone the **torch** around the dark room.
φακός

10.126 out and about (phr) /aʊt ənd əˈbaʊt/ = when you are out and about, you go places where you can meet people. She's always **out and about** with her friends.
εκτός σπιτιού, σε κίνηση

10.127 solar (adj) /ˈsəʊlə/ = using energy from the sun. We use **solar** energy to heat water.
ηλιακός-ή-ό
◆ solar-powered

10.128 charger (n) /ˈtʃɑːdʒə/ = a piece of equipment used to put electricity into a battery. Have you seen my phone **charger** anywhere? ➤ charge (v)
φορτιστής

10.129 on stand-by (prep phr) /ɒn ˈstænd baɪ/ = ready to act or be used if needed. The police are **on stand-by** in case of trouble.
σε ετοιμότητα

10.130 lighting (n) /ˈlaɪtɪŋ/ = the system, arrangement or equipment that lights a place, or the quality of light produced. Better street **lighting** might help prevent crime. ➤ light (n, v)
φωτισμός

10.131 solar panel (n phr) /ˈsəʊlə ˈpænəl/ = a number of solar cells working together. They heat water using energy from **solar panels** on their roof.
ηλιακός συσσωρευτής

10.132 install (v) /ɪnˈstɔːl/ = to put a piece of equipment somewhere and connect it so that you can use it. They **installed** security cameras in the building.
εγκαθιστώ

10.133 bleach (v) /bliːtʃ/ = to make sth white or lighter in colour by using chemicals or the light from the sun. The sun had **bleached** her hair. ➤ bleach (n)
ξεθωριάζω, λευκαίνω

10.134 tissue (n) /ˈtɪʃuː, -sjuː/ = a piece of soft thin paper used for cleaning your nose. a box of **tissues**
χαρτομάντιλο

10.135 petrol (n) /ˈpetrəl/ = a liquid made from petroleum, used for producing power in the engines of cars, etc. Put some **petrol** in the tank.
βενζίνη

10.136 ecological (adj) /ˌiːkəˈlɒdʒɪkəl/ = relating to the relationship of living things to each other and to their environment. The **ecological** balance in the area could be destroyed. ➤ ecology (n), ecologist (n)
οικολογικός-ή-ό

10.137 economical (adj) /ˌekəˈnɒmɪkəl, ˌiː-/ = using money, time, products, etc. carefully and without wasting any. I want to buy a smaller and more **economical** car.
➤ economy (n), economic (adj)
οικονομικός-ή-ό

10.138 uncaring (adj) /ʌnˈkeərɪŋ/ = not caring about other people's feelings. She seemed cold and **uncaring**.
αδιάφορος-η-ο

10.139 renew (v) /rɪˈnjuː/ = to arrange for an agreement or arrangement to continue. You must **renew** your subscription to the magazine. ➤ renewal (n), renewable (adj)
ανανεώνω

10.140 rethink (v) /riːˈθɪŋk/ = to think about a plan or idea again and decide what changes should be made. We need to **rethink** the plan. I don't think it will work.
αναθεωρώ, ξανασκέπτομαι

10.141 lead-free (adj) /ˌled ˈfriː/ = lead-free petrol or paint contains no lead (= a soft, heavy, greyish-blue metal). They use **lead-free** paint on children's toys.
αμόλυβδος-η-ο

10.142 eco-friendly (adj) /ˌiːkəʊ ˈfrendli/ = not harmful to the environment. **eco-friendly** shopping bags
φιλικός-ή-ό προς το περιβάλλον

10.143 water butt (n phr) /ˈwɔːtə bʌt/ = a large container that is kept outside and used for collecting rainwater. We use the rainwater that we collect in **water butts** to water our garden.
βαρέλι περισυλλογής νερού βροχής

10.144 deliver (v) /dɪˈlɪvə/ = to take sth to a place. The postman **delivered** the letters. ➤ delivery (n)
παραδίνω

10.145 insulate (v) /ˈɪnsjʊleɪt/ = to cover sth with a material that stops electricity, sound, heat, etc. from getting in or out. **Insulate** the water pipes so that they don't freeze.
➤ insulation (n)
μονώνω

10.146 tap (n) /tæp/ = a piece of equipment that you turn to control the flow of a liquid or gas. You forgot to turn off the **tap**.
βρύση

10 Planet Earth

10.147 mend (v) /mend/ = to repair sth that is broken or damaged. *mend a broken chair*
επισκευάζω

10.148 trip (n) /trɪp/ = a journey for business or a particular purpose. *She went on a business trip to London.*
ταξίδι
◆ go on a trip

10.149 book (v) /bʊk/ = to arrange in advance to have sth. *Have you booked the tickets yet?* ➤ booking (n)
κλείνω (εισιτήριο, πτήση, θέση, δωμάτιο, κλπ.)

10.150 pack (v) /pæk/ = to put things into cases, bags, etc. ready for a journey. *Don't forget to pack your bags.*
ετοιμάζω αποσκευή

10.151 on holiday (prep phr) /ɒn ˈhɒlədi/ = having a holiday. *Where are you going on holiday?*
σε διακοπές
◆ be/go on holiday

10.152 nail (n) /neɪl/ = the hard flat piece that covers the top end of a finger or toe. *I cut my nails.*
νύχι
Also: fingernail, toenail

10.153 portrait (n) /ˈpɔːtrət/ = a drawing, painting or photograph of a real person or group of people. *The artist painted her portrait.*
πορτρέτο, προσωπογραφία

Writing: Pages 114–115

10.154 project (n) /ˈprɒdʒekt/ = a piece of work that is carefully planned and done over a period of time. *a three-year research project*
μεγάλο έργο

10.155 council (n) /ˈkaʊnsəl/ = a group of people who make rules, laws or decisions, or give advice. *They are members of the town council.*
συμβούλιο

10.156 charity (n) /ˈtʃærəti/ = an organisation that gives money, goods or help to people who are poor, sick, etc. *She gives a lot of money to charities.*
φιλανθρωπικό ίδρυμα

10.157 supporter (n) /səˈpɔːtə/ = sb who supports a person, group or plan. *loyal supporters of the president*
➤ support (n, v)
υποστηρικτής

10.158 sanctuary (n) /ˈsæŋktʃuəri, -tʃəri/ = an area for birds or animals where they are protected and cannot be hunted. *a sanctuary for tigers*
καταφύγιο (άγριων ζώων/πουλιών)

10.159 release (v) /rɪˈliːs/ = to allow sb to be free after you have kept them somewhere. *The bears were released from their cages.* ➤ release (n)
(απ)ελευθερώνω

10.160 free (adj) /friː/ = if sth is free, it does not cost any money. *There's a free gift with this month's magazine.*
➤ free (adv, v), freedom (n)
δωρεάν

10.161 brochure (n) /ˈbrəʊʃə, -ʃʊə/ = a thin book that gives information or advertises sth. *I looked at the holiday brochures.*
διαφημιστικό φυλλάδιο

10.162 pack (n) /pæk/ = several similar things wrapped or packed together in order to sell them or send them to sb. *You can get an information pack from the library.*
πακέτο

10.163 aware (adj) /əˈweə/ = if you are aware of sth, you know about it or realise that it is there. *The children are aware of the danger.* ➤ awareness (n)
◆ aware of. Opp: unaware

10.164 donation (n) /dəʊˈneɪʃən/ = sth, especially money, that you give to help a person or organisation. *Please make a donation to the hospital.* ➤ donate (v)
δωρεά

10.165 affect (v) /əˈfekt/ = to cause a change in sb or sth, or to change the situation they are in. *Help is being sent to areas that were affected by the floods.*
επηρεάζω

10.166 soil (n) /sɔɪl/ = the earth in which plants grow. *The soil here is very poor.*
χώμα, γη

10.167 crop (n) /krɒp/ = a plant such as wheat, fruit, vegetables, etc. that farmers grow and sell. *Our main crops are potatoes and cabbages.*
καλλιέργεια, σοδειά

10.168 raise (v) /reɪz/ = to keep animals or grow crops to sell or eat. *They raise chickens on their farm.*
εκτρέφω

10.169 yearly (adj) /ˈjɪəli/ = happening or appearing every year or once a year. *He has a yearly medical examination.*
➤ yearly (adv), year (n)
ετήσιος-α-ο

10.170 newsletter (n) /ˈnjuːzˌletə/ = a printed report with news about an organisation, sent regularly to its members. *our drama club newsletter*
ενημερωτικό φυλλάδιο

10.171 option (n) /ˈɒpʃən/ = sth that you can choose to do. *What shall we do? We have three options.*
➤ optional (adj)
επιλογή

10.172 benefit (v) /ˈbenəfɪt/ = if you benefit from sth or if it benefits you, it helps you. *Everybody benefits from regular exercise.* ➤ benefit (n)
ωφελώ
◆ benefit from

Planet Earth 10

10.173 in addition (prep phr) /ɪn əˈdɪʃən/ = as well as. *They do a lot of charity work in African countries. **In addition**, they help children in other parts of the world.*
επιπλέον

10.174 in need (prep phr) /ɪn ˈniːd/ = not having enough food or money. *families **in need***
που έχουν ανάγκη

10.175 wooden (adj) /ˈwʊdn/ = made of wood. *a **wooden** box* ➤ wood (n)
ξύλινος-η-ο

10.176 chalet (n) /ˈʃæleɪ/ = a wooden house, especially one in a mountain area. *We stayed in a **chalet** in the mountains.*
σαλέ

10.177 instructor (n) /ɪnˈstrʌktə/ = sb who teaches a sport or activity. *a driving **instructor*** ➤ instruct (v), instruction (n)
εκπαιδευτής

10.178 hire (n) /haɪə/ = an arrangement to borrow sth in exchange for money. *Is this car for **hire**?* ➤ hire (v)
ενοικίαση
◆ for hire

10.179 pass (n) /pɑːs/ = an offical piece of paper with writing on it which shows that you are allowed to do sth like travel on a train without paying or enter a building. *Students can get a rail **pass** and travel all over Europe quite cheaply.*
άδεια

10.180 native (adj) /ˈneɪtɪv/ = belonging to a place from birth. *She is a **native** Londoner.* ➤ native (n)
ντόπιος-α-ο
◆ native speaker = a person who speaks a particular language as their mother tongue

10.181 waterproof (adj) /ˈwɔːtəpruːf/ = not allowing water to enter. ***waterproof** boots*
αδιάβροχος-η-ο

10.182 preference (n) /ˈprefərəns/ = a liking for one thing rather than another. *I don't know your **preferences**, so please choose something yourself.* ➤ prefer (v)
προτίμηση

WORDZONE SPECIAL

Easily confused words: lighting, lightning

lighting
Lighting is the system, arrangement or equipment that lights a place, or the quality of light produced.
*The soft **lighting** gave the room a pleasant atmosphere.*

lightning
Lightning is a bright flash of electrical light in the sky during a storm.
*There was a flash of **lightning** followed by thunder.*

Vocabulary and grammar practice

1 Complete the sentences with these nouns.

desert   drought   floods   frostbite   global warming   mist   planet   temperature

1 The thick .... made it impossible for us to see more than a few metres in front of us.
2 The .... fell below zero and the water in the lake froze.
3 It is hot in the .... and it rarely rains but some animals and plants manage to survive there.
4 In very cold weather, you can get .... on your fingers, toes, nose and ears.
5 Scientists now believe that climate change is a result of ....
6 The Earth is the third .... from the sun.

10 Planet Earth

7 It rained heavily for days and there were serious ....

8 It hadn't rained for months and the animals were suffering from the ....

2 Match the words 1–8 with the words a–h. Then complete the sentences with the correct compound noun.

1 heat ☐   a bag
2 light ☐   b bulb
3 news ☐   c butt
4 rain ☐   d light
5 high ☐   e forest
6 sleeping ☐   f letter
7 water ☐   g life
8 wild ☐   h wave

1 When I go camping, I often sleep on the beach in my ....

2 I would love to go to Australia and photograph kangaroos and other ....

3 We need a new .... for this lamp.

4 A .... is used to collect rainwater.

5 The .... of our holiday was our trip to the rainforest!

6 During the .... it was too hot to sleep at night.

7 More than half the world's animal and plant species live in the ....

8 The charity sends out a monthly ....

3 Choose the correct word to complete the sentences.

1 We can help the environment by *renewing / recycling* plastic, glass and paper.

2 A sudden flash of *lighting / lightning* appeared in the sky.

3 Do you remember our *carefree / uncaring* summer holidays when we were children?

4 We'd better stay in. It's *soaking / pouring* with rain.

5 The farmers in this area *raise / mow* crops like maize and sugar cane.

6 Our goal is to help people *in / on* need.

7 *Installing / Insulating* your house is eco-friendly as it helps you save energy.

8 This is the largest wildlife *enclosure / sanctuary* in the country.

4 Complete the sentences with the correct form of the words in capitals.

1 We found cheap .... for the night in a small hotel.   **ACCOMMODATE**

2 They turned on the heating because it was .... cold.   **FREEZE**

3 Our skiing .... taught us how to move our skis.   **INSTRUCT**

4 I live in a .... area with lots of snow in winter.   **MOUNTAIN**

5 A small car is more .... than a large one.   **ECONOMIC**

6 It's .... in here, so let's open a window to get some fresh air.   **SMELL**

7 If you weren't .... , you wouldn't make so many mistakes.   **CARE**

8 Tigers are now an .... species.   **ENDANGER**

Planet Earth 10

5 **Third conditional; wishes**
Complete the email with the correct form of the verbs in brackets.

Dear Laura,

Sarah and I are having a great time at the Wildlife Camp but I wish you 1) .... (come) with us. If I 2) .... (know) there were so many cool activities, I 3) .... (tell) all my friends about it!

Today we went on a boat trip and saw some dolphins. I wish you 4) .... (be) here to see them – they're so beautiful! Dolphins are in danger because they get caught in nets and die. Fishermen use these nets to catch tuna, which swim together with dolphins. If I 5) .... (realise) this before, I 6) .... (not eat) so many tuna sandwiches last term!

It's time for me to go now. We're going to make a fire and sing songs. I wish we 7) .... (can / do) this every day of the year. We all love to sing, especially Sarah, but I wish she 8) .... (not sing) so loudly – she's got a terrible voice!

See you, Vanessa

6 **have/get something done**
Rewrite the sentences. Use *have* or *get*.

1 Tom's car is being washed at the garage.
   ....

2 Our house has been painted with eco-friendly paint.
   ....

3 The dentist checked my teeth last week.
   ....

4 Maria always cuts my hair.
   ....

5 The gardener planted new trees in their garden.
   ....

6 An expert can insulate your roof.
   ....

7 Somebody is going to build a tree house for them.
   ....

8 The technician is repairing my computer.
   ....

10 Planet Earth

Test yourself!

Choose the word or phrase that best completes the conversation or sentence.

1 If you …… me you were coming, I would have prepared dinner.
   A told
   B would tell
   C would have told
   D had told

2 Be careful you don't burn yourself. The water is …… hot.
   A freezing
   B boiling
   C soaking
   D solar

3 'Where is your computer?'
  'I'm …… at the computer shop.'
   A fixing it
   B having fixed it
   C having fixed
   D getting it fixed

4 Some recyclable materials can be …… up to twenty times.
   A rethought
   B released
   C reused
   D recovered

5 These farmers …… chickens and grow a variety of crops.
   A raise
   B track
   C cross
   D deliver

6 I wish I …… you.
   A join
   B joining
   C could join
   D would join

7 The whole area was …… by the floods.
   A benefited
   B suffered
   C effected
   D affected

8 'It's so cold here!'
  'If you …… some warm clothes, you would have been fine!'
   A brought
   B were bringing
   C had brought
   D would have brought

9 It's not easy to …… with such extreme weather conditions.
   A cope
   B provide
   C strike
   D pack

10 'I'm going to throw away this old radio. It's broken.'
   'Don't do that! You can …… .'
   A have it mended
   B have mended it
   C have it to mend
   D have to mend it

11 They made a huge …… to the charity.
   A project
   B objective
   C effect
   D donation

12 I wish I …… about these eco-friendly products before.
   A knew
   B would know
   C had known
   D would have known

13 I love being out and …… in the countryside.
   A about
   B around
   C in
   D up

14 If you had started recycling a few years ago, you …… a lot of paper.
   A won't waste
   B might not waste
   C hadn't wasted
   D might not have wasted

Time to revise 5 | Units 9–10

1 **Complete the sentences with these adjectives.**

aware   brilliant   creative   ecological   heavy   insensitive   sticky   talkative

1 They felt uncomfortable in the hot and .... weather.
2 The fire was one of the worst .... disasters in the area.
3 That article you wrote about the Amazon was .... ! In fact, it's the best I've ever read about the subject.
4 Gwen is so .... ! She doesn't care about other people's feelings at all.
5 We all need to become more .... of the importance of recycling.
6 You're in a(n) .... mood today. You haven't stopped chatting to people since you arrived!
7 She's a(n) .... person who loves making things with her hands.
8 He stayed at home because of the .... rain.

2 **Choose the correct word to complete the sentences.**

1 What *means / feature* of transport do you use to go to school?
2 Don't tell Fay your secrets! She's a terrible *extrovert / gossip* !
3 My brother has never had any *difficulty / disadvantage* making friends. He's very sociable.
4 This species is *rare / various* and needs protection.
5 I *provide / regret* speaking to you like that. I'm sorry.
6 My best friend and I have many interests *in / with* common.
7 It was very exciting! We saw some lions in the *wild / wildlife* !
8 'I wish I could be a *careless / carefree* child again with no worries!' said the old lady.

3 **Complete the second sentence so that it has a similar meaning to the first sentence, using the word given. Do not change the word given. You must use between two and five words, including the word given.**

1 'Have you spoken to Oscar yet?' asked Zoe.   I
   Zoe asked me .... to Oscar yet.
2 You will never have the opportunity to take part in an expedition like that again.   CHANCE
   Taking part in an expedition like that .... lifetime.
3 I can't wait to see the animals in their natural habitat.   FORWARD
   I'm really .... the animals in their natural habitat.
4 Please don't throw those CDs away.   HOLD
   Please .... those CDs.
5 Unfortunately, I have to leave now.   NOT
   I wish .... leave now.
6 It was raining very heavily, so they stayed home.   WITH
   It was .... , so they stayed home.
7 They are going to repair our roof next week.   REPAIRED
   We are going to .... next week.
8 Claude has a friendly relationship with his neighbours.   ON
   Claude .... with his neighbours.

11 Get fit, have fun

Reading: Pages 118–119

11.1 fit (adj) /fɪt/ = healthy and strong, especially because you exercise regularly. *I am **fit** because I exercise every day.* ➤ fitness (n)
σε φόρμα
Opp: unfit

11.2 junior (adj) /ˈdʒuːniə/ = relating to sport for young people below a particular age. *He plays for the **junior** football team.* ➤ junior (n)
παίδων

11.3 triathlon (n) /traɪˈæθlən/ = a sports competition in which competitors run, swim and cycle long distances. *Will you be competing in the **triathlon**?*
τρίαθλο

11.4 sex (n) /seks/ = all women considered as a group or all men considered as a group. *There are people of both **sexes** in the team.*
γένος, φύλο

11.5 competitor (n) /kəmˈpetɪtə/ = sb that takes part in a competition. *Eight **competitors** took part in the race.* ➤ compete (v), competition (n), competitive (adj)
ανταγωνιστής-ρια

11.6 exhausting (adj) /ɪgˈzɔːstɪŋ/ = making you feel extremely tired. *It was a long and **exhausting** flight.* ➤ exhaust (v), exhaustion (n), exhausted (adj)
εξαντλητικός-ή-ό

11.7 out of breath (prep phr) /ˌaʊt əv ˈbreθ/ = having difficulty breathing, especially after exercise. *Erica had been running and was **out of breath**.*
λαχανιασμένος-η-ο

11.8 champion (n) /ˈtʃæmpiən/ = sb who has won a competition, especially in sport. *She's a **champion** tennis player.* ➤ championship (n)
πρωταθλητής-ρια

11.9 triathlete (n) /traɪˈæθliːt/ = sb who competes in a triathlon. *He is a trained **triathlete**.*
αθλητής του τρίαθλου

11.10 up for sth (phr) /ˈʌp fə ˌsʌmθɪŋ/ = willing to do sth or interested in doing sth. *We're going to play football later – are you **up for** it?*
πρόθυμος-η-ο

11.11 daily (adj) /ˈdeɪli/ = happening, done or produced every day. *This is a popular **daily** newspaper.* ➤ daily (adv), day (n)
καθημερινός-ή-ό

11.12 routine (n) /ruːˈtiːn/ = the usual way that you do things or the things you do regularly. *Making the beds is part of her daily **routine**.*
καθημερινότητα, ρουτίνα

11.13 workout (n) /ˈwɜːkaʊt/ = a period of physical exercise done to make your body stronger. *I have a daily **workout** in the gym.* ➤ work out (phr v)
σωματική άσκηση, προπόνηση

11.14 build up (phr v) /ˌbɪld ˈʌp/ = if sth builds up, it gradually increases. *Regular exercise will **build up** your strength.*
καθίσταμαι μεγαλύτερος-η-ο/πολυπληθέστερος-η-ο, κλπ.

11.15 muscle (n) /ˈmʌsəl/ = one of the pieces of flesh inside your body that you use in order to move. *These exercises make your leg **muscles** stronger.* ➤ muscular (adj)
μυς

11.16 stamina (n) /ˈstæmɪnə/ = physical or mental strength that lets you continue doing sth for a long time. *He showed me some exercises to improve my speed and **stamina**.*
αντοχή

11.17 run out of (phr v) /ˌrʌn ˈaʊt əv, ɒv/ = to use all of sth so that there is none left. *We've **run out of** sugar.*
ξεμένω από

11.18 tale (n) /teɪl/ = a story about things that happened long ago or things that did not really happen. *Grandad told us some **tales** about his life when he was young.*
αφήγημα, ιστορία
◆ tell a tale

11.19 step out (phr v) /ˌstep ˈaʊt/ = to leave your home or office for a short time. *She isn't here. She's **stepped out** for a few minutes.*
βγαίνω

11.20 smack (adv) /smæk/ = with a lot of force. *The van ran **smack** into a wall.*
ξαφνικά και βίαια, με φόρα
◆ smack into

11.21 cyclist (n) /ˈsaɪklɪst/ = sb who rides a bicycle. *Watch out for the **cyclists** on the road.* ➤ cycle (v)
ποδηλάτης

11.22 elbow (n) /ˈelbəʊ/ = the joint where your arm bends. *I hurt my **elbow** playing tennis.*
αγκώνας

11.23 goggles (n pl) /ˈgɒgəlz/ = a pair of glasses that protect your eyes, with an edge that fits against your skin. *He put on his **goggles** and went skiing.*
προστατευτικά ματογυάλια

Get fit, have fun 11

11.24 pull (v) /pʊl/ = to use force to take sth from the place where it is fixed or held. *The little girl **pulled** the arm off her doll.*
τραβώ

11.25 black eye (n phr) /blæk 'aɪ/ = an area of dark skin around sb's eye that is the result of them being hit. *He has been fighting and he has a **black eye**.*
μαυρισμένο μάτι

11.26 split (v) /splɪt/ = to make sb's head or lip have a cut in it as a result of a fall or hit. *She fell against the table and **split** her lip.*
προκαλώ ή υφίσταμαι σχίσιμο
Irr v: split–split–split

11.27 lip (n) /lɪp/ = one of the two edges of your mouth where the skin is redder or darker. *She gave him a kiss on the **lips**.*
χείλος

11.28 equipment (n) /ɪˈkwɪpmənt/ = the things that you need to do a job or sport. *They bought new computer **equipment**.* ➤ equip (v), equipped (adj)
εξοπλισμός

11.29 put sb off (phr v) /ˌpʊt sʌmbədi ˈɒf/ = to make you dislike sth or not want to do sth. *Don't let the title **put** you **off** the book – it's really good.*
δημιουργώ αρνητικές εντυπώσεις

11.30 look on the bright side (phr) /lʊk ɒn ðə ˈbraɪt saɪd/ = to see the good points in a situation that seems to be bad. *Don't be upset. Try to **look on the bright side**.*
βλέπω την καλή όψη των πραγμάτων

11.31 take care of (v phr) /teɪk ˈkeər əv/ = to do the work or make the arrangements that are necessary for sth to happen. *Relax! I'll **take care of** everything.*
αναλαμβάνω, φροντίζω για

11.32 technical (adj) /ˈteknɪkəl/ = connected with knowledge of how machines work. *He's good with machines and can solve any **technical** problems you have.*
➤ technician (n), technique (n), technology (n)
τεχνικός-ή-ό

11.33 maintenance (n) /ˈmeɪntənəns/ = the work that is necessary to keep sth in good condition. *They were doing some routine **maintenance** work.* ➤ maintain (v)
συντήρηση

11.34 swimsuit (n) /ˈswɪmsuːt, -sjuːt/ = a piece of clothing that people, usually girls and women, wear for swimming. *She put on her **swimsuit** and dived into the pool.*
μαγιό
Also: swimming costume

11.35 tight (adj) /taɪt/ = fitting part of your body very closely. *These shoes aren't comfortable. They're too **tight**.*
➤ tighten (v)
εφαρμοστός-ή-ό, στενός-ή-ό
Opp: loose

11.36 Lycra (n) /ˈlaɪkrə/ = a material that is used especially for making sports clothes that fit tightly, because it moves with your body. ***Lycra** sportswear is very popular.*
λύκρα (είδος υφάσματος)

11.37 wonder (v) /ˈwʌndə/ = to think about sth you do not know and want to know it. *I **wonder** where she lives.*
➤ wonder (n), wonderful (adj)
αναρωτιέμαι
❖ wonder who/what/where/why/if, etc.

11.38 addictive (adj) /əˈdɪktɪv/ = an activity that is addictive is so enjoyable that you do not want to stop. *He started painting as a hobby but it was so **addictive** that now he paints every day.* ➤ addicted (adj), addict (n)
εθιστικός-ή-ό

11.39 go (n) /gəʊ/ = an attempt to do sth. *I'm not sure if I'll like it but I'll give it a **go**.*
προσπάθεια
❖ give sth a go

11.40 instant (adj) /ˈɪnstənt/ = happening immediately. *The song became an **instant** success.*
άμεσος-η-ο

11.41 hit (n) /hɪt/ = a very successful and popular film, song, play, etc. *The show was a huge **hit** in London.*
επιτυχία

11.42 medallist (n) /ˈmedl-ɪst/ = sb who has won a medal in a competition. *She is an Olympic silver **medallist**.*
κάτοχος μεταλλίου
❖ gold/silver/bronze medallist

11.43 unhealthy (adj) /ʌnˈhelθi/ = likely to make you ill or less healthy. *They eat a lot of **unhealthy** junk food.*
ανθυγιεινός-ή-ό
Opp: healthy

11.44 snack (n) /snæk/ = a small amount of food eaten between meals or instead of a meal. *I'm hungry. I think I'll have a **snack**.*
σνακ

11.45 combine (v) /kəmˈbaɪn/ = to join or mix two or more things together. ***Combine** the flour with the milk and eggs.* ➤ combination (n)
συνδυάζω-ομαι

11.46 stage (n) /steɪdʒ/ = one part of a process or one time in the development of sth. *At this **stage**, I'm not sure what will happen. Let's wait and see.*
στάδιο

Vocabulary: Page 120

11.47 health (n) /helθ/ = the general condition of your body and how healthy you are. *Good **health** is very important.*
➤ healthy (adj)
υγεία

11 Get fit, have fun

11.48 fitness (n) /ˈfɪtnəs/ = when you are healthy and strong enough to play sports or do physical work. *Regular exercise will improve your physical fitness.*
καλή φυσική κατάσταση, φόρμα

11.49 diet (n) /ˈdaɪət/ = the kind of food that you eat each day. *A healthy diet is important for good health.* ➤ diet (v)
δίαιτα

11.50 particularly (adv) /pəˈtɪkjʊləli/ = much more than other people or things; especially. *We like all sports but we're particularly interested in athletics.* ➤ particular (adj)
ιδιαίτερα

11.51 catch a bus (phr) /ˌkætʃ ə ˈbʌs/ = to get on a bus in order to travel on it, or to be in time to get on a bus before it leaves. *I caught the bus to Thessaloniki.*
προλαβαίνω και επιβιβάζομαι σε λεωφορείο
◈ catch a bus/train/plane, etc.

11.52 extreme sport (n phr) /ɪkˌstriːm ˈspɔːt/ = an extreme sport is one that is done in a way that has much more risk and so is more dangerous than an ordinary form of the sport. *Extreme sports are becoming popular.*
ριψοκίνδυνο άθλημα

11.53 contact sport (n phr) /ˈkɒntækt spɔːt/ = a sport such as American football, rugby, etc. in which players have physical contact with each other. *Some people think contact sports are dangerous.*
άθλημα κατά το οποίο τα σώματα των αντιπάλων έρχονται σε επαφή

11.54 spectator sport (n phr) /spekˈteɪtə ˌspɔːt/ = a sport that people go and watch. *Football is one of the most popular spectator sports in the world.*
θεαματικό άθλημα

11.55 category (n) /ˈkætɪɡəri/ = a group of people or things that have the same qualities or features. *There are two categories of workers: those who earn a lot of money and those who earn a little.*
κατηγορία

11.56 sportsperson (n) /ˈspɔːtsˌpɜːsən/ = sb who takes part in sports or a sport. *Can you give me the name of a famous Greek sportsperson?*
αθλητής-ρια

11.57 athletics (n) /æθˈletɪks, əθ-/ = sports such as running and jumping. *I love watching athletics.* ➤ athletic (adj), athlete (n)
στίβος

11.58 athlete (n) /ˈæθliːt/ = sb who competes in sports such as running or jumping. *Pete is a top athlete.*
αθλητής-ρια (του στίβου)

11.59 gymnastics (n) /dʒɪmˈnæstɪks/ = a sport in which skilful physical exercises and movements are performed. *Are you good at gymnastics?* ➤ gymnast (n), gym (n)
ενόργανη γυμναστική

11.60 gymnast (n) /ˈdʒɪmnæst/ = sb who is good at gymnastics and competes against other people in competitions. *She is a talented gymnast and has won several medals.*
αθλητής -ρια ενόργανης γυμναστικής

11.61 hockey (n) /ˈhɒki/ = a game played on grass, in which two teams of players use long curved sticks to hit a ball. *We play hockey at school.*
χόκεϊ

11.62 boxing (n) /ˈbɒksɪŋ/ = a game in which two men fight by hitting each other wearing big leather gloves. *I think boxing is a violent sport.* ➤ box (v), boxer (n)
πυγμαχία

11.63 motor racing (n phr) /ˈməʊtə ˌreɪsɪŋ/ = a sport in which there are races between people in cars. *Motor racing is an exciting sport to watch.*
αυτοκινητοδρομία

11.64 snowboarding (n) /ˈsnəʊbɔːdɪŋ/ = the sport of coming down snowy mountains standing on a board. *The children go snowboarding in winter.* ➤ snowboard (n)
κατάβαση χιονισμένης πλαγιάς με σανίδα

11.65 disaster (n) /dɪˈzɑːstə/ = sth that is a complete failure. *It rained and our garden party was a disaster.* ➤ disastrous (adj)
αποτυχία, καταστροφή

11.66 total (n) /ˈtəʊtəl/ = the final number or amount of sth after everything has been included or all the parts have been added together. *They spent a total of a thousand euros.* ➤ total (adj)
σύνολο

11.67 bottom (n) /ˈbɒtəm/ = the lowest position in an organisation or company. *The football team is at the bottom of the league this year.*
πάτος, κατώτατη θέση αξιολόγησης
◈ the bottom of

11.68 bounce (v) /baʊns/ = if sth such as a ball bounces or if you bounce it, it hits a surface and then immediately moves away from it. *The ball bounced off the post and into the goal.* ➤ bounce (n)
προκαλώ ή υφίσταμαι γκελάρισμα

Grammar: Page 121

11.69 obligation (n) /ˌɒblɪˈɡeɪʃən/ = a moral or legal duty to do sth. *The company has an obligation to provide a safe working environment.* ➤ oblige (v)
υποχρέωση

11.70 regulation (n) /ˌreɡjʊˈleɪʃən/ = an official rule or order. *There are so many rules and regulations at this school!*
κανονισμός, κανόνας

Get fit, have fun 11

11.71 crisp (n) /krɪsp/ = a thin, flat round piece of potato cooked in very hot oil and eaten cold as a snack. *I ate a packet of **crisps**.*
τηγανητό πατατάκι, τσιπ

11.72 marathon (n) /ˈmærəθən/ = a race in which people run just over 26 miles. *They want to take part in a **marathon**, so they must get very fit.*
μαραθώνιος (δρόμος)

11.73 length (n) /leŋθ/ = the distance from one end of a swimming pool to the other. *She swims twenty **lengths** a day.*
μήκος πισίνας
◆ swim/do a length

11.74 permit (v) /pəˈmɪt/ = to allow sth to happen or sb to do sth. *Smoking is not **permitted** inside the building.*
➤ permit (n), permission (n)
επιτρέπω
◆ permit sb to do sth

11.75 helmet (n) /ˈhelmɪt/ = a hard hat that covers and protects your head. *You must wear a **helmet** when you are riding a motorbike.*
κράνος

Listening: Page 122

11.76 zorbing (n) /ˈzɔːbɪŋ/ = an activity where you get into a large plastic ball and roll along the ground, on water or down hills. *Have you ever tried **zorbing**?*
άθλημα όπου ο συμμετέχων προχωρά στο έδαφος μέσα σε μια φουσκωτή μπάλα

11.77 origin (n) /ˈɒrədʒɪn/ = where, when or how sth began. *the **origin** of life on Earth* ➤ originate (v), original (adj)
προέλευση

11.78 maximum (adj) /ˈmæksɪməm/ = the maximum amount, speed, number, etc. is the biggest that is possible. *The car has a **maximum** speed of 200 kilometres per hour.*
➤ maximum (n)
μέγιστος-η-ο, ανώτατος-η-ο
Opp: minimum

Speaking: Page 123

11.79 sporty (adj) /ˈspɔːti/ = sb who is sporty likes sport and is good at it. *I've never been a **sporty** person.*
καλός-ή-ό στα σπορ, που ενδιαφέρεται για τα σπορ

11.80 yoga (n) /ˈjəʊgə/ = a system of exercises which helps you to relax your body and mind. *We do **yoga** to relax.*
γιόγκα

11.81 keep sth going (v phr) /kiːp sʌmθɪŋ ˈgəʊɪŋ/ = to make sth continue. *She tried to **keep** the conversation **going**.*
δίνω ώθηση σε κάτι, συνεχίζω κάτι

Use your English: Pages 124–125

11.82 kayaking (n) /ˈkaɪækɪŋ/ = the sport of travelling in a small boat called a kayak. *Chris has gone **kayaking** in the river.* ➤ kayak (n)
καγιάκ

11.83 cycle path (n phr) /ˈsaɪkəl pɑːθ/ = a path for bicycles, for example beside a road or in a park. *We rode along the **cycle path** in the park.*
ποδηλατόδρομος

11.84 pick (v) /pɪk/ = to choose sth or sb. *The coach **picked** me for the volleyball team!*
διαλέγω, επιλέγω

11.85 unfit (adj) /ʌnˈfɪt/ = not in a good physical condition. *She never does any exercise – she's really **unfit**.*
σε κακή φυσική κατάσταση

11.86 talk (n) /tɔːk/ = a speech on a particular subject. *Professor Mason is giving a **talk** on the environment tomorrow.* ➤ talk (v), talkative (adj)
ομιλία
◆ give a talk

11.87 motivated (adj) /ˈməʊtɪveɪtɪd/ = very keen to do sth or achieve sth, especially because you find it interesting or exciting. *The students were all **motivated** to succeed.*
➤ motivate (v), motivation (n)
που έχει κίνητρο

11.88 costume (n) /ˈkɒstjʊm/ = a swimsuit. *We're going swimming tomorrow, so bring your **costume** with you.*
μαγιό
Also: swimming costume

11.89 pity (n) /ˈpɪti/ = used when you are disappointed about a situation and wish it was different. *'We're leaving tomorrow.' 'What a **pity**!'*
κρίμα
◆ what a pity

Writing: Pages 126–127

11.90 conclude (v) /kənˈkluːd/ = to end a meeting, speech, book or event by doing or saying one final thing, or to end in this way. *To **conclude**, I'd like to thank my family for their support.* ➤ conclusion (n)
τελειώνω, ολοκληρώνω
◆ to conclude

11.91 horse-riding (n) /ˈhɔːs ˌraɪdɪŋ/ = the activity of riding a horse. *The girls go **horse-riding** every week.*
ιππασία

11.92 contrast (v) /kənˈtrɑːst/ = to compare two people, ideas, objects, etc. and show how they are different from each other. *The speaker **contrasted** the two methods of doing things.* ➤ contrast (n)
αντιπαραβάλλω, συγκρίνω

11 Get fit, have fun

11.93 composition (n) /ˌkɒmpəˈzɪʃən/ = a short piece of writing about a subject by a student. *I wrote a **composition** about the Olympic Games.*
έκθεση

11.94 function (n) /ˈfʌŋkʃən/ = the purpose that sth has. *One of the **functions** of the museum is education.*
➤ function (v)
λειτουργία, σκοπός

11.95 to begin with (phr) /tə bɪˈɡɪn wɪð, wɪθ/ = used to introduce the first and most important point you want to make. *The accident was his fault. **To begin with**, he shouldn't have borrowed my car without asking me.*
κατ' αρχήν

11.96 as well as (phr) /əz ˈwel əz, æz/ = in addition to sth else. *She's learning the piano **as well as** the guitar.*
επιπλέον

11.97 introductory (adj) /ˌɪntrəˈdʌktəri/ = said or written at the beginning of a book, piece of writing or speech in order to explain what it is about. *Please read the short **introductory** paragraph.* ➤ introduction (n), introduce (v)
εισαγωγικός-ή-ό

11.98 argument (n) /ˈɑːɡjʊmənt/ = a set of reasons that show that sth is true or untrue, right or wrong, etc. *They presented some good **arguments** against the plan.*
➤ argue (v)
επιχείρημα

WORDZONE SPECIAL

British English and American English: medallist, athletics, hockey

There are some differences between British English and American English. Sometimes there are differences in spelling. For example:

medallist = British English
medalist = American English

Sometimes different words are used for the same thing. For example:
athletics (British English) = *track and field* (American English)
hockey (British English) = *field hockey* (American English)
ice hockey (British English) = *hockey* (American English)

Vocabulary and grammar practice

 Choose the correct word to complete the sentences.

1 It is difficult to predict who will win the match at this *stage / stay*.
2 He gave an excellent *tale / talk* about exercise and fitness.
3 Megan's composition presented several *arguments / functions* against the use of drugs in sport.
4 What a *disaster / pity* you forgot to bring your swimming costume!
5 If you exercise regularly every day, you will *build / increase* up your stamina.
6 That looks like fun! Can I *have / make* a go?
7 I was bad at sports when I was at school and that *did / put* me off exercise for years.
8 How many *competitions / competitors* took part in the race?
9 They managed to finish the marathon but it was a really *exhausted / exhausting* race.
10 Why are you out of *breath / breathing*? Have you been running?

Get fit, have fun 11

2 Complete the sentences with the correct form of these verbs.

bounce   catch   conclude   contrast   permit   pick   pull   split   take   wonder

1 I was ………………………… if you could do me a favour.
2 Eating in the gym is not ………………………… .
3 The player ………………………… the ball a few times before throwing it into the basket.
4 I must leave now. I have to ………………………… the six o'clock train to Manchester.
5 She ………………………… her speech by thanking the people who had come to listen to her.
6 The boy ………………………… his lip when he fell against the kitchen table.
7 Our coach ………………………… Helen to be the captain of the team.
8 Can you compare and ………………………… the two pictures?
9 My poor father had a bad tooth, so he went to the dentist and he had it ………………………… out.
10 Our neighbours are going away on holiday and they've asked us to ………………………… care of their cats.

3 Complete the sentences with the correct form of the words in capitals.

1 John says that exercise is ………………………… and he runs every day.	**ADDICT**
2 I love swimming and I do ten ………………………… a day in the summer.	**LONG**
3 Running a marathon is an ………………………… experience.	**EXHAUST**
4 For an athlete, exercise is part of his or her ………………………… routine.	**DAY**
5 The players were ………………………… and practised hard every day.	**MOTIVATE**
6 Did you have a good ………………………… at the gym today?	**WORK**
7 The ………………………… rode along the path through the forest.	**CYCLE**
8 Do you need a lot of expensive ………………………… to play golf?	**EQUIP**
9 How many Greek athletes do you think will be gold ………………………… at the next Olympic Games?	**MEDAL**
10 All that junk food is very bad for you. No wonder you're so ………………………… !	**HEALTHY**
11 I don't want to watch ………………………… on television tonight! It's too violent!	**BOX**
12 George likes watching football but he prefers ………………………… .	**ATHLETE**

Read the text below and think of the word which best fits in each blank. Use only one word in each blank.

Would you like to 1) ………………… fit but are not sure how to begin? Here are some tips to help you.

To begin 2) ………………… , start slowly! If you haven't done any exercise for a long time, you'll soon get 3) ………………… of breath, so don't overdo it. It's better to build 4) ………………… your strength and stamina gradually. Always warm up first. If you don't, you will injure yourself!

A healthy diet is also important or you will 5) ………………… out of energy. Drink plenty of water.

Do you think you are up 6) ………………… to it? Then start exercising! You may be unfit now but 7) ………………… on the bright side: you can only get fitter!

112

11 Get fit, have fun

5 Match the statements and questions 1–6 with the responses a–f.

1. Nina and I are thinking of taking part in the marathon.
2. Do you have to be very strong to run a marathon?
3. Where's Harry? I can't find him anywhere in the building.
4. It rained all day and the event was a disaster.
5. Diana doesn't want to play tennis or go swimming.
6. Can you explain why your team did badly in the competition?

a. Actually, I think stamina is more important.
b. He must have stepped out for a minute.
c. Perhaps she isn't a sporty person.
d. Really? Are you up to it?
e. Well, to begin with, they hadn't practised enough.
f. What a pity!

6 Obligation: *must, have to, don't have to, mustn't*
Complete the sentences with the correct form of *must* or *have to*.

1. You really .... see the new gym. It's great!
2. Ben .... leave early for swimming practice yesterday evening.
3. You .... wear a helmet when you are riding a motorbike. It's the law.
4. You .... be a top athlete to enjoy sport. You can have fun even if you aren't very good.
5. We .... forget to bring our running shoes tomorrow.
6. Mary .... wear a uniform at school but Rachel can wear anything she likes.
7. He's much better than us, so he .... practise so hard.
8. You .... talk during the exam. It's not allowed.

7 *could/must/should* + *have* + past participle
Choose the correct word to complete the sentences.

1. They won the race. They *could / must* have been very excited!
2. Why didn't you tell me you needed a car? I *could / should* have lent you mine.
3. Gina *should / shouldn't* have been late. She kept everybody waiting.
4. Joe didn't answer the phone when I called. He *must / should* have been out.
5. My sister is in Canada on holiday. You *couldn't / mustn't* have seen her yesterday.
6. I'm freezing! I *must / should* have put on warmer clothes this morning.
7. What a pity you didn't try harder! You *could / must* have won the match.
8. I thought I heard somebody at the door but I *must / should* have been wrong.

Get fit, have fun 11

Test yourself!

Choose the word or phrase that best completes the conversation or sentence.

1. The aerobics DVD was very popular. In fact, it was an instant ....
   - A tale
   - B order
   - C routine
   - D hit

2. 'I'm exhausted.'
   'Well, you .... have gone to bed so late last night.'
   - A must
   - B mustn't
   - C should
   - D shouldn't

3. Our swimming instructor wants us to swim ten .... every day.
   - A lengths
   - B helmets
   - C workouts
   - D stages

4. Are you .... hockey again tonight?
   - A doing
   - B going
   - C playing
   - D making

5. 'I forgot to bring money to pay for the gym.'
   'You .... pay now. You can do it next time.'
   - A must
   - B mustn't
   - C have to
   - D don't have to

6. The swimming pool is closed this week as they are doing .... work.
   - A function
   - B maintenance
   - C regulation
   - D equipment

7. Fran .... wait in the rain for an hour yesterday.
   - A must
   - B have to
   - C has to
   - D had to

8. 'Saul won a gold medal last year.'
   'Really? His family .... have been proud of him!'
   - A must
   - B may
   - C could
   - D should

9. Gabriella is a talented ....
   - A athletic
   - B athletics
   - C athlete
   - D triathlon

10. These are the .... and we all have to obey them.
    - A arguments
    - B origins
    - C regulations
    - D practices

11. You .... park here. It's forbidden.
    - A must
    - B mustn't
    - C have to
    - D don't have to

12. Our skiing trip was fun. You .... have come with us!
    - A must
    - B may
    - C should
    - D would

13. Mike is a boxer, so he is used to getting .... eyes.
    - A brown
    - B blue
    - C red
    - D black

14. You .... to become a member of the gym if you want to work out here.
    - A must
    - B mustn't
    - C have
    - D haven't

12 Thrills and chills

Reading: Pages 128–129

12.1 chill (n) /tʃɪl/ = a sudden feeling of fear. *The strange sound sent a **chill** through her.* ➤ chill (v), chilly (adj)
παγωμάρα

12.2 be located (v phr) /bi ləʊˈkeɪtɪd/ = to be in a particular place or position. *The castle **is located** at the top of the hill.*
βρίσκομαι

12.3 historic (adj) /hɪˈstɒrɪk/ = a historic place or event is famous or important in history. *It was a **historic** speech.* ➤ history (n), historical (adj), historian (n)
ιστορικής σημασίας

12.4 ride (n) /raɪd/ = a large machine that people ride on for fun at a fair. *They went on lots of **rides** at the theme park.*
μηχάνημα σε λούνα παρκ

12.5 stroll (v) /strəʊl/ = to walk in a slow and relaxed way. *We **strolled** along the beach.* ➤ stroll (n)
βολτάρω
◈ stroll along/around, etc.

12.6 tour (n) /tʊə/ = a journey for pleasure in which you visit several different towns, areas, etc. *We went on a two-week **tour** of Egypt.* ➤ tour (v), tourist (n)
γύρος, περιήγηση

12.7 spine-chilling (adj) /ˈspaɪn ˌtʃɪlɪŋ/ = very frightening in a way that you enjoy. *It's a **spine-chilling** thriller.*
τρομακτικός-ή-ό συνάμα ευχάριστος-η-ο

12.8 off (adv) /ɒf/ = away from or out of a place or position. *They said goodbye and they were **off**.*
be off = φεύγω

12.9 futuristic (adj) /ˌfjuːtʃəˈrɪstɪk/ = sth which is futuristic looks unusual and modern as if it belongs in the future instead of the present. *She showed us her **futuristic** design for the new sports stadium.* ➤ future (n)
φουτουριστικός-ή-ό

12.10 arena (n) /əˈriːnə/ = a building with a large flat central area surrounded by raised seats, used for sports or entertainment. *a sports **arena***
αρένα

12.11 archaeological (adj) /ˌɑːkiəˈlɒdʒɪkəl/ = related to archaeology (= the study of ancient societies by examining what remains of their buildings, tools, places where people were buried, etc.). *It was an important **archaeological** discovery.* ➤ archaeology (n), archaeologist (n)
αρχαιολογικός-ή-ό

12.12 excavation (n) /ˌekskəˈveɪʃən/ = the careful digging of an area of land in order to find ancient objects. *The archaeologist in charge of the **excavation** was Greek.* ➤ excavate (v)
ανασκαφή, εκσκαφή

12.13 experience (v) /ɪkˈspɪəriəns/ = to be affected by sth. *I've never **experienced** anything so frightening before.* ➤ experience (n), experienced (adj)
γεύομαι, βιώνω

12.14 massive (adj) /ˈmæsɪv/ = very big. *The dog was **massive** and the child was scared.*
ογκώδης-ες, τεράστιος-α-ο

12.15 sailing ship (n phr) /ˈseɪlɪŋ ʃɪp/ = a large ship with sails. *The **sailing ships** of the eighteenth century were very beautiful.*
ιστιοφόρο

12.16 impressive (adj) /ɪmˈpresɪv/ = making you admire sth. *The castle is large and **impressive**.* ➤ impress (v), impression (n)
εντυπωσιακός-ή-ό

12.17 entrance (n) /ˈentrəns/ = a door or gate that you go through to enter a place. *We waited at the **entrance** to the building.* ➤ enter (v)
είσοδος

12.18 water-coaster (n) /ˈwɔːtə ˌkəʊstə/ = a water slide that is like a roller coaster and moves up and down on water. *The children loved the ride on the **water-coaster**.*
είδος νεροτσουλήθρας

12.19 shipbuilding (n) /ˈʃɪpˌbɪldɪŋ/ = the industry of making ships. *He works in a **shipbuilding** yard.*
ναυπηγείο

12.20 cabin (n) /ˈkæbɪn/ = a small room on a ship where you sleep. *We slept in a tiny **cabin** on the boat.*
καμπίνα

12.21 check out (phr v) /tʃek ˈaʊt/ = to visit a place or look at sth or sb to see if you like them. ***Check out** our new website.*
επισκέπτομαι/κοιτάζω για να δω αν μου αρέσει

12.22 suit (v) /suːt, sjuːt/ = to be acceptable, right or suitable for sb. *Let's arrange a meeting on a day that **suits** everybody.* ➤ suitable (adj)
εξυπηρετώ, βολεύω

12.23 adventurous (adj) /ədˈventʃərəs/ = wanting to do new, exciting or dangerous things. *Andy is very **adventurous** and he loves extreme sports.* ➤ adventure (n)
περιπετειώδης-ες

Thrills and chills 12

12.24 guest (n) /gest/ = sb who is staying in a hotel or rented accommodation. *The **guests** enjoyed their stay at the hotel.*
επισκέπτης, φιλοξενούμενος-η

12.25 Wild West (n phr) /ˌwaɪld ˈwest/ = the western part of the United States in the nineteenth century, used especially when referring to the time before there were many laws there. *We watched a film about the **Wild West**.*
Άγρια Δύση

12.26 scenery (n) /ˈsiːnəri/ = the natural features of a place such as the mountains, forests, etc. *You can look at the **scenery** from the top of the hill.* ➤ scene (n)
(φυσικό) τοπίο

12.27 caravan (n) /ˈkærəvæn/ = a vehicle that can be pulled by a car and that people can live and sleep in. *We slept in a **caravan** near the beach.*
τροχόσπιτο

12.28 site (n) /saɪt/ = a place that is used for a particular purpose. *a camp **site***
χώρος, τοποθεσία

12.29 comfort (n) /ˈkʌmfət/ = a way of living in which you have all the things you need. *I enjoy the **comfort** of staying at a luxury hotel.* ➤ comfortable (adj)
άνεση, κομφόρ
Opp: discomfort

12.30 medieval (adj) /ˌmediˈiːvəl/ = relating to the Middle Ages. *a **medieval** castle*
μεσαιωνικός-ή-ό

12.31 charming (adj) /ˈtʃɑːmɪŋ/ = very pleasing or attractive. *They live in a **charming** little village.* ➤ charm (n, v)
χαριτωμένος-η-ο, γοητευτικός-ή-ό

12.32 monastery (n) /ˈmɒnəstəri/ = a place where monks live. *We visited the beautiful old church at the **monastery**.*
μοναστήρι

12.33 souvenir (n) /ˌsuːvəˈnɪə, ˈsuːvənɪə/ = an object that you keep to remind yourself of a special occasion or place that you have visited. *The tourists bought some **souvenirs** to remind them of their stay.*
αναμνηστικό

12.34 free of charge (phr) /ˌfriː əv ˈtʃɑːdʒ/ = without payment. *All these services are **free of charge**.*
δωρεάν, χωρίς χρέωση

12.35 cash dispenser (n phr) /ˈkæʃ dɪˌspensə/ = a machine that you get money from using a plastic card, especially in a wall outside a bank or supermarket. *You can get money from the **cash dispenser** at the mall.*
αυτόματο μηχάνημα ανάληψης μετρητών

12.36 first aid (n phr) /ˌfɜːst ˈeɪd/ = simple medical treatment that is given as soon as possible to sb who is injured or who suddenly becomes ill. *They gave him **first aid** and saved his life.*
πρώτες βοήθειες

12.37 opening hours (n phr) /ˈəʊpənɪŋ ˌaʊəz/ = the hours when a shop, bank, bar, etc. is open to the public. *Before we go there, let's check the **opening hours**.*
ώρες λειτουργίας

12.38 peak (adj) /piːk/ = the peak time, period or season is when the greatest number of people are doing the same thing, using the same service, etc. *Hotel prices are higher during **peak** season.*
περίοδος αιχμής
◈ peak time/season/period

12.39 admission (n) /ədˈmɪʃən/ = the price charged when you go to a film, sports event, concert, etc. *The price of **admission** is printed on the brochure.*
είσοδος

12.40 senior citizen (n phr) /ˌsiːniə ˈsɪtəzən/ = sb who is over the age of sixty. ***Senior citizens** can travel on buses without a ticket.*
συνταξιούχος, υπερήλικας

12.41 height (n) /haɪt/ = how tall sb or sth is. *The boys are about the same **height**.* ➤ high (adj, adv)
ύψος

12.42 restriction (n) /rɪˈstrɪkʃən/ = a rule or law that limits what you are allowed to do. *There are **restrictions** on the sale of guns.* ➤ restrict (v)
περιορισμός

12.43 minimum (n) /ˈmɪnəməm/ = the smallest number or amount that is possible or needed. *A car like that will cost a **minimum** of £10,000.*
ελάχιστο όριο, μίνιμουμ

12.44 track (n) /træk/ = a special path or road used for races. *The cars raced around the **track**.*
πίστα
◈ racing track

12.45 safety (n) /ˈseɪfti/ = the state of being safe from danger or harm. *Parents worry about their children's **safety**.*
➤ safe (adj)
ασφάλεια

Vocabulary: Page 130

12.46 journey (n) /ˈdʒɜːni/ = the time spent travelling from one place to another, especially over a long distance. *It was a long **journey** by car.*
(απόσταση που διανύεται σε συνήθως χερσαίο) ταξίδι

12.47 pleasure (n) /ˈpleʒə/ = a feeling of happiness, satisfaction or enjoyment. *I am looking forward to my holiday with **pleasure**.* ➤ please (v), pleasant (adj)
ευχαρίστηση

12.48 vehicle (n) /ˈviːɪkəl/ = a thing such as a car or bus that is used for carrying people or things from one place to another. *There were many **vehicles** on the road.*
όχημα

12 Thrills and chills

12.49 midnight (n) /ˈmɪdnaɪt/ = twelve o'clock at night. *We came home at midnight.*
μεσάνυχτα

12.50 rest (n) /rest/ = a period of time when you can relax or sleep. *You look tired. Why don't you have a rest?*
➤ rest (v)
ξεκούραση

12.51 sightseeing (n) /ˈsaɪtˌsiːɪŋ/ = the activity of visiting famous or interesting places, especially as a tourist. *The tourists went sightseeing.*
περιήγηση αξιοθέατων, ξενάγηση σε αξιοθέατα

12.52 hurry (v) /ˈhʌri/ = to do sth or go somewhere quickly. *If we hurry, we'll be on time.* ➤ hurry (n)
βιάζομαι, σπεύδω

Grammar: Page 131

12.53 equal (adj) /ˈiːkwəl/ = the same in size, value or amount. *Let's divide the cake into equal parts.* ➤ equality (n)
ίσος-η-ο

12.54 ideal (adj) /ˌaɪˈdɪəl/ = the best that sth could possibly be. *This is an ideal place for a picnic.*
ιδανικός-ή-ό

Listening: Page 132

12.55 sick (adj) /sɪk/ = if you feel sick, you feel as if food is going to come up from your stomach and out of your mouth. *The child ate too much chocolate and felt sick.*
be sick = κάνω εμετό

12.56 height (n) /haɪt/ = a place or position that is a long way above the ground. *Rachel has always been scared of heights.*
ύψος, υψόμετρο
◆ scared of heights

12.57 dizzy (adj) /ˈdɪzi/ = feeling that you are losing your balance, for example because you have been spinning around or you are ill. *She felt dizzy when she stood up.*
➤ dizziness (n)
ζαλισμένος-η-ο

12.58 thrilled (adj) /θrɪld/ = very excited and pleased. *We're thrilled with our results.* ➤ thrill (v, n), thrilling (adj)
ενθουσιασμένος-η-ο

Speaking: Page 133

12.59 sporting (adj) /ˈspɔːtɪŋ/ = relating to sports. *sporting events*
αθλητικός-ή-ό

12.60 bungee-jumping (n) /ˈbʌndʒi ˌdʒʌmpɪŋ/ = a sport in which you jump off sth very high with a long length of elastic tied to your legs so that you do not hit the ground. *Who wants to go bungee-jumping with me?*
ελεύθερη πτώση με ελαστικό προστατευτικό σκοινί

12.61 record (n) /ˈrekɔːd/ = the facts about how good, bad, etc. sb or sth has been in the past. *It is an airline with a good safety record.*
καλό παρελθόν, ιστορικό

12.62 head (v) /hed/ = to go in a particular direction. *The explorers are heading for the mountains.*
κατευθύνομαι, οδεύω
◆ head for/towards

12.63 sunbathe (v) /ˈsʌnbeɪð/ = to sit or lie outside in the sun in order to become brown. *Jenny is sunbathing near the pool.*
κάνω ηλιοθεραπεία

12.64 racket (n) /ˈrækɪt/ = a piece of equipment that you use for hitting the ball in games such as tennis. *Where is my tennis racket?*
ρακέτα
Also: racquet

12.65 windsurfing (n) /ˈwɪndˌsɜːfɪŋ/ = the sport of sailing across water by standing on a special board and holding onto a large sail. *Windsurfing is my favourite water sport.* ➤ windsurfer (n)
ιστιοσανίδα

12.66 dive (v) /daɪv/ = to jump into the water with your head and arms first. *Harry dived into the pool.* ➤ dive (n), diver (n)
βουτώ (με το κεφάλι)

Use your English: Pages 134–135

12.67 astonished (adj) /əˈstɒnɪʃt/ = very surprised. *We were astonished at the size of the place.*
➤ astonish (v), astonishing (adj), astonishment (n)
έκπληκτος-η-ο, κατάπληκτος-η-ο
◆ astonished at/by

12.68 hilarious (n) /hɪˈleəriəs/ = very funny. *We watched a hilarious programme on TV.*
ξεκαρδιστικός-ή-ό

12.69 mind-blowing (adj) /ˈmaɪnd ˌbləʊɪŋ/ = very exciting or strange. *Bungee-jumping is a mind-blowing experience.*
φοβερός-ή-ό, καταπληκτικός-ή-ό

12.70 risky (adj) /ˈrɪski/ = involving a risk that sth bad or dangerous will happen. *Travelling alone can be risky.*
➤ risk (n, v)
ριψοκίνδυνος-η-ο, επικίνδυνος-η-ο

117

Thrills and chills 12

12.71 hectic (adj) /ˈhektɪk/ = very busy or full of activity. *It had been a hectic day at work and I was exhausted.*
πολυτάραχος-η-ο, πυρετώδης-ες

12.72 wicked (adj) /ˈwɪkɪd/ = very good. *That's a wicked bike!*
φοβερός-ή-ό, καταπληκτικός-ή-ό

12.73 petrified (adj) /ˈpetrɪfaɪd/ = very frightened. *I'm petrified of heights.* ➤ petrify (v), petrifying (adj)
κοκαλωμένος-η-ο από τρόμο
◆ petrified of

12.74 alarmed (adj) /əˈlɑːmd/ = worried or frightened. *He was alarmed when he heard the news.* ➤ alarm (v, n), alarming (adj)
θορυβημένος-η-ο

12.75 whisper (v) /ˈwɪspə/ = to say sth very quietly using your breath rather than your voice. *He whispered something but I couldn't hear him.* ➤ whisper (n)
ψιθυρίζω

12.76 moan (v) /məʊn/ = to make a long low sound expressing pain or unhappiness. *She lay on the bed and moaned with pain.* ➤ moan (n)
βογκώ, στενάζω

12.77 yell (v) /jel/ = to shout sth very loudly. *Somebody yelled at her to stop.* ➤ yell (n)
κραυγάζω, φωνάζω

12.78 mumble (v) /ˈmʌmbəl/ = to say sth very quietly so that it is difficult to understand you. *Carol mumbles when she talks, so I don't always understand her.*
μουρμουρίζω (κατά τρόπο στερούμενο ευκρίνειας)

12.79 gossip (v) /ˈɡɒsɪp/ = to talk or write about other people's behaviour and private lives. *The old ladies sat in the kitchen and gossiped about their neighbours.*
➤ gossip (n)
κουτσομπολεύω

12.80 shriek (v) /ʃriːk/ = to shout in a high voice, especially because you are afraid, excited or in pain. *'Stop it!' she shrieked.* ➤ shriek (n)
τσιρίζω, στριγκλίζω

12.81 sob (v) /sɒb/ = to cry noisily while taking short breaths. *The child was sobbing and it was clear that he was very unhappy.* ➤ sob (n)
κλαίω με λυγμούς

12.82 crossly (adv) /ˈkrɒsli/ = in a way that shows you are annoyed or angry. *'Leave me alone!' he said crossly.*
➤ cross (adj)
θυμωμένα

12.83 grumble (v) /ˈɡrʌmbəl/ = to complain. *They grumbled about the bad food.* ➤ grumble (n)
γκρινιάζω, παραπονούμαι
◆ grumble about

12.84 pour (v) /pɔː/ = if people or things pour into or out of a place, a lot of them arrive or leave at the same time. *Letters of complaint poured in.*
συρρέω
◆ pour in/out of

12.85 gate (n) /ɡeɪt/ = a door in a fence or outside wall. *The fans stood outside the gates of the stadium.*
πύλη

12.86 run off (phr v) /ˌrʌn ˈɒf/ = to leave a place or person when you should not. *The children ran off to play with their friends.*
φεύγω χωρίς άδεια, το σκάω

12.87 chase (v) /tʃeɪs/ = to quickly follow sb or sth, especially to catch them. *The dog chased the rabbit but couldn't catch it.* ➤ chase (n)
κυνηγώ

12.88 false teeth (n phr) /ˌfɔːls ˈtiːθ/ = a set of artificial teeth worn by sb who has lost their natural teeth. *The old man had false teeth.*
ψεύτικα δόντια

12.89 yuck! (interjection) /jʌk/ = said when you think sth looks or tastes very unpleasant. *Yuck! I hate mayonnaise!*
(για έκφραση αποστροφής) αηδία!

12.90 client (n) /ˈklaɪənt/ = sb who pays a person or organisation for a service. *An important client called and wanted to speak to the manager.*
πελάτης

12.91 patient (n) /ˈpeɪʃənt/ = sb who is being treated by a doctor, nurse, etc. *How many patients have you seen today, Doctor?*
ασθενής

12.92 dim (adj) /dɪm/ = not bright, clear or easy to see. *The light outside was dim, so we turned on some more lights.*
αμυδρός-ή-ό, σκοτεινός-ή-ό

12.93 pale (adj) /peɪl/ = pale light is not bright. *the pale light of dawn*
ασθενικός-ή-ό, ωχρός-ή-ό

12.94 ferry (n) /ˈferi/ = a boat that regularly carries people, often with their cars, across a narrow area of water. *We went to Aigina by ferry.*
πορθμείο, φέρι μποτ

12.95 generally (adv) /ˈdʒenərəli/ = usually. *I generally get to school early.* ➤ general (adj)
γενικώς

12.96 hopefully (adv) /ˈhəʊpfəli/ = used when you are saying what you hope will happen. *Hopefully, I'll be home early on Monday.* ➤ hopeful (adj), hope (n, v)
ευελπίστως

12 Thrills and chills

Writing: Pages 136–137

12.97 eventually (adv) /ɪˈventʃuəli, -tʃəli/ = after a long time. *Eventually, he got a job.* ➤ eventual (adj)
τελικά

12.98 all of a sudden (phr) /ˌɔːl əv ə ˈsʌdn/ = suddenly. *All of a sudden, the lights went out.*
εντελώς αναπάντεχα

12.99 at once (prep phr) /ət ˈwʌns/ = immediately. *They recognised her at once.*
αμέσως

12.100 horror (n) /ˈhɒrə/ = a strong feeling of shock and worry. *She stared at him in horror.* ➤ horrify (v), horrifying (adj), horrified (adj)
φρίκη
◆ in horror

12.101 beneath (adv) /bɪˈniːθ/ = under or below sth. *I could feel the warm sand beneath my feet.*
ακριβώς από κάτω

12.102 apartment (n phr) /əˈpɑːtmənt/ = a set of rooms on one floor of a large building, where sb lives. *Let's meet at your apartment.*
διαμέρισμα

12.103 Canary Islands (n phr) /kəˈneəri ˌaɪləndz/ = a group of islands near northwest Africa which belong to Spain and are popular with tourists. *We're going to the Canary Islands for our holiday.*
Κανάριοι Νήσοι
Also: Canaries

12.104 olive tree (n phr) /ˈɒlɪv triː/ = a tree that produces olives, grown especially in Mediterranean countries. *Farmers grow olive trees on the sides of the hills.*
ελαιόδεντρο

12.105 goat (n) /ɡəʊt/ = a common farm animal with horns and with long hair under its chin. *The goat climbed the rocks easily.*
κατσίκα

12.106 ring (v) /rɪŋ/ = if a bell or telephone rings, it makes a sound. *I heard the church bells ringing.*
κουδουνίζω

12.107 grab (v) /ɡræb/ = to take hold of sb or sth suddenly or violently. *He grabbed my bag and ran away with it.*
αρπάζω

12.108 set the scene (phr) /ˌset ðə ˈsiːn/ = to describe the situation before you tell a story. *She wrote a few sentences to set the scene of the story.*
δίνω την ατμόσφαιρα (εποχής, κλπ.)

12.109 coach (n) /kəʊtʃ/ = a bus with comfortable seats used for long journeys. *We went to Paris by coach.*
τουριστικό λεωφορείο, πούλμαν

12.110 fly (v) /flaɪ/ = if time flies, it seems to pass very quickly. *Time flew by and before we knew it, our holidays were over.*
γοργοδιαβαίνω
◆ time flies (by)

12.111 block of flats (n phr) /ˌblɒk əv ˈflæts/ = a large building with many flats in it. *Karen lives in the block of flats across the road.*
πολυκατοικία

12.112 queue (v) /kjuː/ = to wait in a line of people in order to do sth. *They queued for hours outside the theatre to get tickets.* ➤ queue (n)
σχηματίζω ουρά, μπαίνω ή περιμένω σε ουρά

12.113 suspense (n) /səˈspens/ = the feeling you have when waiting for sth exciting to happen. *Don't keep us in suspense. What happened?*
αγωνία, αγωνιώδης προσμονή

12.114 curiosity (n) /ˌkjʊəriˈɒsəti/ = the desire to know about sth. *I opened the box to satisfy my curiosity.*
➤ curious (adj)
περιέργεια

12.115 on the part of sb (phr) /ɒn ðə pɑːt əv ˈsʌmbədi/ = used when describing a particular person's feelings or actions. *It was an accident on the part of the doctor.*
εκ μέρους κάποιου/κάποιας
Also: on sb's part

12.116 bring sth alive (phr) /ˌbrɪŋ ˈsʌmθɪŋ əˈlaɪv/ = to make sth interesting and real. *The way he describes his characters brings them alive.*
ζωντανεύω, δίνω ζωή σε κάτι

WORDZONE SPECIAL

Easily confused words: historic, historical

historic
Historic places, events, speeches, etc. are important or famous in history.
*The French Revolution was a **historic** event that changed the world.*

historical
Historical people or things existed in the past.
*Christopher Columbus is a **historical** character but Robin Hood is a character from a legend.*

Thrills and chills 12

Vocabulary and grammar practice

1 Choose the correct word to complete the sentences.

1 Shall we wait for you at the *entrance / entry* to the cinema?
2 Sylvia lives in a modern *monastery / apartment* in the centre of town.
3 The children loved the *rides / arenas* at the theme park.
4 Space Zone is a *medieval / futuristic* theme park with spaceships and aliens.
5 *Particularly / Hopefully*, if we get there early, we won't have to queue.
6 I was *alarmed / petrified* when I saw the child crying.
7 All of a *sudden / suddenly*, the lights when out.
8 Why don't you check *off / out* their website for more information?

2 Rewrite the sentences replacing the words in italics. Use these verbs.

grumbled   moaned   mumbled   shrieked   sobbed   strolled   whispered   yelled

1 'Oh, no! There's a mouse!' she *shouted in a high, frightened voice*.
   ....
2 The man *complained* that the tickets were too expensive.
   ....
3 The couple *walked in a leisurely way* around the park.
   ....
4 'Come back here!' I *shouted loudly*.
   ....
5 The injured child *made a low sound of pain*.
   ....
6 He *spoke unclearly* and I didn't understand him.
   ....
7 The little girl *cried noisily* when her doll broke.
   ....
8 'Don't wake up the children,' she *said very quietly*.
   ....

3 Complete the sentences with the correct form of the words in capitals.

1 I was .... to hear that he had left the country.   **ASTONISH**
2 That's a very .... building!   **IMPRESS**
3 Make sure you follow the .... instructions carefully.   **SAFE**
4 The price of .... for children is five euros.   **ADMIT**
5 Nathan is petrified of .... and he hates flying!   **HIGH**
6 Are there any age .... for this ride?   **RESTRICT**
7 Elaine is .... and she likes activities like bungee-jumping.   **ADVENTURE**
8 It was a long journey but we .... reached our destination.   **EVENTUAL**

12 Thrills and chills

4 **Adjectives: comparatives and superlatives**
Complete the email with the correct form of the adjectives in brackets.

Hi, Amy!

It was great to hear from you! We're all fine here.

Last week we went to Dorney Park and Wildwater Kingdom, one of 1) ………………… (popular) theme parks in the United States. It has some fantastic rides and it also has 2) ………………… (large) water park in the country!

I'd heard great things about it but it was even 3) ………………… (amazing) than I expected! I loved the ride on the Mega Coaster, which was 4) ………………… (fast) than any ride I've ever been on. My parents preferred 5) ………………… (relaxing) rides but that's because they aren't as 6) ………………… (adventurous) as me! When you come to the States, you must visit Dorney Park. It's 7) ………………… (cheap) to buy tickets online than at the gate, so book in advance.

Well, I'd better go now. I have to study for an exam tomorrow!

Love, Kayla

5 **Future continuous and future perfect simple**
Choose the correct verbs to complete the sentences.

1. Joe *will be finishing / will have finished* reading the book by the end of the week.
2. Barbara *will be showing / will have shown* you around town tomorrow.
3. This time next week, I *'ll be sunbathing / 'll have sunbathed* on a beautiful beach in Corfu.
4. I'm sure they *'ll be opening / 'll have opened* the new theme park by June.
5. I can give the CD to Emily. I *'ll be seeing / 'll have seen* her later this evening.
6. By the end of their holiday, they *'ll be spending / 'll have spent* all their money.
7. Between six and eight tonight, I *'ll be working / 'll have worked* on the computer.
8. Jonathan *will be completing / will have completed* his homework by eight and then he'll watch TV for an hour.

Thrills and chills 12

Test yourself!

Choose the word or phrase that best completes the conversation or sentence.

1 The Supercoaster is …… ride I've ever been on.
   A better
   B the best
   C the more good
   D more better

2 We admired the beautiful …… of Scotland.
   A arena
   B entrance
   C site
   D scenery

3 …… to the museum is free for children under seven.
   A Tour
   B Restriction
   C Admission
   D Opening hours

4 'My plane leaves at seven tonight.'
   'Have a great trip. I …… of you.'
   A 'll think
   B 'll be thinking
   C 'll have thought
   D 'll have been thinking

5 As soon as the gates opened, people started …… in.
   A pouring
   B chasing
   C diving
   D flying

6 By tomorrow, they …… from their trip.
   A return
   B will return
   C will be returning
   D will have returned

7 'Why can't you give me the tickets tomorrow?'
   'Because I …… them yet.'
   A won't buy
   B won't be buying
   C won't have bought
   D won't have been buying

8 The hotel is …… in a beautiful garden.
   A locate
   B located
   C location
   D locating

9 Staying in a tent is not …… as staying in a hotel.
   A comfortable
   B more comfortable
   C as comfortable
   D most comfortable

10 Lizzy has always been scared of …… .
   A high
   B highs
   C height
   D heights

11 The film was so …… that we couldn't stop laughing.
   A hilarious
   B wicked
   C pale
   D dizzy

12 Francesca looks …… now than she did before she went on holiday.
   A happier
   B happiest
   C more happy
   D most happy

13 It was a …… day and they were exhausted.
   A hectic
   B ideal
   C peak
   D equal

14 'I'm arriving at eight tomorrow.'
   'I …… for you at the station.'
   A wait
   B waited
   C 'll be waiting
   D 'll have waited

Time to revise 6 | Units 11–12

1 Complete the sentences with these nouns.

caravan champions competitors guests journey medallist patient rides

1 We always stay in a .... when we go camping. It's more comfortable than a tent.
2 The children enjoyed all the .... at the theme park.
3 Who were the European Football .... last year?
4 I met Sam on the train .... from Paris to Madrid.
5 She's a brilliant athlete! In fact, she's a gold ....
6 About twenty .... took part in the quiz show.
7 Only .... staying at the hotel can use the swimming pool.
8 The doctor is busy. She's examining a .... at the moment.

2 Complete the sentences with these adjectives.

annual daily dizzy equal hilarious historic massive maximum sick tight

1 They are going away on their .... summer holiday next week.
2 I looked down from the tenth-floor balcony and I suddenly felt ....
3 I like this shirt but it's too .... Do you have a bigger size?
4 Thousands of tourists visit this .... site every year.
5 Mum cut the cake into eight .... pieces.
6 The train was moving very fast. In fact, it was going at .... speed.
7 Their house is .... It's got over fifteen rooms!
8 A swim in the pool is part of his .... routine.
9 I ate too many cherries and I felt ....
10 The new comedy series on TV is .... ! You should watch it.

3 Read the text below and think of the word which best fits each blank. Use only one word in each blank.

Last summer I had 1) .... best holiday of my life. It all started in June when my friend Nicole told me that she had won two Eurail tickets in a competition.

'I'm going to explore Italy by train!' she said. 'And guess what! I can take a friend with me 2) .... of charge! Are you up 3) .... it? You don't 4) .... to answer me today,' she said, 'but let me know soon.'

'Are you joking? Of course I'll come!' I yelled. 'I just can't believe that in a few weeks I'll 5) .... travelling around Italy!'

Eventually, the big day arrived for us to leave on our journey. As we got on the train, I felt more excited 6) .... I had ever been in my life. My first trip abroad together with my best friend! Of course, our parents must 7) .... been worried about us and we 8) .... to promise to call them every day so that they would know we were safe. But for Nicole and me a great adventure was about to begin.

Wordlist

A

a pain (n, phr)	5.122
abbreviation (n)	7.107
ability (n)	1.59
abolish (v)	2.88
absolutely (adv)	8.54
abstract (adj)	6.135
academically (adv)	6.87
accept (v)	9.38
acceptable (adj)	3.99
access (n)	6.76
accessible (adj)	8.121
accidentally (adv)	5.4
accommodation (n)	10.5
according to (prep)	2.98
ache (v)	7.137
act (n)	4.16
act (v)	8.51
act out (phr v)	9.70
action-packed (adj)	6.34
active (adj)	6.113
activity (n)	1.143
actually (adv)	1.170, 6.159
AD (abbreviation)	7.48
add (v)	9.31
addictive (adj)	11.38
admission (n)	12.39
admit (v)	1.19
adult (n)	2.13
advantage (n)	7.74
adventurous (adj)	12.23
advert (n)	2.11
advice (n)	3.37
advise (v)	3.38
affect (v)	3.120, 10.165
affirmative (adj)	8.126
afford (v)	3.46
after all (phr)	5.137
afterwards (adv)	5.79
against the law (phr)	5.61
ages (n pl)	5.17
aggressive (adj)	8.27
ahead (adv)	1.177
aim (n)	2.15
alarmed (adj)	12.74
alive (adj)	8.26
all of a sudden (phr)	12.98
along with (phr)	4.5
alternative (adj)	4.107
amazed (adj)	1.115
amazing (adj)	1.116
ambitious (adj)	9.39
amount (n)	4.51
amphitheatre (n)	4.44
announcement (n)	9.100
annoyed (adj)	1.111
annoying (adj)	1.112
annual (adj)	4.27
anxious (adj)	2.92
anyway (adv)	5.23
apartment (n phr)	12.102
apologise (v)	5.6
apparently (adv)	4.69
appeal (v)	8.100
appear (v)	9.18
appearance (n)	1.88
application (n)	3.133
apply (v)	1.102
appreciate (v)	2.130
approach (v)	9.20
appropriate (adj)	3.100
approve (v)	5.57
archaeological (adj)	12.11
archaeology (n)	7.100
Arctic (n)	10.4
arena (n)	12.10
argue (v)	5.78
argument (n)	9.97, 11.98
around (adv)	7.104
arrange (v)	1.45
arrangement (n)	3.63
arrogant (adj)	9.19
arrow (n)	7.97
artificial intelligence (n phr)	6.43
arts (n pl)	4.39
as a result (phr)	6.164
as far as I'm concerned (phr)	9.69
as well as (phr)	11.96
assembly (n)	2.31
assertive (adj)	9.48
assistant (n)	3.135
association (n)	4.85
astonished (adj)	12.67
astronomer (n)	8.78
at last (prep phr)	1.50
at least (prep phr)	5.64
at once (prep phr)	12.99
at the time (prep phr)	7.111
at times (prep phr)	7.15
athlete (n)	11.58
athletics (n)	11.57
atmosphere (n)	2.135
attack (v)	7.8
attention (n)	1.101, 10.116
attitude (n)	6.89
attract (v)	8.7
attraction (n)	4.95
attractive (adj)	1.62
audible (adj)	8.62
audience (n)	1.42
author (n)	6.138
available (adj)	3.137
average (adj)	3.10
avoid (v)	8.116
awake (adj)	1.152
aware (adj)	10.163
awareness (n)	8.97
awful (adj)	6.90

B

background (n)	6.8, 9.10
backstage (adj)	4.8
baggy (adj)	9.94
band (n)	4.14
bang (v)	5.32
bank account (n phr)	5.72
bargain (n)	3.81
base on (phr v)	3.60
battery (n)	8.92
battle (n)	6.26
BC (abbreviation)	7.65
be a laugh (phr)	9.65
be about to do sth (v phr)	1.22
be bothered (v phr)	2.101
be coming up (v phr)	1.65
be fitted with sth (phr)	8.29
be in for (v phr)	1.25
be in the wrong (phr)	5.131
be into (v phr)	1.107, 9.47
be located (v phr)	12.2
be out of order (phr)	5.112
beard (n)	2.175
beat (v)	8.45
because of sb/sth (phr)	7.30
beep (v)	3.118
beg (v)	2.43
behave (v)	1.87
belong to (phr v)	2.146
beneath (adv)	12.101
benefit (v)	10.172
best-selling (adj)	6.14
big (adj)	5.110
big-head (n)	9.57
birth certificate (n phr)	5.76
bit (n)	10.99
black eye (n phr)	11.25
blame (v)	5.103
bleach (v)	10.133
blizzard (n)	10.7
block (n)	8.53
block of flats (n phr)	12.111
blow (v)	4.99
blush (v)	1.132
board (n)	1.71
body painting (n phr)	4.17
body piercing (n phr)	5.66
boiling (adj)	10.43
bone (n)	7.90
boo (v)	4.75
book (v)	4.13, 10.149
bookworm (n)	6.38
bored (adj)	1.108
boring (adj)	1.117
borrow (v)	5.136
bossy (adj)	9.41
bother (v)	5.47
bottom (n)	11.67
bounce (v)	11.68
bowl (n)	7.86
boxing (n)	11.62
brain (n)	1.144
brave (adj)	5.116
break dancing (n phr)	2.3
break down (phr v)	4.97
break up (phr v)	8.107
breakdown (n)	8.1
breeze (n)	7.132
brick (n)	8.39
briefly (adv)	5.144
bright (adj)	1.133
brilliant (adj)	10.34
bring sth alive (phr)	12.116
bring up (phr v)	6.158
broadband (n)	8.132
brochure (n)	10.161
bug (n)	4.83
build up (phr v)	4.22, 11.14
bully (n)	5.14
bully (v)	5.16
bump into (phr v)	2.155
bungee-jumping (n)	12.60
burst (v)	9.17
burst out (phr v)	2.176
busk (v)	7.145
by the time (prep phr)	7.112
by the way (prep phr)	1.176

C

cabin (n)	12.20
cage (n)	10.52
calculate (v)	7.78
call out (phr v)	6.81
call sb names (phr)	5.45
calm (adj)	1.93
camp (n)	10.90
can't help (v phr)	9.51
can't stand (v phr)	1.113
Canary Islands (n phr)	12.103
cancel (v)	4.93
canoe (v)	10.23
captain (n)	1.181
caravan (n)	12.27
card (n)	8.103
carefree (adj)	10.111
careless (adj)	10.110
caretaker (n)	2.72
Caribbean (n)	7.20
carnival (n)	4.56
carry on (phr v)	2.35
case (n)	8.86
cash (n)	3.43
cash dispenser (n phr)	12.35
catch a bus (phr)	11.51
catch up (phr v)	3.122
category (n)	11.55
cause (n)	3.106, 4.61
cause (v)	5.87
celebration (n)	10.24
celebrity (n)	1.156
cello (n)	1.27
centimetre (n)	6.66
century (n)	7.2
certain (adj)	1.145
certainly (adv)	7.16
certainty (n)	3.111
chalet (n)	10.176
challenge (n)	1.13
challenging (adj)	6.88
champion (n)	11.8
chance (n)	1.161
change (n)	3.44, 3.87, 5.128
change your mind (phr)	5.93
character (n)	6.49
charge (v)	8.151
charger (n)	10.128
charity (n)	10.156
charming (adj)	12.31
chase (v)	12.87
chat (v)	2.29
chatty (adj)	4.124
check (v)	1.183
check out (phr v)	12.21
cheeky (adj)	9.44
cheer (v)	4.73
cheerful (adj)	6.110
chef (n)	1.1
Chemistry (n)	2.147
cheque (n)	3.28
chew (v)	1.120
chill (n)	12.1
chill out (phr v)	3.27
chip (n)	8.4
chlorine (n)	10.112
chocolate-coated (adj)	4.82
choice (n)	2.137
circumstances (n pl)	6.162
clap (v)	4.58
class (n)	5.48
clear up (phr v)	2.73
clearly (adv)	7.4
click (v)	6.67
client (n)	12.90
climate (n)	7.124
close (adj)	5.140
cloth (n)	4.48
clothing (n)	10.19
clutter (n)	3.131
coach (n)	1.48, 12.109
coast (n)	4.34
cockroach (n)	10.91
coin (n)	7.91
column (n)	5.132
combine (v)	11.45
come along (phr v)	4.123
come from (phr v)	9.9
come on (phr v)	4.57
come out (phr v)	6.21
come round (phr v)	3.9
comfort (n)	12.29
comment (n)	5.8
commercial (adj)	8.17
common (adj)	1.135
communication (n)	6.56
companion (n)	7.36
compete (v)	4.102
competition (n)	8.11
competitive (adj)	9.40
competitor (n)	11.5
complain (v)	2.28
complaint (n)	8.134
complete (adj)	1.60
completely (adv)	1.23
complicated (adj)	6.71
composition (n)	11.93
compound noun (n phr)	4.76
computer gaming (n phr)	2.5
concentrate (v)	2.48
concentration (n)	6.30
conclude (v)	11.90
conclusion (n)	2.93

condition (n)	7.59
conference (n)	3.143
confident (adj)	1.49
confirm (v)	5.90
connected (adj)	6.59
connection (n)	8.111
conservation (n)	10.60
console (n)	3.11
contact (v)	3.139, 8.93
contact sport (n phr)	11.53
contain (v)	6.128
content (n)	6.84
contestant (n)	1.14
continue (v)	4.78
contrast (v)	11.92
control (v)	7.71
convenient (adj)	3.138
conversation (n)	1.90
conversational (adj)	4.127
convince (v)	1.16
cool (adj)	2.16
cope (v)	10.67
copy (v)	5.75
corridor (n)	2.68
costume (n)	4.43, 11.88
cotton (n)	8.101
council (n)	10.155
couple (n)	1.40
course (n)	1.85, 9.21
court (n)	5.68
cousin (n)	9.199
cover (v)	8.137
covered (adj)	1.155
coz (conjunction)	5.125
craft (n)	4.18
cramped (adj)	7.22
create (v)	1.70
creative (adj)	9.82
credit card (n phr)	3.45
crew (n)	4.9
criminal (n)	7.129
crisp (n)	11.71
criticism (n)	6.45
crop (n)	10.167
cross (adj)	3.57, 8.142
cross (v)	10.44
crossly (adv)	12.82
crowd (n)	4.15
cruise ship (n phr)	7.18
culture (n)	9.11
curiosity (n)	12.114
curriculum (n)	2.17
cushion (n)	3.26
customer (n)	8.90
cut off (phr v)	8.108
cycle path (n phr)	11.83
cyclist (n)	11.21

D

daily (adj)	11.11
damage (n)	10.87
date from (phr v)	7.72
dead (adj)	8.129
deadly (adj)	6.129
deal with (phr v)	2.30
death (n)	6.163
decade (n)	7.64
decision (n)	1.75
de-clutter (v)	3.136
decorate (v)	5.101
decrease (v)	8.115
definite (adj)	6.82
definitely (adv)	3.114
definition (n)	2.84
delay (v)	3.110
deliver (v)	10.144
demand (v)	5.28
depart (v)	3.145
dependent (adj)	3.93
desert (n)	10.35
deserted (adj)	7.106
design (n)	5.98
design (v)	8.5
desperately (adv)	6.161
destination (n)	7.122
destroy (v)	10.27
detail (n)	2.7
detailed (adj)	6.9
detect (v)	8.20
detention (n)	2.38
develop (v)	8.10
development (n)	6.74
device (n)	6.60
dialect (n)	8.84
diary (n)	5.129
diet (n)	11.49
difference (n)	3.105
difficulty (n)	9.32
dim (adj)	12.92
dip (v)	4.36
direction (n)	8.33
directly (adv)	9.37
director (n)	7.131
disadvantage (n)	9.80
disagree (v)	5.56
disappoint (v)	2.80
disappointed (adj)	6.92
disapprove (v)	5.37
disaster (n)	4.72, 11.65
disbelief (n)	1.30
discotheque (n)	3.72
discount (n)	3.80
discover (v)	6.155
discuss (v)	2.6
dish (n)	4.86
dislike (v)	5.91
display (n)	8.85
display (v)	6.83
distance (n)	7.79
dive (v)	12.66
divide (v)	7.146
dizzy (adj)	12.57
DJ (n)	1.11
do well (phr)	1.72
do without (phr v)	9.36
do your best (phr)	1.53
donation (n)	10.164
download (v)	6.78
dramatic (adj)	6.115
dress (v)	5.107
dress up (phr v)	6.95
drive sb mad (phr)	9.50
drop (v)	2.156
drought (n)	10.68
dry (adj)	7.31, 10.74
dull (adj)	6.17
dung (n)	10.37
during (prep)	7.54
Dutch (n)	2.142
dye (v)	5.80
dynamic (adj)	6.99

E

earn (v)	3.31
eco-friendly (adj)	10.142
ecological (adj)	10.136
economical (adj)	10.137
Ecuador (n)	10.49
educate (v)	2.76
educational (adj)	2.56
effect (n)	10.9
elbow (n)	11.22
electricity (n)	10.76
electronics (n)	8.77
elegant (adj)	1.61, 6.108
embarrassment (n)	2.77
emergency (n)	2.125
emperor (n)	7.126
emphasise (v)	5.117
enclosure (n)	10.32
encourage (v)	6.173
end up (phr v)	3.13, 9.88
endanger (v)	10.40
enemy (n)	6.169
energetic (adj)	6.114
energy (n)	1.99
energy-saving (adj)	10.121
engine (n)	8.74
enormous (adj)	4.121
enter (v)	8.9
entertaining (adj)	5.146
enthusiasm (n)	4.111
enthusiastic (adj)	1.105
entrance (n)	2.81, 12.17
entry (n)	2.172
environment (n)	8.30, 10.2
environmentally-friendy (adj)	10.122
equal (adj)	12.53
equip (v)	3.69
equipment (n)	11.28
escape (v)	7.56
especially (adv)	1.167
essay (n)	2.50
essential (adj)	8.12
event (n)	4.28, 6.157
eventually (adv)	12.97, 6.39
everyday (adj)	6.117
evil (n)	6.36
exactly (adv)	5.95
examination (n)	2.21
excavation (n)	12.12
except (prep)	9.27
excuse (n)	2.20
exhausted (adj)	9.62
exhausting (adj)	11.6
exhibition (n)	4.91
exist (v)	6.35
exotic (adj)	7.46
expect (v)	1.91, 5.24
expedition (n)	10.59
experience (n)	1.164
experience (v)	12.13
experienced (adj)	1.73
experiment (n)	8.43
expert (n)	1.86
explore (v)	8.72
express (v)	5.108
expression (n)	1.130
extra (adj)	6.57
extract (n)	8.96
extreme (adj)	5.1
extreme sport (n phr)	11.52
extrovert (n)	9.42
eye contact (n phr)	9.13
eyebrow (n)	5.81

F

fabulous (adj)	4.80
face-to-face (adj)	8.117
fact (n)	3.127
factory (n)	4.38
fade (v)	5.85
fail (v)	2.149
fair (adj)	2.78
fair (n)	5.121
fairly (adv)	6.142
fake (v)	1.9
fall apart	8.106
fall asleep (v phr)	2.103
fall down (phr v)	2.162
fall over (phr v)	5.5
false teeth (n phr)	12.88
fame (n)	3.50
fare (n)	3.146
fascinate (v)	7.142
fascinating (adj)	1.169
fashion statement (n phr)	5.86
fashionable (adj)	1.38
fasten (v)	5.60
fault (n)	2.154
feature (n)	6.47
fed up (adj)	1.119
feed (v)	1.171
female (adj)	8.80
ferry (n)	12.94
festival (n)	4.1
fever (n)	4.2
fight back (phr v)	5.36
filmmaker (n)	7.3
filthy (adj)	7.21
final (adj)	1.51
finalist (n)	4.112
financial (adj)	4.94
find out (phr v)	1.141
findings (n pl)	6.94
fine (n)	5.62
fire brigade (n phr)	3.75
firework (n)	4.29
first aid (n phr)	12.36
fit (adj)	3.95, 11.1
fitness (n)	4.71, 11.48
five-star (adj)	10.103
fix (v)	4.118
fixed (adj)	3.62
flash (n)	10.75
flea (n)	7.39
flex (v)	6.3
flirt (v)	8.122
flood (n)	10.69
fluently (adv)	7.141
fly (v)	12.110
for sale (prep phr)	8.56
force (v)	7.81
foreign (adj)	8.98
form (n)	3.134, 5.139
form (v)	1.146
formal (adj)	2.171
fort (n)	7.102
fortnight (n)	7.67
fortunately (adv)	10.88
forward (v)	8.140
fountain (n)	4.26
freaky (adj)	9.83
free (adj)	10.160
free of charge (phr)	12.34
freedom (n)	2.138
freezing (adj)	6.111, 10.56
frequently (adv)	1.148
fried (adj)	4.84
frightened (adj)	1.57
frightening (adj)	1.109
from time to time (prep phr)	7.114
frostbite (n)	10.20
frozen (adj)	10.64
full stop (interjection)	5.94
fully (adv)	3.70
fun (adj)	1.5
function (n)	2.152, 11.94
function (v)	3.71
funky (adj)	2.19
furthermore (adv)	8.153
futuristic (adj)	12.9

G

gadget (n)	3.7
gallery (n)	7.108
gate (n)	12.85
gather (v)	4.24
generally (adv)	12.95
genre (n)	6.146
get (v)	5.9, 5.29
get a life (phr)	3.16
get dressed (v phr)	2.113
get into trouble (phr)	5.39
get involved in sth (phr)	5.13
get on (phr v)	7.88, 9.1
get on like a house on fire (phr)	9.89
get to know (phr)	9.8
get up (phr v)	9.93
giant (adj)	1.162
giggle (v)	2.34
give sb a hand (phr)	3.65
give up (phr v)	5.25, 6.143
glacier (n)	10.8
global warming (n phr)	10.10
go (n)	11.39
go back (phr v)	5.82
go free (v phr)	10.54
go off (phr v)	4.74
go out with (phr v)	9.60
go through (phr v)	5.123
go well (phr)	1.84
goat (n)	12.105
goggles (n pl)	11.23
gossip (n)	9.58
gossip (v)	12.79
grab (v)	12.107
gradually (adv)	2.46
graffiti (n)	2.122
graphics (n pl)	6.41
gross (adj)	3.22
ground (n)	1.134
grow up (phr v)	1.173
grown-up	2.52
grumble (v)	12.83
guarantee (n)	8.138
guard (n)	7.118
guest (n)	4.122, 12.24
guide (n)	7.135, 8.89
guidelines (n pl)	6.86
guilty (adj)	5.35
gum (n)	1.121
gymnast (n)	11.60
gymnastics (n)	11.59

H

| habit (n) | 1.79 |

Wordlist

habitat (n)	10.53	
half price (n phr)	3.78	
hall (n)	2.67	
hand over (phr v)	5.26	
harbour (n)	7.83	
hard (adj)	5.142	
hard-working (adj)	9.55	
harm (n)	3.51	
harmful (adj)	5.97	
harmless (adj)	10.113	
have sth in common (phr)	9.12	
head (n)	8.99	
head (v)	12.62	
head teacher (n phr)	2.9	
headache (n)	5.119	
heading (n)	6.5	
headphones (n pl)	2.41	
headquarters (n pl)	6.168	
health (n)	11.47	
hearing (n)	8.63	
heart rate (n phr)	1.138	
heat (n)	1.140	
heat wave (n phr)	10.70	
heavy (adj)	10.104	
hectic (adj)	12.71	
height (n)	12.41, 12.56	
helmet (n)	11.75	
helpline (n)	8.135	
henna (n)	5.83	
hidden (adj)	5.130	
highlight (n)	10.11	
hilarious (n)	12.68	
hire (n)	10.178	
historian (n)	7.49	
historic (adj)	12.3	
historical (adj)	7.1	
hit (n)	11.41	
hi-tech (adj)	6.116	
hockey (n)	11.61	
hold on to (phr v)	9.33	
honest (adj)	1.126	
honestly (adv)	3.66	
honesty (n)	6.136	
hooked (adj)	6.13	
hopefully (adv)	12.96	
hormone (n)	3.104	
horrible (adj)	1.83	
horror (n)	12.100	
horse-riding (n)	11.91	
house music (n phr)	1.20	
housemate (n)	9.7	
however (adv)	2.55	
human (adj)	7.23	
human (n)	1.172	
humanoid (adj)	8.16	
humid (adj)	7.125	
humorous (adj)	9.45	
hunter (n)	10.31	
hurricane (n)	10.71	
hurry (v)	12.52	
husky (n)	10.14	
hut (n)	10.36	

I

ice (n)	10.6
icy (adj)	6.112
ID card (n phr)	5.74
ideal (adj)	12.54
identify (v)	8.95
identity (n)	3.2
ignore (v)	5.11
illegal (adj)	5.42
illegally (adv)	7.50
image (n)	1.39
imaginative (adj)	2.100
immature (adj)	2.36
immediate (adj)	8.120
immediately (adv)	2.32
impact (n)	3.124
impress (v)	4.109
impression (n)	1.18
impressive (adj)	12.16
improvement (n)	2.47
in addition (prep phr)	10.173
in advance (prep phr)	4.92
in case of (prep phr)	2.124
in connection with (prep phr)	8.136
in contrast (prep phr)	7.130
in danger (prep phr)	10.30
in fact (prep phr)	1.179, 6.18
in need (prep phr)	10.174
in progress (prep phr)	2.82
in secret (prep phr)	5.141
in spite of (phr)	6.167
in the end (prep phr)	2.178
in the wild (prep phr)	10.29
in time (prep phr)	3.115
include (v)	2.18
including (prep)	1.81
increase (n)	10.66
increase (v)	8.114
independence (n)	9.75
independent (adj)	4.113
individual (adj)	6.132
individuality (n)	5.109
indoor (adj)	2.126
industry (n)	4.105
inexpensive (adj)	3.92
influence (v)	5.89
ingredient (n)	6.12
injured (adj)	7.80
ink (n)	6.145
input (n)	6.33
insecure (adj)	5.44
insensitive (adj)	9.53
inspect (v)	7.84
install (v)	10.132
instant (adj)	11.40
instruction (n)	5.134
instructor (n)	10.177
insulate (v)	10.145
insult (n)	5.111
intelligent (adj)	6.37
intend (v)	3.76
intention (n)	3.61
interact (v)	8.82
interactive (adj)	6.31
international (adj)	4.41
interrupt (v)	2.83
interviewer (n)	6.139
intonation (n)	2.97
introduce (v)	1.180
introductory (adj)	11.97
invent (v)	2.64
inventor (n)	8.81
involve (v)	6.25
iPod (n)	3.4
ironing (n)	9.61
irregular (adj)	5.52
irresponsible (adj)	5.55
it's no good (phr)	7.10
it's time (phr)	9.71
item (n)	3.40

J

jammed (adj)	4.125
jaw (n)	8.34
jealous (adj)	5.135
jewel (n)	7.13
jewellery (n)	7.93
join (v)	7.139
join in (phr v)	5.143
journalist (n)	4.126
journey (n)	12.46
joypad (n)	8.28
judge (n)	5.69
judge (v)	4.104, 5.104
junior (adj)	11.2

K

kayaking (n)	11.82
keen (adj)	1.32
keep an eye on sb/sth (phr)	2.105
keep on (phr v)	2.111
keep sth going (v phr)	11.81
keep up with (phr v)	2.118
keyboard (n)	6.61
keypad (n)	8.149
kick (v)	8.2
knock (v)	10.83

L

lab (n)	2.70
lack (n)	3.108
laid-back (adj)	4.7
land (n)	7.47
laptop (n)	6.62
last (v)	2.144
latest (adj)	5.105
laugh at (phr v)	5.40
laureate (n)	6.172
law (n)	5.43
lawn (n)	10.81
laziness (n)	3.103
lazy (adj)	2.59
lead (v)	6.40
lead-free (adj)	10.141
league (n)	2.145
leap (v)	8.40
leather (n)	6.103
legal (adj)	5.54
legend (n)	7.63
lend (v)	3.47
length (n)	2.24, 11.73
let (v)	1.154
liar (n)	1.131
licence (n)	5.71
lie (n)	1.125
lie detector (n phr)	1.136
life-size (adj)	8.49
lifetime (n)	9.6
light bulb (n phr)	10.120
light up (phr v)	4.59
lighting (n)	10.130
lightning (n)	10.72
lightning bolt (n phr)	6.125
likeable (adj)	9.15
limit (v)	8.35
line (n)	4.50, 8.118
lip (n)	11.27
liquid (n)	7.58
litter (n)	10.119
lively (adj)	1.95
loads of (phr)	5.19
local (adj)	1.97
local (n)	4.23
location (n)	7.128
lock (n)	2.168, 5.138
logical (adj)	5.51
long-term (adj)	5.88
loo (n)	2.166
look (n)	2.143
look after (phr v)	1.168
look forward to (phr v)	1.166, 3.140
look on the bright side (phr)	11.30
lover (n)	4.81
loyalty (n)	4.110
luckily (adv)	2.157
luggage (n)	10.48
luxury (n)	7.17
Lycra (n)	11.36
lyrics (n pl)	1.114

M

madness (n)	3.117
magically (adv)	9.84
main (adj)	1.6
maintenance (n)	11.33
major (adj)	3.123
majority (n)	6.53
make (v)	2.123
make a fool of yourself (phr)	2.33
make for (phr v)	2.110
make history (phr)	6.4
make it (phr)	3.74
make out (phr v)	7.110
make sure (v phr)	2.116
make up (phr v)	2.39, 2.117
makeover (n)	3.129
male (adj)	6.54
manager (n)	1.2
manufacture (v)	8.76
marathon (n)	11.72
march (v)	5.27
maritime (adj)	7.51
mark (n)	3.56
mark (v)	5.99
marking (n)	10.51
mass (n)	6.133
massage (n)	4.37
massive (adj)	12.14
mate (n)	5.21
material (n)	6.102
matter (v)	3.3
mature (adj)	3.96
maximum (adj)	11.78
mayor (n)	4.98
mean (adj)	6.109
means (n)	10.21
meanwhile (adv)	2.131
measure (v)	1.142
medallist (n)	11.42
media (n pl)	8.105
medicine (n)	7.75
medieval (adj)	12.30
melt (v)	10.84
member (n)	10.108
memorise (v)	1.77
memory stick (n phr)	6.63
mend (v)	10.147
mention (v)	2.95
menu (n)	7.34
mercury (n)	10.123
messy (adj)	2.74
metal (n)	6.104
method (n)	7.77
MI6 (abbreviation)	6.165
microchip (n)	6.72
mid (prefix)	7.73
Middle Ages (n phr)	7.69
midnight (n)	12.49
mile (n)	10.106
millennium (n)	7.66
mind (n)	8.79
mind (v)	5.49
mind-blowing (adj)	12.69
minimum (n)	12.43
misbehave (v)	2.40
miss (v)	2.102, 10.96
mist (n)	10.57
mixed (adj)	2.60
moan (v)	12.76
monastery (n)	12.32
mood (n)	1.92
moody (adj)	3.109
moreover (adv)	6.160
mosquito (n)	10.98
most of the time (phr)	7.115
motivated (adj)	11.87
motor racing (n phr)	11.63
mountaineer (n)	8.73
mountainous (adj)	10.63
mouse (n)	6.64
move (n)	2.49
move (v)	7.143
movement (n)	1.47
mow (v)	10.80
mumble (v)	12.78
murderer (n)	7.7
muscle (n)	11.15

N

nag (v)	3.20
nail (n)	10.152
Namibian (adj)	10.42
nan (n)	1.165
narrative (n)	2.179
nasty (adj)	3.35
native (adj)	10.180
naughty (adj)	2.85
navigation (n)	7.41
nearly (adv)	2.177
neat (adj)	6.107
necessary (adj)	8.55
needle (n)	7.61
neon (n)	4.77
nervous (adj)	1.52
net (n)	10.28
New England (n phr)	7.99
newsletter (n)	10.170
nick (v)	5.124
nickname (n)	1.104
nightmare (n)	9.5
no way! (phr)	10.101
no wonder (phr)	3.24
noisy (adj)	1.63
none (pronoun)	6.15
non-fiction (n)	6.147
northern (adj)	7.98
not at all (phr)	7.5
note (n)	5.148, 6.97
notice (v)	3.52
novel (n)	6.144
nowadays (adv)	7.19
numerical (adj)	6.69

126

O

obey (v)	5.53
object (n)	7.89
objective (n)	6.27
obligation (n)	11.69
obvious (adj)	4.108
occasionally (adv)	1.150
odd (adj)	4.62
off (adv)	3.82, 12.8
offer (n)	3.77
old-fashioned (adj)	2.141
olive tree (n phr)	12.104
omit (v)	2.140
on board (prep phr)	7.25
on foot (prep phr)	10.38
on holiday (prep phr)	10.151
on horseback (prep phr)	10.50
on stand-by (prep phr)	10.129
on the other hand (phr)	9.14
on the part of sb (phr)	12.115
on the whole (phr)	9.78
on time (prep phr)	7.116
on your own (prep phr)	1.41
on your way (prep phr)	7.53
once (adv)	8.37
online (adv)	6.23
opening hours (n phr)	12.37
operate (v)	6.70
operation (n)	6.119
opponent (n)	6.28
opportunity (n)	4.60
optimistic (adj)	6.174
option (n)	3.148, 10.171
orchestra (n)	2.69
order (n)	1.147
ordinal number (n phr)	7.68
organise (v)	1.66
organised (adj)	9.91
organiser (n)	4.12
origin (n)	11.77
out and about (phr)	10.126
out of breath (prep phr)	11.7
out of order (prep phr)	2.170
outdoor (adj)	2.127
outdoors (adv)	1.68
outlet (n)	8.91
outspoken (adj)	9.96
over (adj)	9.35
owe (v)	3.48
own (v)	8.75
own goal (n phr)	8.36

P

pack (n)	10.162
pack (v)	10.150
package (n)	8.146
pain (n)	4.53
pale (adj)	12.93
palm tree (n phr)	7.120
panther (n)	10.100
pants (n pl)	2.163
parade (n)	4.42
pardon (interjection)	9.68
participant (n)	4.64
particular (adj)	1.76
particularly (adv)	11.50
part-time (adj)	3.68
pass (n)	10.179
pass (v)	2.54
passage (n)	8.94
past (prep)	2.173
patience (n)	6.46
patient (adj)	3.102
patient (n)	12.91
pattern (n)	3.121
PE (abbreviation)	2.159
peace (n)	6.137
peak (adj)	12.38
penalty (n)	8.22
per (prep)	3.147
percent (n)	6.50
perfect (adj)	7.121
perhaps (adv)	7.14
period (n)	10.73
permanent (adj)	5.92
permanently (adv)	1.78
permission (n)	5.67
permit (v)	11.74
personality (n)	1.89
personally (adv)	5.96
persuade (v)	3.84
petrified (adj)	12.73
petrol (n)	10.135
phobia (n)	1.122
physical (adj)	7.119
pick (v)	11.84
pick up (phr v)	1.137
pierce (v)	5.120
pinch (v)	5.127
pity (n)	11.89
plain (adj)	6.118, 8.104
planet (n)	10.1
plant (n)	1.69
pleasure (n)	12.47
plenty (pronoun)	6.98
plot (n)	6.120
pocket money (n phr)	3.25
point (v)	5.102
point of view (n phr)	5.115
poisonous (adj)	7.38
polite (adj)	1.182, 3.142
poor (adj)	2.79
porridge (n)	10.93
port (n)	7.12
portable (adj)	6.24
portrait (n)	10.153
posh (adj)	5.18
positive (adj)	5.147
possession (n)	3.85
possibility (n)	3.113
postage (n)	3.141
poster (n)	4.128
pottery (n)	7.92
pour (v)	10.77, 12.84
power (n)	6.127
powerful (adj)	8.21
powerfully (adv)	7.101
practical (adj)	3.97
practical joke (n phr)	1.123
predictable (adj)	6.52
prediction (n)	3.58
prefer (v)	4.55
preference (n)	10.182
press (v)	4.54
pressure (n)	1.36, 2.106
print (v)	3.41
prison (n)	5.70
prisoner (n)	7.117
privacy (n)	7.27
private (adj)	2.86
probability (n)	3.112
process (n)	7.113
produce (v)	7.60, 8.13
producer (n)	3.132
professional (adj)	1.17
professional (n)	1.37
program (n)	8.8
programmable (adj)	8.15
programme (v)	6.44
project (n)	10.154
promise (v)	2.45
prompt (n)	7.140
proof (n)	5.77
properly (adv)	8.58
protect (v)	5.20
proud (adj)	10.33
prove (v)	4.89
provide (v)	10.94
PS (abbreviation)	1.175
public (adj)	1.157
publisher (n)	6.19
pull (v)	10.13, 11.24
punctuation (n)	1.184
punish (v)	2.37
purpose (n)	6.55
put on (phr v)	2.112
put out (phr v)	6.16
put sb off (phr v)	11.29
put up (phr v)	4.3
put up with (phr v)	2.120
put your heart into sth (phr)	2.121

Q

quad bike (n phr)	6.106
quality (n)	3.125, 8.148
quarter (n)	8.124
queue (n)	4.6
queue (v)	12.112
quite (adv)	1.7

R

rack (n)	3.91
racket (n)	12.64
radar (n)	8.18
rainforest (n)	10.26
raise (v)	10.168
raise money (phr)	3.86
raise your voice (phr)	8.112
range (n)	6.48
rare (adj)	10.46
rarely (adv)	1.149
rat (n)	7.35
rating (n)	6.85
react (v)	5.2
reactions (n pl)	6.29
realise (v)	2.160
realistic (adj)	6.175
real-life (adj)	2.14
recent (adj)	4.79
recently (adv)	2.87
receptionist (n)	8.87
recharge (v)	8.130
recognise (v)	6.2
recommend (v)	6.171
recommendation (n)	6.6
record (v)	1.33, 2.119, 12.61
recover (v)	10.89
recruit (v)	7.82
rectangular (adj)	8.52
recycle (v)	10.114
reduce (v)	4.52
refer to (phr v)	2.139
reflect (v)	9.28
refund (n)	8.144
refuse (v)	3.83
register (n)	4.129
regret (v)	10.95
regular (adj)	2.65
regulation (n)	11.70
relate (v)	6.58
relationship (n)	8.113
relaxed (adj)	2.136
release (v)	10.159
relevant (adj)	6.152
reliable (adj)	3.101
Religion (n)	2.148
religious (adj)	4.65
remain (v)	9.34
remainder (n)	7.136
remote (adj)	7.127
remote control (n phr)	8.61
remote-controlled (adj)	8.24
remove (v)	2.109
renew (v)	10.139
repair (v)	8.139
repeat (v)	5.46
repeated (adj)	1.80
replace (v)	8.23
replacement (n)	8.47
reply (n)	3.149
report (n)	2.91
require (v)	4.46
research (n)	3.119
researcher (n)	8.44
reserve (v)	4.116
respond (v)	3.88, 6.32
responsible (adj)	5.30
rest (n)	12.50
restriction (n)	12.42
result (n)	1.128
rethink (v)	10.140
reuse (v)	10.109
review (v)	6.7
revise (v)	2.53
revolting (adj)	5.33
reward (n)	3.29
rhino (n)	10.41
ride (n)	12.4
ridiculous (adj)	2.27
right (n)	5.58
ring (v)	12.106
risky (adj)	12.70
robber (n)	7.6
robotic (adj)	8.25
robotics (n)	8.48
roller coaster (n phr)	10.15
rollerblading (n)	2.128
Roman (n)	7.103
romance (n)	6.148
room for improvement (phr)	3.1
rope (n)	4.49
rotten (adj)	7.33
route (n)	7.42
routine (n)	11.12
rude (adj)	5.7
ruin (v)	9.98
rule (n)	9.30
rule (v)	2.1
rumble (v)	2.151
run (v)	4.11
run off (phr v)	12.86
run out of (phr v)	11.17
rush (v)	2.167

S

safety (n)	12.45
sail (v)	7.70
sailing ship (n phr)	12.15
sale (n)	3.79
sample (n)	4.68
sanctuary (n)	10.158
sand (n)	10.45
satellite (n)	7.40
sauce (n)	7.87
sausage (n)	7.85
save up (phr v)	3.39
scare (v)	3.53
scared (adj)	9.16
scary (adj)	3.14
scenery (n)	12.26
scent (n)	8.64
scientific (adj)	7.76
scissors (n pl)	8.59
scratch (v)	3.55
scream (v)	4.32
screen (n)	6.65
scruffy (adj)	2.174
seat (n)	5.50
seatbelt (n)	5.59
secondary school (n phr)	2.10
second-hand (adj)	3.8
section (n)	6.149
semi (prefix)	3.150
senior citizen (n phr)	12.40
sensation (n)	4.101
sense (n)	1.82, 3.54, 8.70
sense of humour (n phr)	1.100
sensible (adj)	9.87
sensibly (adv)	2.75
sensitive (adj)	6.75, 8.71, 9.46
sensor (n)	8.3
separate (adj)	2.133
separately (adv)	2.107
series (n)	1.15, 6.154, 6.156
serious (adj)	1.94, 10.3
serve (v)	4.120
service (n)	8.141
set off (phr v)	4.33
set the scene (phr)	12.108
set up (phr v)	4.96, 8.131
several (determiner)	2.89
severe (adj)	10.86
sew (v)	7.45
sex (n)	11.4
shape (n)	6.101
shaped (adj)	8.38
sheet (n)	10.62
shelter (n)	4.47
shipbuilding (n)	12.19
shocking (adj)	2.158
shove (v)	5.22
show (v)	2.164
show off (phr v)	9.43
shower (n)	4.31, 10.97
shriek (v)	12.80
shy (adj)	1.54
sick (adj)	12.55
sight (n)	8.67
sightseeing (n)	12.51
sign (n)	2.165
sign (v)	3.42
sign up (phr v)	8.145
signal (n)	8.60
silk (n)	8.102
silly (adj)	2.58

Word	Ref
similar (adj)	3.33
simulated (adj)	9.25
sit around (phr v)	7.44
site (n)	7.105, 12.28
situation (n)	1.58
size (n)	6.100
skateboard (n)	9.74
skill (n)	1.10
skin (n)	1.139
skull (n)	7.94
sledge (n)	10.12
sleeping bag (n phr)	10.102
slim (adj)	9.86
slow down (phr v)	2.8
smack (adv)	11.20
smart (adj)	1.26
smell (n)	8.68
smelly (adj)	10.47
smoke (n)	3.73
snack (n)	11.44
snob (n)	9.59
snowboarding (n)	11.64
soaking (adj)	10.78
soap opera (n phr)	9.73
sob (v)	12.81
sociable (adj)	9.2
social (adj)	8.125
soft toy (n phr)	3.17
soil (n)	10.166
solar (adj)	10.127
solar panel (n phr)	10.131
solution (n)	3.126
solve (v)	2.63
sonic (adj)	8.32
sort out (phr v)	3.19, 5.12
sound (v)	4.130
souvenir (n)	12.33
space (n)	5.126
spare (adj)	2.161
speak up (phr v)	7.138
specially (adv)	8.50
species (n)	10.61
specific (adj)	2.96
spectacles (n pl)	6.124
spectator (n)	4.63
spectator sport (n phr)	11.54
speech (n)	8.119
speed (n)	6.51
speedboat (n)	7.52
spine-chilling (adj)	12.7
splash (v)	4.25
split (v)	11.26
spoil (v)	6.131
sporting (adj)	12.59
sportsperson (n)	11.56
sporty (adj)	11.79
spot (n)	1.96
spot (v)	1.127
spray (v)	4.30
spread (v)	6.73
spy (n)	6.121
square (n)	4.20
staff (n)	2.71
stage (n)	4.45, 11.46
stall (n)	4.35
stallholder (n)	4.119
stamina (n)	11.16
stand (v)	3.23
stare (v)	1.29
state (v)	8.152
statement (n)	1.98
statue (n)	7.109
stay (n)	7.55
stay behind	2.66
stay in (phr v)	6.1
stay out (phr v)	9.66
stay up (phr v)	1.21
step out (phr v)	11.19
stew (n)	4.87
sticky (adj)	10.79
stomach (n)	7.28
stomachache (n)	7.29
stone (n)	7.57
straight (adv)	8.41, 10.107
strength (n)	6.150
stress (v)	2.104
stressed (adj)	9.92
strike (v)	10.82
strip sb of sth (phr v)	9.29
stroll (v)	12.5
strongly (adv)	6.170
structure (n)	6.77
stuck (adj)	1.158, 2.169
stuff (n)	3.90
stunning (adj)	6.96
stupid (adj)	9.63
subject (n)	2.4
substance (n)	6.134
succeed (v)	4.106
success (n)	1.34
suffer (v)	3.107, 10.85
suggest (v)	6.91
suggestion (n)	3.64
suit (v)	12.22
suitable (adj)	2.153
summarise (v)	1.64
summary (n)	6.176
sunbathe (v)	12.63
supply (n)	10.115
support (n)	4.114
support (v)	5.100
supporter (n)	10.157
suppose (v)	9.67
surely (adv)	6.11
surfer (n)	1.3
surname (n)	1.103
surprised (adj)	1.110
surprising (adj)	1.56
surround (v)	7.123
survey (n)	2.99
survival (n)	10.17
survive (v)	7.133
suspense (n)	12.113
suspiciously (adv)	4.115
swallow (v)	1.159
swap (v)	5.149
sweat (n)	7.24
sweet (n)	1.151
swimsuit (n)	11.34
switch off (phr v)	3.116
switch on (phr v)	6.126

T

Word	Ref
take action (phr)	8.154
take care of (v phr)	2.115, 11.31
take it in turns (phr)	6.80
take off (phr v)	2.108
take part (v phr)	1.55
take place (v phr)	9.64
take up (phr v)	2.114, 3.30, 6.166
tale (n)	11.18
talk (n)	11.86
talk show (n phr)	1.160
talkative (adj)	9.49
tap (n)	10.146
tarantula (n)	10.105
task (n)	3.36
taste (n)	8.69
tasteless (adj)	7.32
tasty (adj)	4.90
tattoo (n)	5.65
tear (n)	1.44
tease (v)	5.15
technical (adj)	11.32
technician (n)	4.117
technique (n)	10.18
teen (adj)	9.4
tell a joke (phr)	9.79
temperature (n)	10.16
temporary (adj)	5.84
tension (n)	4.21
tent (n)	4.4
terrified (adj)	1.43
terror (n)	3.49
text-messaging (n)	2.2
the outside world (phr)	9.26
theme park (n phr)	4.67
there's no going back (phr)	1.31
think up (phr v)	9.52
third (n)	8.123
thoroughly (adv)	8.83
though (adv)	2.51
thoughts (n pl)	1.28
thread (n)	7.62
three-quarter (adj)	2.23
thrill (n)	6.10
thrilled (adj)	12.58
thrilling (adj)	7.134
throw away (phr v)	10.118
throw out (phr v)	3.21
thump (n)	5.34
thunderstorm (n)	8.127
tidy up (phr v)	5.133
tight (adj)	11.35
timetable (n)	2.134, 3.144
timid (adj)	9.54
tiny (adj)	1.129
tip (n)	6.140
tissue (n)	10.134
title (n)	6.153
to begin with (phr)	11.95
tone (n)	6.93
tongue (n)	8.65
tool (n)	7.95, 8.6
top (adj)	8.147
top (n)	2.25
top mark (n phr)	2.61
top up (phr v)	8.150
topic (n)	1.8
torch (n)	10.125
total (n)	11.66
totally (adv)	5.113
touch (n)	8.31
tough (adj)	10.58
tour (n)	8.88, 12.6
towards (prep)	2.42
track (n)	12.44
track (v)	10.39
tradition (n)	4.66
train (v)	1.67
trainer (n)	2.26
transform (v)	1.24
transformation (n)	1.12
transport (n)	10.22
treasure (n)	7.11
trendy (adj)	9.95
triathlete (n)	11.9
triathlon (n)	11.3
tribal (adj)	10.25
trip (n)	10.148
tropical (adj)	7.37
troublemaker (n)	5.106
trumpet (n)	7.144
truth (n)	1.124
tummy (n)	2.150
tune (n)	3.5
tune up (phr v)	4.10
turn down (phr v)	8.110
turn into (phr v)	4.40
turn off (phr v)	2.44
turn up (phr v)	8.109
twin (n)	9.76
twist (n)	2.12
typical (adj)	3.34

U

Word	Ref
unable (adj)	3.98
unacceptable (adj)	5.114
unattractive (adj)	9.56
unblock (v)	9.24
uncaring (adj)	10.138
uncomfortable (adj)	9.3
underline (v)	3.130
underneath (prep)	1.153
understanding (adj)	9.90
understanding (n)	5.145
undone (adj)	5.63
unexpected (adj)	2.62
unfair (adj)	5.3
unfit (adj)	11.85
unforgettable (adj)	1.163
unfortunately (adv)	5.31
unhealthy (adj)	11.43
uni-cycling (n)	2.129
uniform (n)	2.22
unimaginable (adj)	7.26
university (n)	2.90
unless (conjunction)	5.41
unlikely (adj)	10.117
unplanned (adj)	3.59
unpopular (adj)	2.57
untidy (adj)	6.105
up for sth (phr)	11.10
up to (sth) (phr)	9.77
upset (adj)	5.10
urgently (adv)	8.14
use (n)	8.57
useless (adj)	8.143

V

Word	Ref
vacuum clean (v phr)	3.67
valuable (adj)	7.9
varied (adj)	2.132
various (adj)	9.22
vary (v)	9.23
vehicle (n)	12.48
versatile (adj)	6.22
version (n)	6.42
vet (n)	1.174
villain (n)	6.122
violence (n)	5.38
virus (n)	6.130
visible (adj)	3.94
vision (n)	8.19
visual (adj)	8.66
voice (n)	1.46
volcano (n)	10.55
volume (n)	8.133
vote (n)	3.128
vote (v)	5.73
vowel (n)	9.72
voyage (n)	7.43

W

Word	Ref
wake up (phr v)	9.85
wannabe (n)	4.103
wardrobe (n)	3.18
wash up (phr v)	2.94
waste (v)	3.12
water butt (n phr)	10.143
water slide (n phr)	4.70
water-coaster (n)	12.18
waterproof (adj)	10.181
way (n)	1.74
weakness (n)	6.151
weapon (n)	7.96
wearily (adv)	1.35
web designer (n phr)	1.4
website (n)	8.42
weird (adj)	5.118
well (interjection)	1.178
well-dressed (adj)	9.81
well-known (adj)	6.68
What is … like? (phr)	3.6
wherever (adv)	6.79
whichever (determiner)	8.46
whisper (v)	12.75
white lie (n phr)	1.106
whole (adj)	3.15
wicked (adj)	12.72
wide (adj)	4.88
wig (n)	4.100
Wild West (n phr)	12.25
wildlife (n)	10.65
windsurfing (n)	12.65
wind-up (adj)	10.124
wire (n)	8.128
wire-framed (adj)	6.123
wonder (v)	11.37
wooden (adj)	10.175
work out (phr v)	3.32
workout (n)	11.13
workshop (n)	4.19
worldwide (adv)	6.20
worm (n)	10.92
worried (adj)	1.118
would rather (phr)	3.89
would-be (adj)	6.141

Y

Word	Ref
yearly (adj)	10.169
yell (v)	12.77
yoga (n)	11.80
yuck! (interjection)	12.89

Z

Word	Ref
zorbing (n)	11.76